# Fundamentals of
# **iPhone**
## iOS 12 Edition

## Kevin Wilson

**elluminet Press**
www.elluminetpress.com

# Fundamentals of iPhone: iOS 12 Ed

Publisher: Elluminet Press
Director: Kevin Wilson
Lead Editor: Steven Ashmore
Technical Reviewer: Mike Taylor, Robert Ashcroft
Copy Editors: Joanne Taylor, James Marsh
Proof Reader: Mike Taylor
Indexer: James Marsh
Cover Designer: Kevin Wilson

eBook versions and licenses are also available for most titles. Any source code or other supplementary materials referenced by the author in this text is available to readers at

www.elluminetpress.com/resources

For detailed information about how to locate your book's resources, go to

www.elluminetpress.com/resources

# Table of Contents

# About the Author

Kevin Wilson has made a career out of technology and showing others how to use it. After earning a master's degree in computer science, software engineering, and multimedia systems, Kevin worked as a tutor and college instructor, helping students master such subjects as multimedia, computer literacy and information technology. He currently serves as Elluminet Press Publishing's senior writer and director, he periodically teaches computing at college in South Africa and serves as an IT trainer in England.

Kevin's motto is clear: "If you can't explain something simply, you haven't understood it well enough." To that end, he has created the Computer Essentials series, in which he breaks down complex technological subjects into smaller, easy-to-follow steps that students and ordinary computer users can put into practice.

# Acknowledgements

Thanks to all the staff at Luminescent Media & Elluminet Press for their passion, dedication and hard work in the preparation and production of this book.

To all my friends and family for their continued support and encouragement in all my writing projects.

To all my colleagues, students and testers who took the time to test procedures and offer feedback on the book

Finally thanks to you the reader for choosing this book. I hope it helps you to use your iPhone with greater ease.

# iPhones

iPhones run iOS. iOS is mobile, multitasking operating system designed specifically for iPads and iPhones. iOS 12 is the latest release for iPhones and iPads.

An Operating System is a program that manages the device's hardware resources such as memory, processor and storage. The Operating System also provides a platform for you to run apps such as web browsers, maps, email, photos, games and so on.

The iOS user interface is a touch screen, meaning you can directly manipulate sliders, switches, buttons and icons on screen using your finger.

iOS has a main screen called the home screen containing icons that represent apps. You can download countless apps from the App Store - you'll find an app for almost anything you can think of.

Security has improved on these devices, you can unlock just with a finger print - no need to keep remembering a PIN.

Finally there's Siri, the voice activated personal assistant that uses natural language AI to interpret voice commands you speak out loud. You can ask Siri to send messages, dial a number, as well as search the web, and answer certain questions.

# iPhone Models

In this guide, we'll be taking a look at the iPhone 6 / 6 Plus, iPhone 6S / 6S Plus, iPhone 7 / 7 Plus, and iPhone 8 / 8 Plus.

| iPhone 8 | iPhone 8 Plus | iPhone 7 | iPhone 7 plus |
|---|---|---|---|

I'll spare you all the boring technical differences between the phones, Apple's website has plenty of information about their product if you want to read in more detail. There are however, a few differences worth pointing out. The major difference between the standard model and the 'plus' model is the physical size. The plus model is a larger phone with a 5.5" screen rather than a 4.7" screen. The plus model also has some additional features such as dual rear cameras that allows for higher quality photos, 4K video, better zoom, and portrait photo effects. The iPhone 7 and later does away with the 3.5mm headphone jack in favour of Airpods or bluetooth headphones, and introduces image stabilisation for recording better video. The iPhone 8 introduces wireless charging.

The iPhone 6 series had 4 iterations. The 'plus' model has a larger screen.

| iPhone 6 | iPhone 6 Plus | iPhone 6s | iPhone 6s Plus |
|---|---|---|---|

The main differences between the 'S' model and the standard model are minor. The 'S' model has better cameras, 4K video, a slightly faster processor, and 3D touch

**11**

# What's New in iOS 12?

With iOS 12, Apple have concentrated on improving performance - meaning apps load faster, and are generally more responsive.

iBooks has been renamed Apple Books and makes it easier to find and read your ebooks.

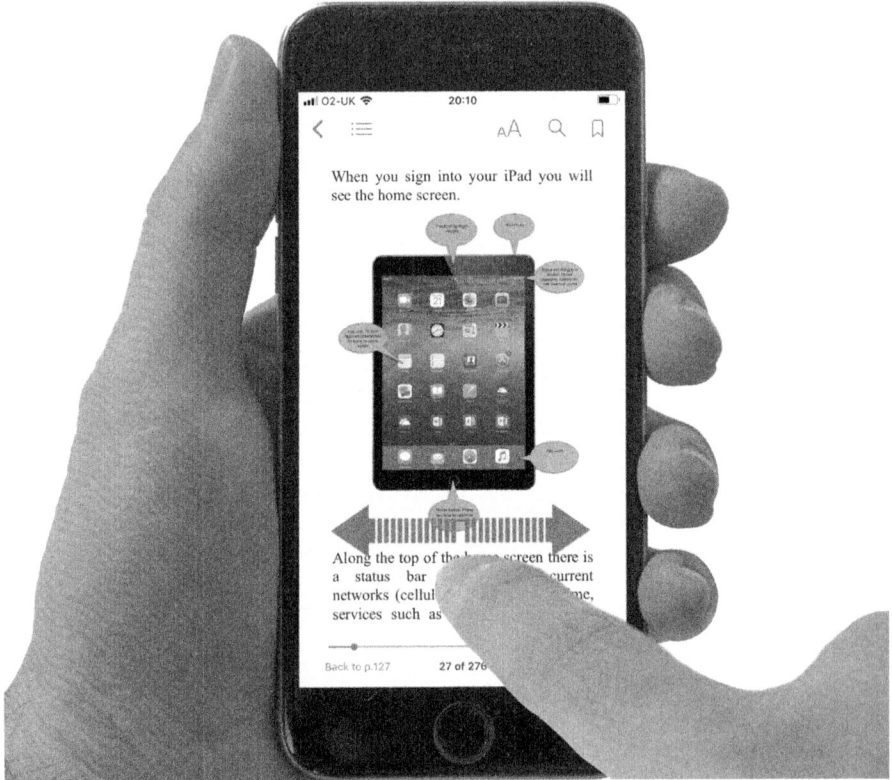

Apple News app has been redesigned, making it easier to keep up with the news that interests you.

FaceTime has also had a few updates. You can now talk to multiple people using Group FaceTime, as well as liven up your chat using various camera effects.

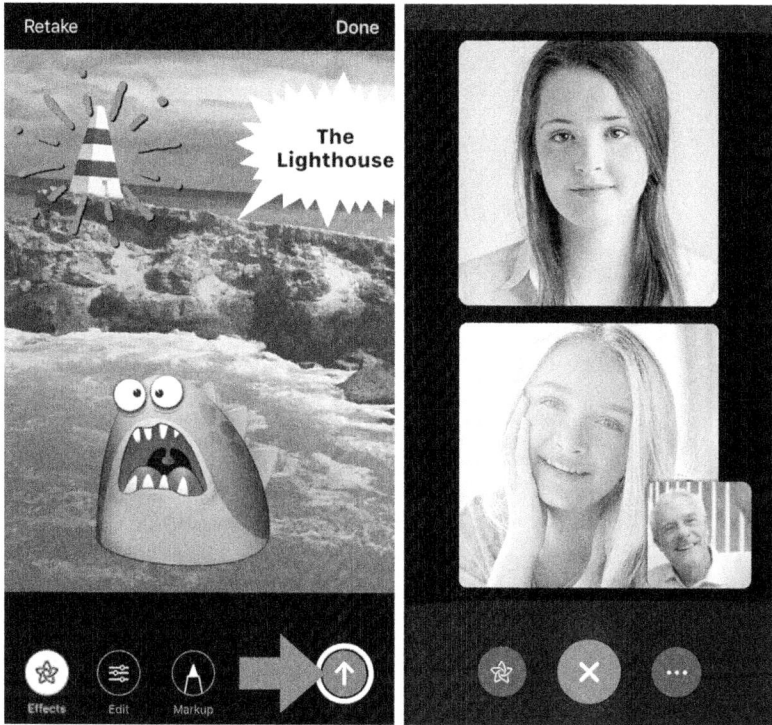

Screen Time is a new feature that allows you to keep track of your iPhone usage, as well as giving you stats and reports on your child's online activity

Also in the mix are new ways to share photos, Siri has a few new shortcuts, as well as the usual security tweaks and other enhancements.

# Setting up Your iPhone

If you've just bought your new iPhone and taken it out the box, the process to set it up to use for the first time is very simple. You don't even have to connect it to your computer.

With iOS 12, Apple have dropped support for the iPhone 4 series.

iOS 12 will run on these devices:

- iPhone XS
- iPhone XS Max
- iPhone XR
- iPhone X
- iPhone 8
- iPhone 8 Plus
- iPhone 7
- iPhone 7 Plus
- iPhone 6s
- iPhone 6s Plus
- iPhone 6
- iPhone 6 Plus
- iPhone SE
- iPhone 5s

In this section we'll take a look at the processes of setting up your iPhone when you turn it on for the first time.

# Insert your SIM

**Make sure your device is off before doing this.** Insert the SIM card from your network provider.

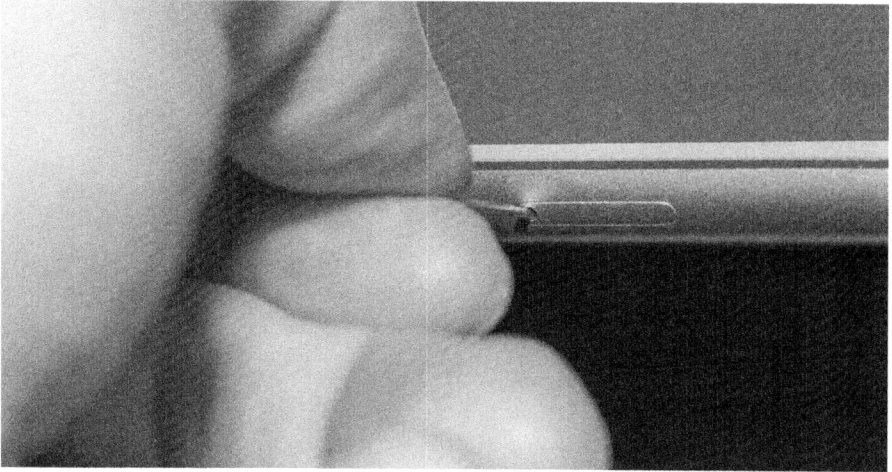

Push the end of a paper clip into the release hole on the side of your device. Pull out the little tray and insert your SIM.

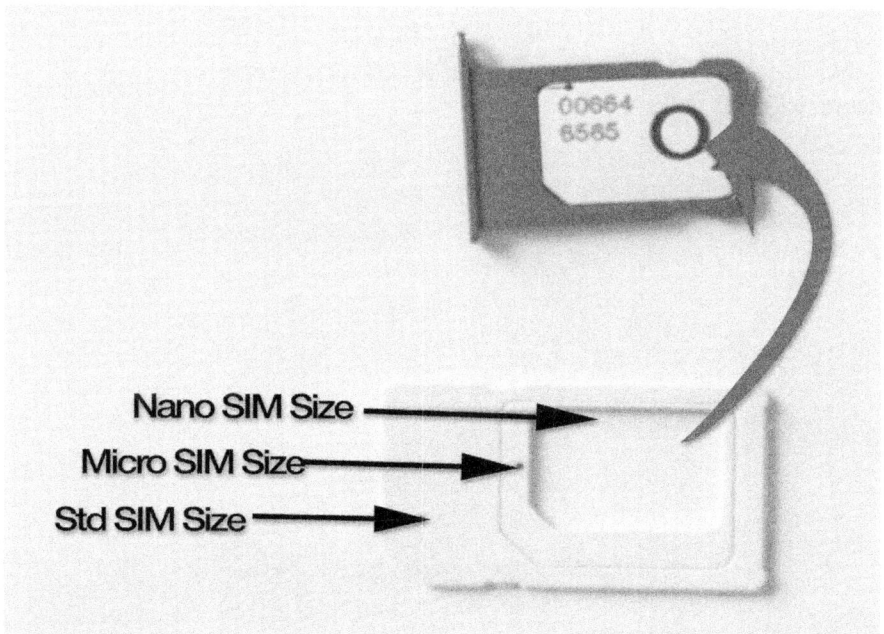

You'll need to punch out the nano SIM in the centre of the SIM card as shown above.

**Chapter 2: Setting up Your iPhone**

Slide the little tray back into your device, until it fits firmly into place against the side.

You're now ready to power on your iPhone. To do this, hold down the power button located on the right edge of your device, until you see the Apple logo on the screen.

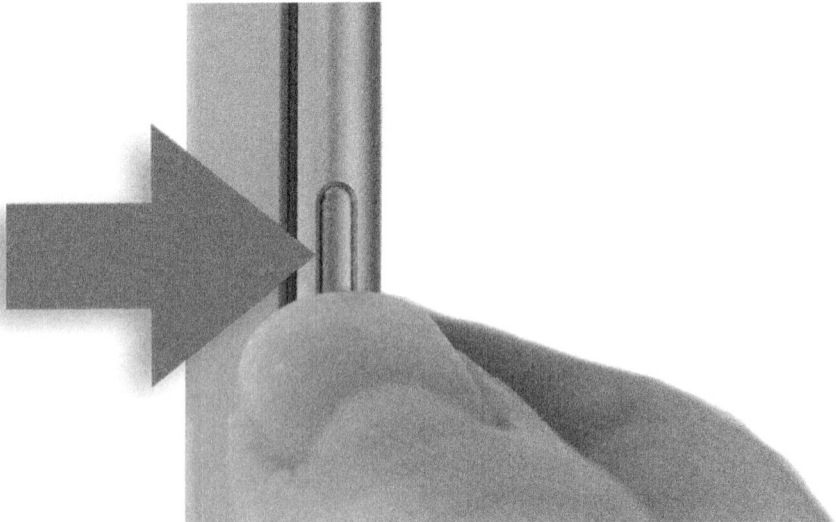

Give your iPhone a few seconds to start up.

16

# Power Up & Power Down

Once your iPhone battery is fully charged, press and hold the power button on the right edge, for a couple of seconds until you see the apple logo.

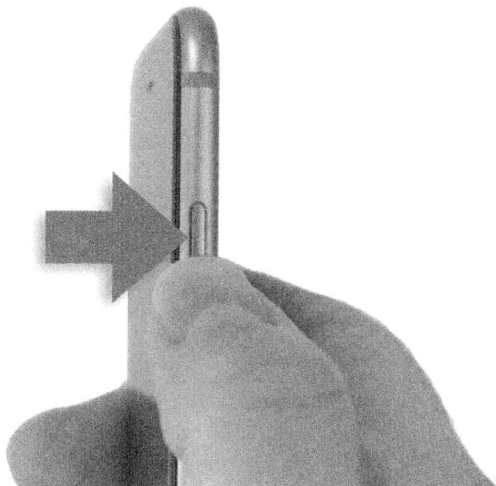

To completely shut down your iPhone, press and hold the power button for a few seconds, until you see the shut down slider on your screen. Slide your finger across the slider to shut down your iPhone.

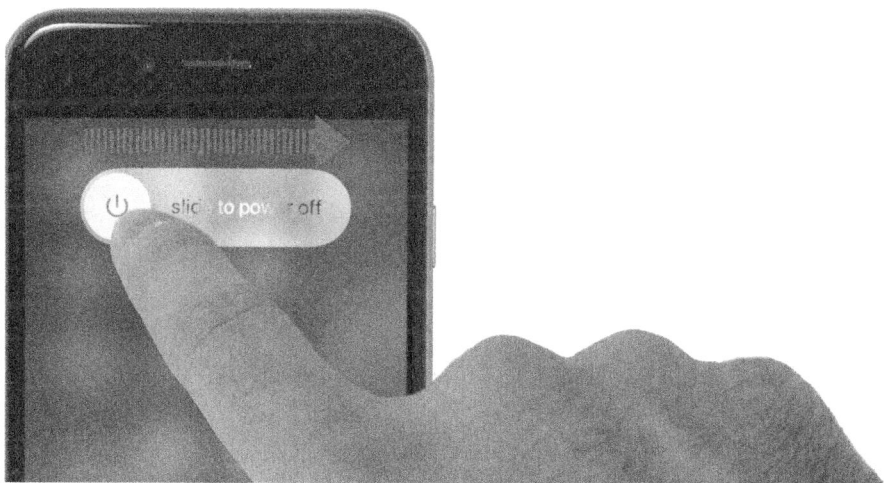

It's a good a idea to completely power down your iPhone from time to time to reset its resources - this can help when your iPhone seems to be running slower than usual. Most of the time your iPhone goes into sleep mode when in normal use.

**17**

# Unlock & Wake iPhone

The home button also contains a finger print scanner and is usually set up during the initial setup.

Place your finger on the button so your thumb fits snugly into the button's indent, then press & release the button once to unlock your iPhone while resting your finger on the button - **don't** hold the button down.

If you haven't set up your finger print scanner, you'll be prompted for your passcode. This is the code you enter during the initial setup procedure.

# Force Shutdown

Sometimes your iPhone can become unresponsive or freeze. When this happens you can force a shutdown.

To do this, hold down the power button on the right edge, and the home button at the same time until the screen goes blank.

Once the screen has gone blank, wait a few seconds, then press and hold the power button for a couple of seconds, until the apple logo appears on screen.

Your iPhone will start up.

# Upgrading your iPhone to iOS 12

Make sure your iPhone is plugged into a power charger and that it is connected to your WiFi.

Once you have done that, go to the settings app and tap 'General', then select 'Software Update'.

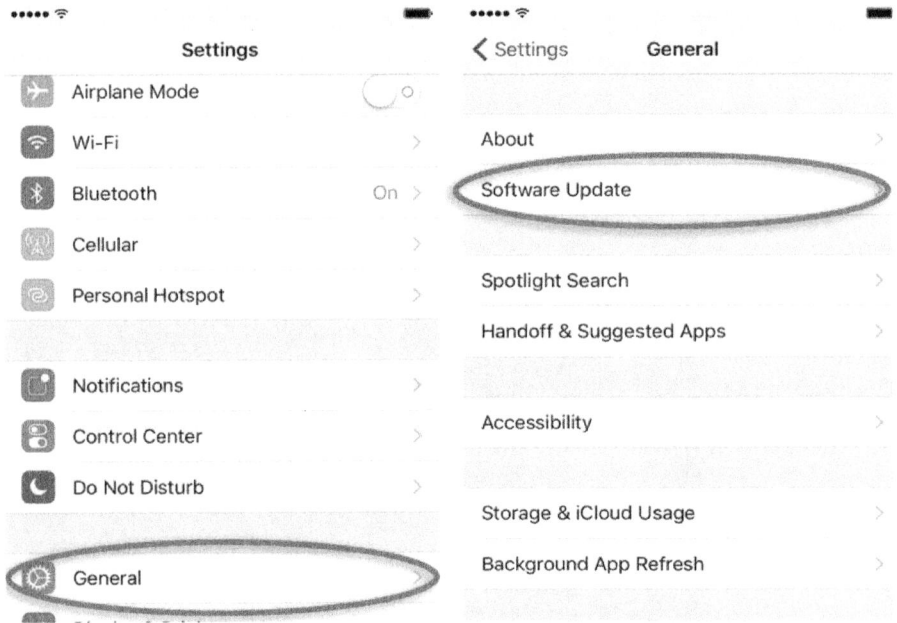

| Settings | | Settings General | |
|---|---|---|---|
| ✈ Airplane Mode | ○ | About | > |
| 🛜 Wi-Fi | > | Software Update | |
| ⁑ Bluetooth | On > | | |
| 📶 Cellular | > | Spotlight Search | > |
| 📶 Personal Hotspot | > | Handoff & Suggested Apps | > |
| 🔲 Notifications | > | | |
| 🔲 Control Center | > | Accessibility | > |
| 🌙 Do Not Disturb | > | | |
| | | Storage & iCloud Usage | > |
| ⚙ General | > | Background App Refresh | > |

Tap 'Download and Install'.

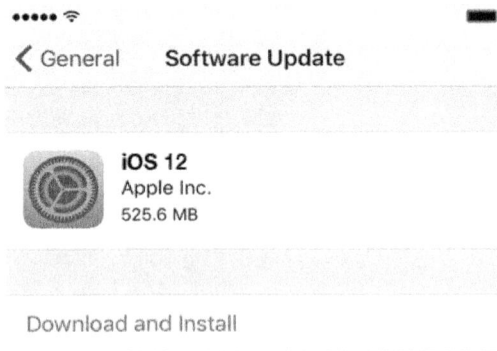

< General    **Software Update**

**iOS 12**
Apple Inc.
525.6 MB

Download and Install

To update now, tap 'download and install'. Enter your passcode when prompted. Your iPhone will restart and the update will install. This might take a while.

# Initial Setup

To use iPhone, you need an internet connection and your Apple ID. For iOS 11 & iOS 12, Apple have introduced an automated setup feature that allows you to transfer settings from another device, such as an iPhone. Both devices must be running iOS 11 or iOS 12. If you don't have this, you can still set up your iPhone manually. First lets take a look at the auto setup feature.

## Auto Setup

If you have iOS11 or iOS12 set up on another device such as an iPhone, you can use it to transfer your settings to your new iPhone.

On your iPhone, slide or press the home button to start, then select your language

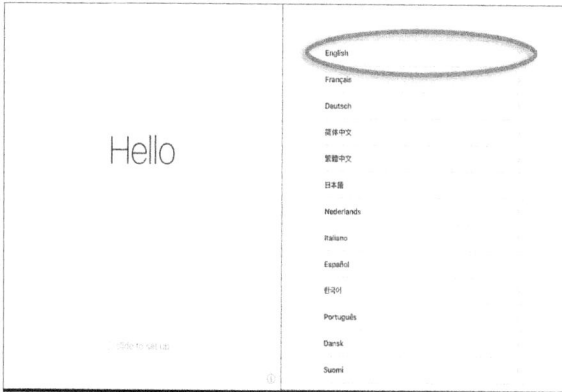

Select your region or country.

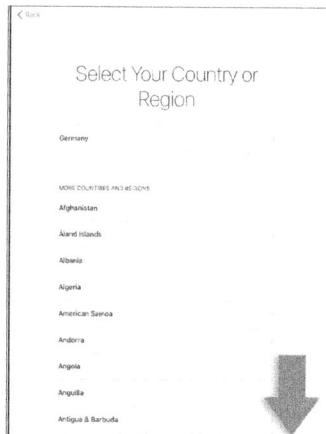

Now, if you have iOS 11 or 12 set up on your old iPhone, bring it over to your new iPhone. You'll see a prompt on your old iPhone. Tap 'continue'.

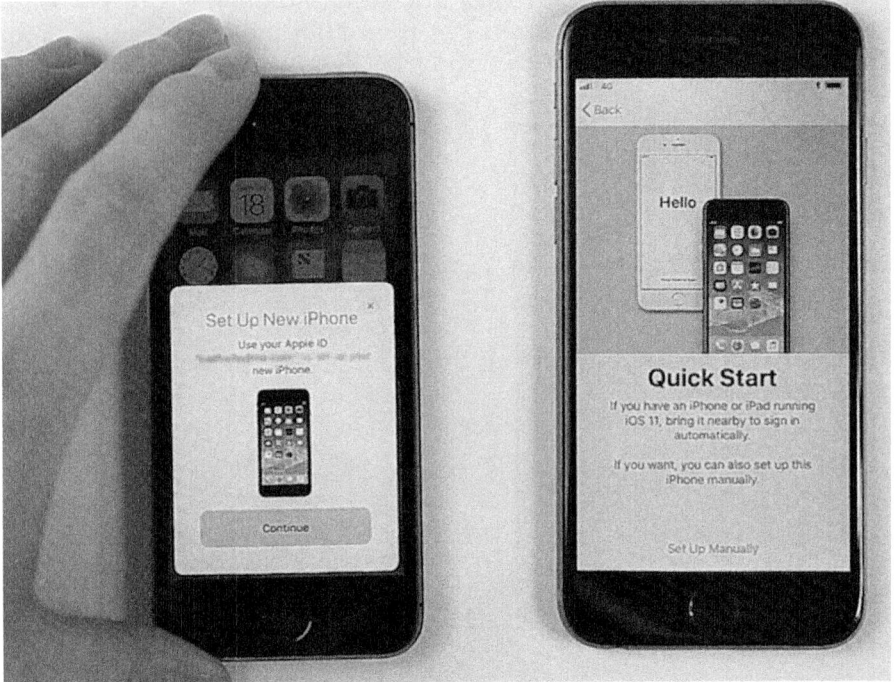

Your iPhone will display a strange pattern, like the one shown below.

Use the camera on your old iPhone, and position the blue pattern shown on your new phone, in the circle shown on the bottom of your old iPhone screen.

Use the camera on your old phone and position the blue pattern in the circle

Hold Your New iPhone Up to the Camera
Position the pattern in the circle

Now leave your iPhone next to your new iPhone until the set up process is complete. Your new iPhone will activate, you may need to enter your passcode, the same one you use to unlock your iPhone.

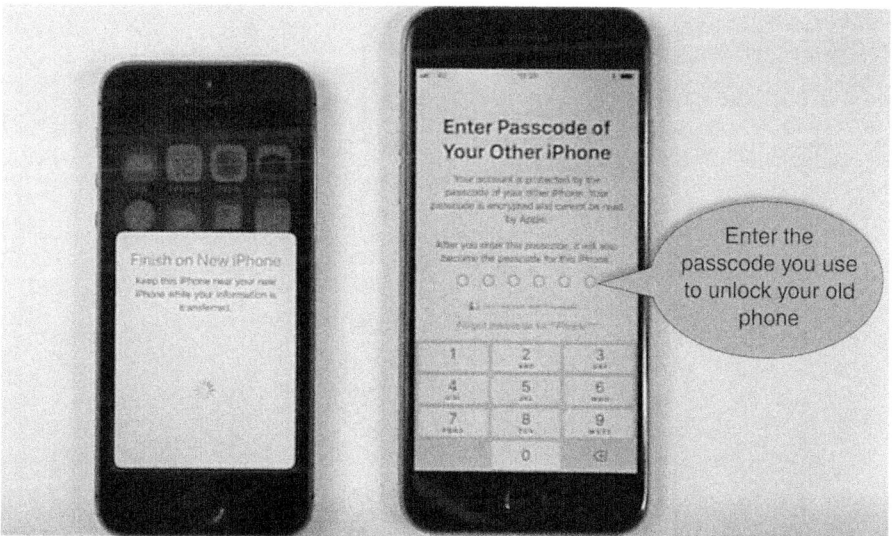

Enter Passcode of Your Other iPhone

Finish on New iPhone

Enter the passcode you use to unlock your old phone

Follow the prompts on your iPhone to set up touch ID if required

## Manual Setup

Turn iPhone on and follow the Setup Assistant. This will guide you through the process

Swipe your finger across the bottom of the screen.

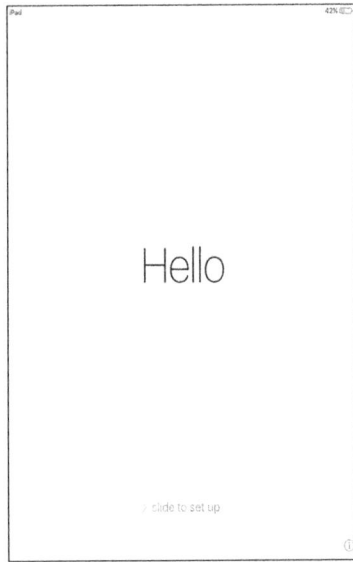

Select Language, scroll down and Select Country or Region.

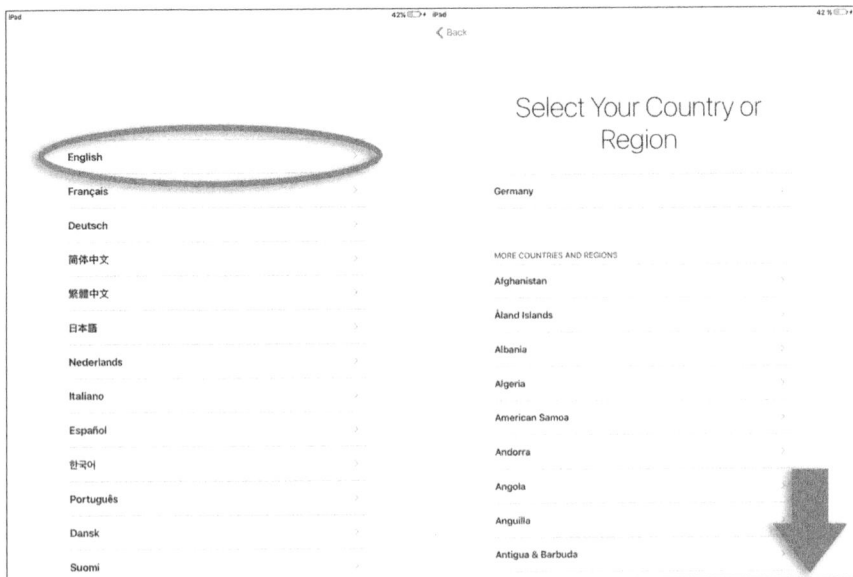

Tap 'set up manually' at the bottom of the screen.

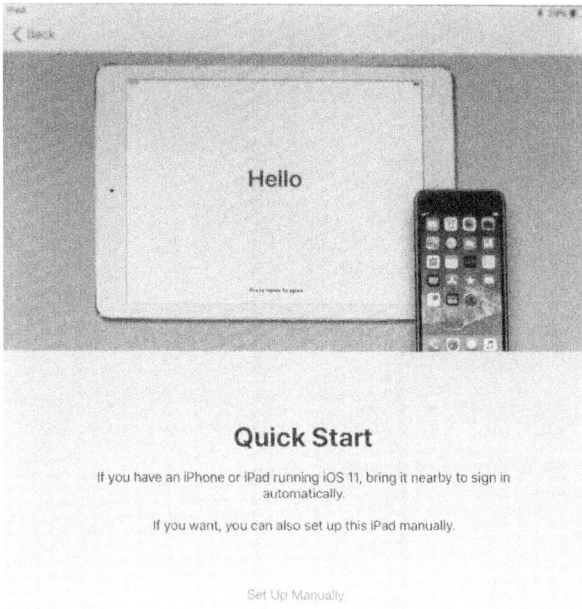

Tap on the name of your WiFi Network. Enter your WiFi password or network key when prompted.

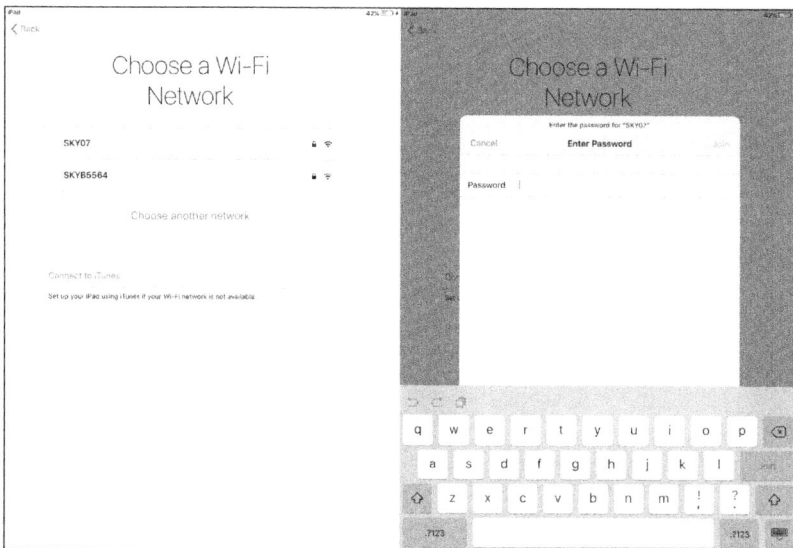

Tap 'Enable Location Services'. The location services allow your iPhone to determine your current physical location. Some apps require this; maps and other apps that provide local information.

Enter a passcode and set up touch ID if you have it. This is used to lock your iPhone and you will be prompted for this code when you open your iPhone from the lock screen.

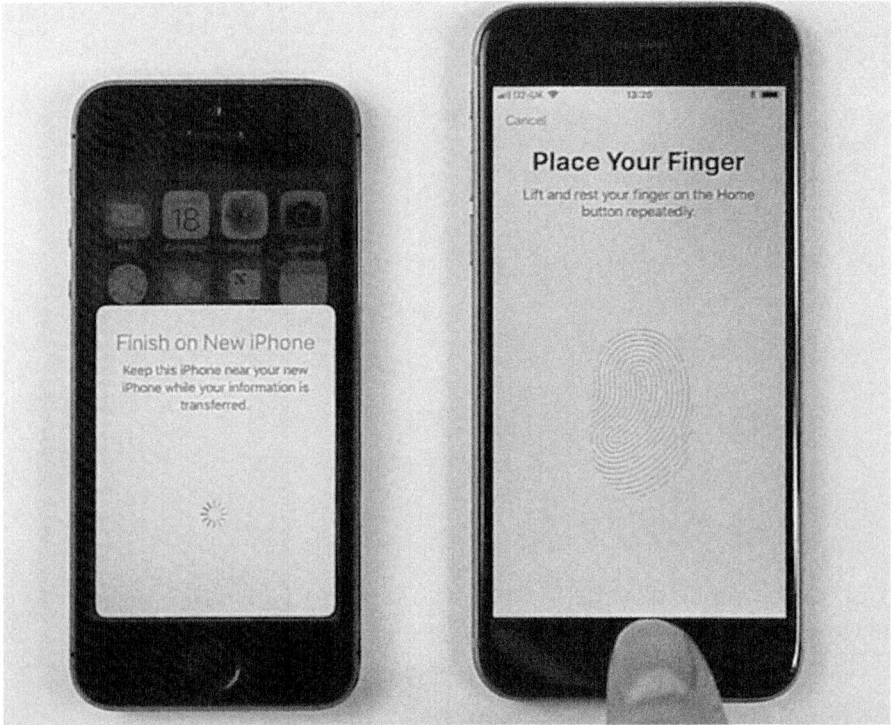

For touch ID, scan the finger you are most likely to use to press the home button with. In most cases this is your thumb, so it makes sense to scan this finger. Follow the instructions on the screen.

You'll need to scan your finger a few times, so the system can account for different variations, as you wont always put your thumb on the pad in exactly the same position every time. Do what it says on the screen. When you're done, tap 'next'.

Tap 'set up as New iPhone'. This will create a clean iPhone. *If you have upgraded to a new iPhone, you can tap 'restore from iCloud backup' and select the latest backup. This will set up your iPhone using your previous settings and data.*

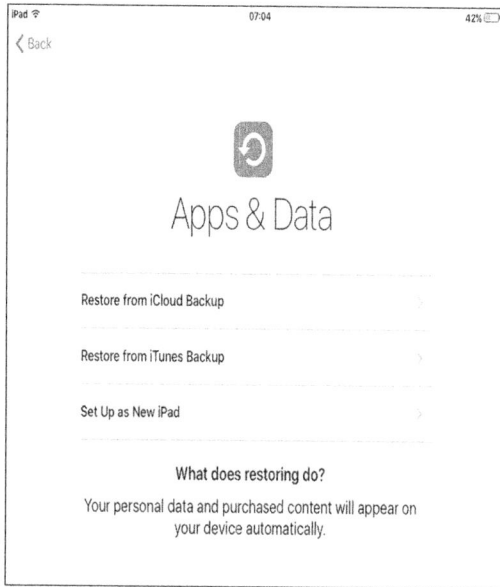

Tap sign in with your Apple ID. Enter your username and password.

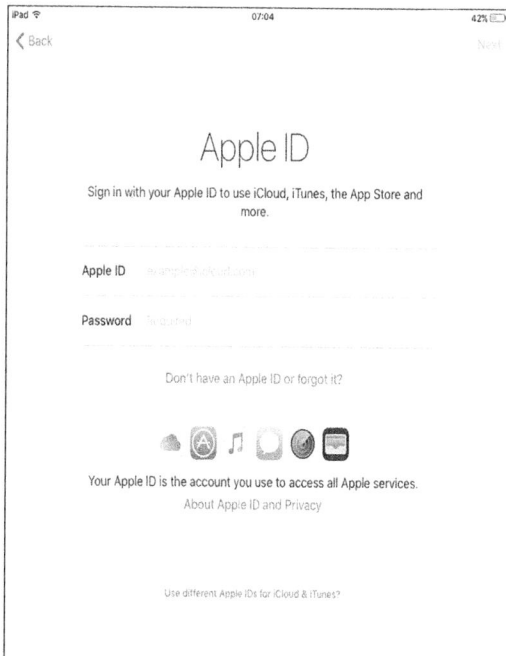

Hit 'continue' to set up Siri. Follow the instructions on the screen to initialise Siri.

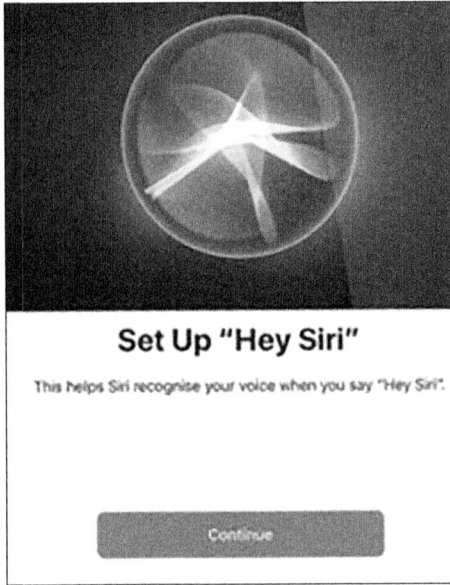

Tap "don't send" or "don't share" on 'Apple Diagnostics' and 'App Analytics'.

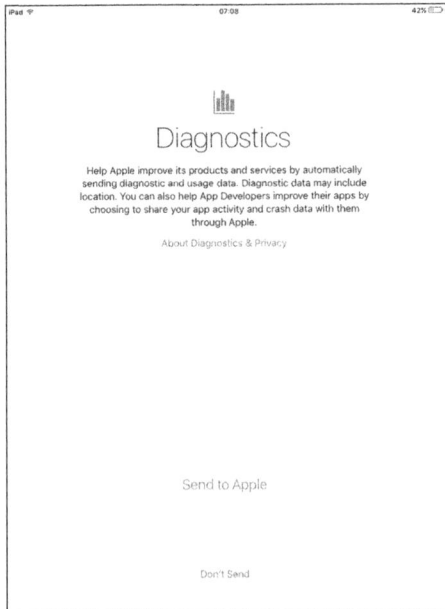

Tap OK to get started.

When you sign into your iPhone, you will see the home screen. Lets take a closer look at the screen. Along the top of the home screen there is a status bar that displays current networks (cellular or WiFi), current time, services such as bluetooth and battery life.

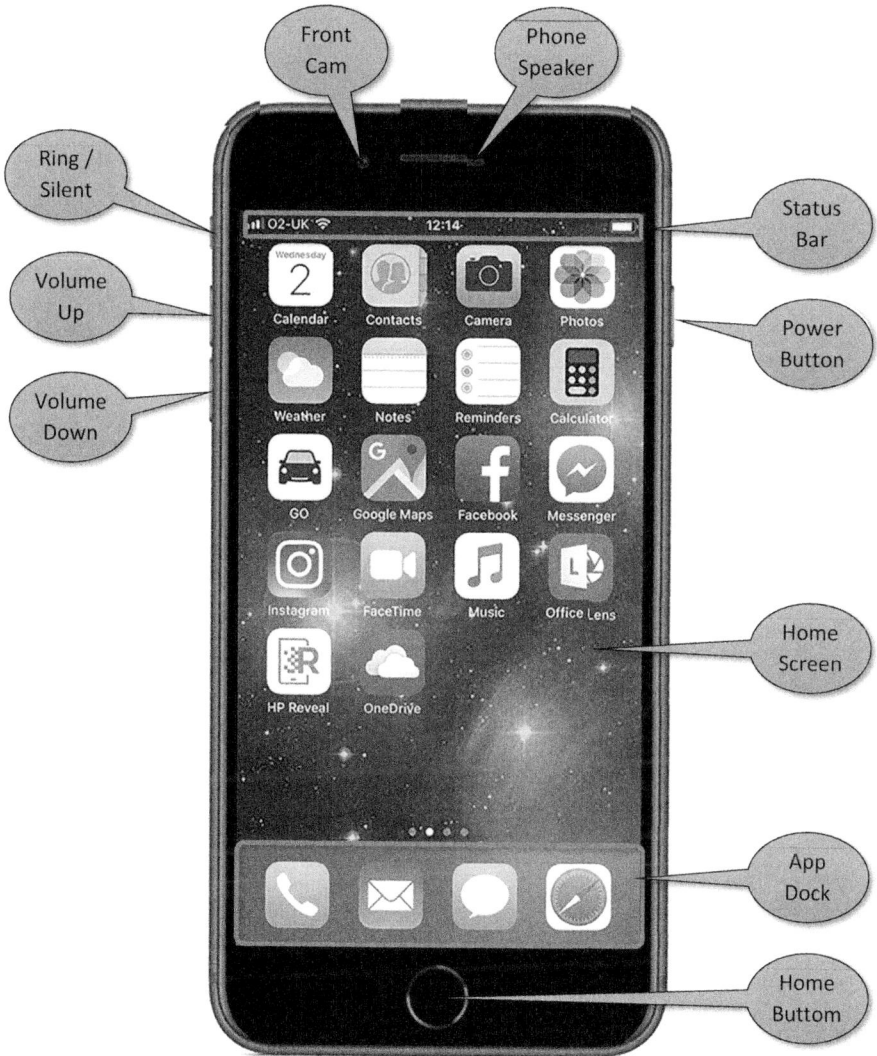

In the centre of the screen are icons representing apps that are currently installed on iPhone. Some are installed already but many can be downloaded from the app store.

Along the bottom of the screen is the Dock. At the bottom of the iPhone itself, we have the home button. Whenever you want to get back to the home screen from any app, just press this button.

## Chapter 2: Setting up Your iPhone

On the back you'll see your rear camera, and camera flash / flash light.

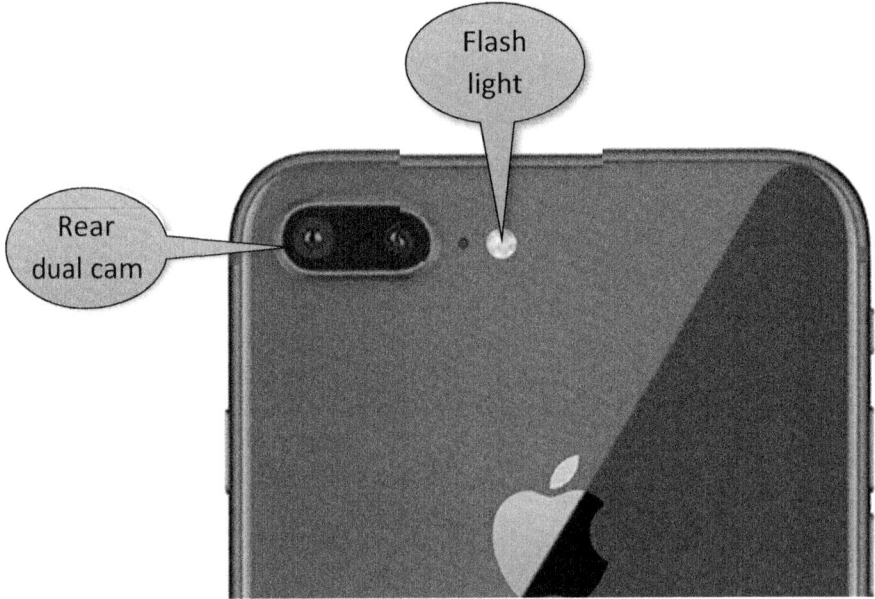

Along the bottom edge, you'll see your lightning dock connector. You can use this to charge your phone, connect to a computer, or connect your ear pods on iPhone 7 & 8. You also have two speakers either side for audio alerts, music and any call you put on speaker phone.

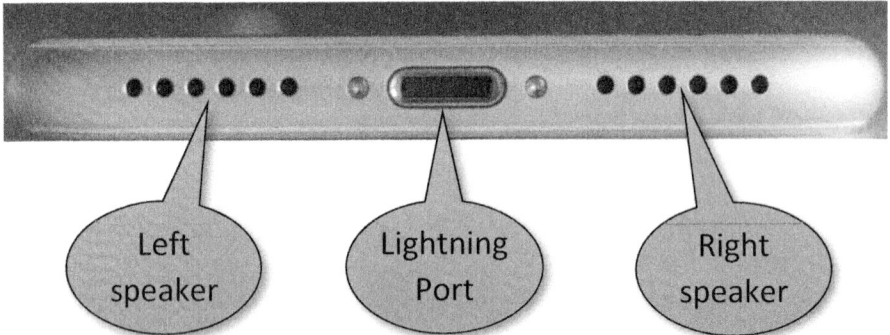

On the iPhone 5s & 6 you'll also have a 3.5mm headphone jack. This feature was dropped on the iPhone 7 and later.

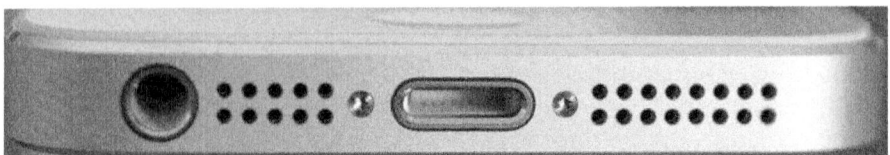

# Charging your iPhone's Battery

You can plug your iPhone directly into the charger to charge the battery, without having to go through a computer.

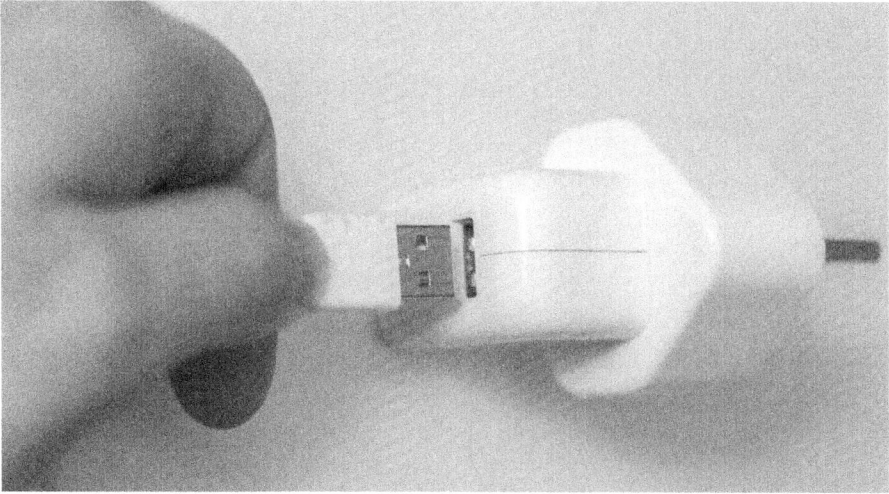

Plug the other end of the lightning cable into the port on the bottom of your iPhone.

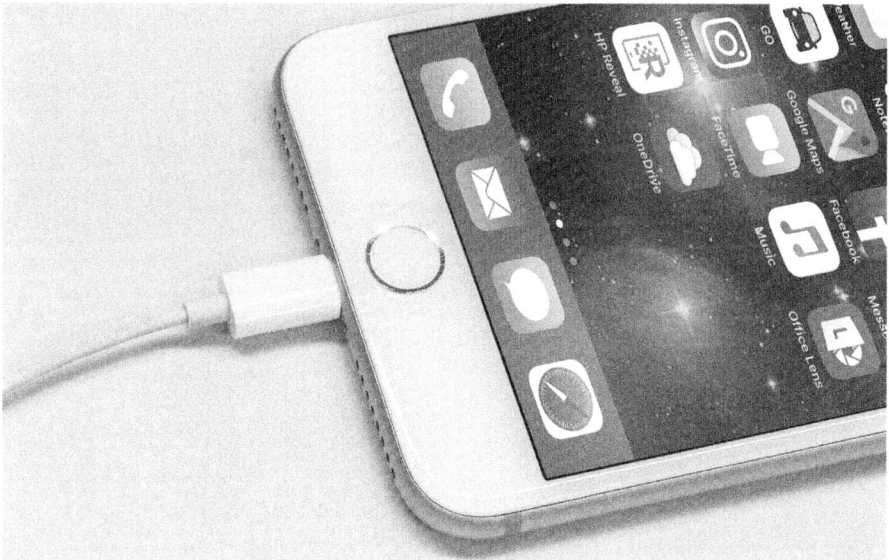

Your battery will take a few hours to charge. Best practice is not to let your battery deplete completely, charge it up when you still have about 20% charge left.

# Connecting your iPhone to a Mac/ PC

Your iPhone lightning cable connects to the port on the bottom of your iPhone.

The other end of the cable can be plugged into a PC or Mac to allow you to load on music, photos, apps etc.

# Using iTunes

To access iPhone from your computer you will need to have iTunes installed. If you are using a Mac, iTunes will already be installed. If you are on a PC then you need to download the software from Apple's website.

You can download it from

`www.apple.com/itunes`

On iTunes' website, click the download link on the top right.

iTunes.

Then on the next page remove the ticks from the two boxes shown below.

### Download iTunes

X   iTunes 11.3.1 for Mac OS X

☐ Send me iTunes updates, news, and special offers.

☐ Keep me up to date with Apple news, software updates, and the latest information on products and services.

Apple Customer Privacy Policy

**Email Address**

**Location**
◉ United Kingdom
○ Other

Why do we need this?

**Download Now** ⊙

If you want apple to send you lots of notifications via email, enter email address. Otherwise leave it blank.

Click the 'download now' button. Go to your downloads folder and double click the iTunes installer. It is usually called 'iTunes6464Setup'

**33**

## Chapter 2: Setting up Your iPhone

Once iTunes has installed, sign in with your Apple ID and password.

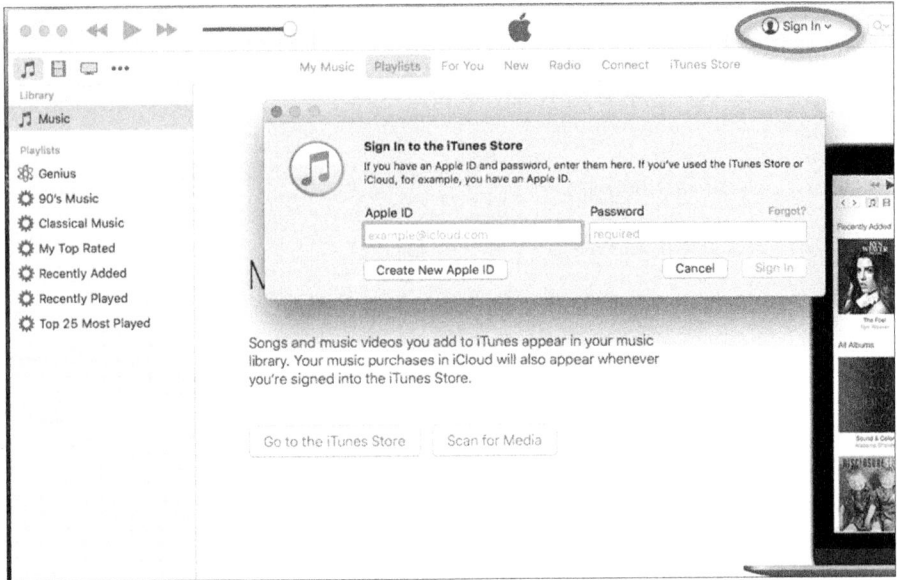

# Syncing your iPhone with your Mac/PC

Plug your iPhone into your computer, iTunes will take a few moments to recognise your device.

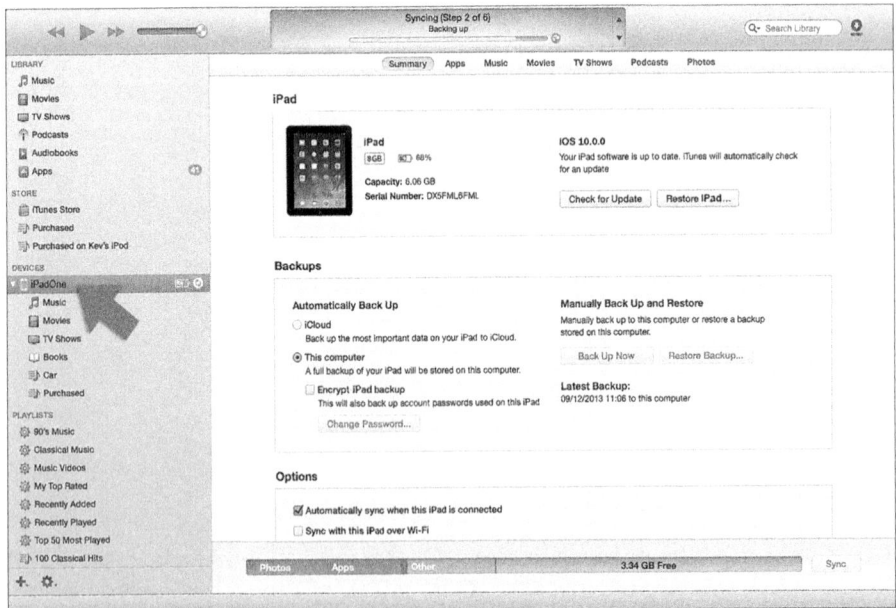

# Connecting to the Internet

With an iPhone, you can connect to the internet two ways: one is using WiFi and the other is using a cellular connection if you've inserted a SIM card. In this section, we'll take a look at connecting using WiFi

## WiFi

WiFi is often faster than cellular data networks, but may not be available in many locations.

To locate nearby WiFi networks, tap Settings on your home screen.

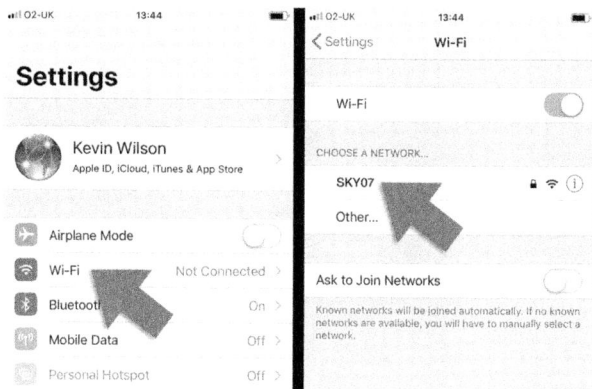

Tap WiFi, then tap the name of the network you want to join

Enter the WiFi password or network key.

Once you have done that tap Join.

# Chapter 2: Setting up Your iPhone

For your home WiFi, the network key or password, is usually printed on the back of your router.

The network name is sometimes called an SSID.

Use the same procedure if you are on a public hotspot such as in a cafe, library, hotel, airport and so on. You'll need to find the network key if they have one. Some are open networks and you can just connect.

When using public hotspots, keep in mind that most of them don't encrypt the data you send over the internet and aren't secure. So don't start checking your online banking account or shop online while using an unsecured connection, as anyone who is on the public WiFi hotspot can potentially gain access to anything you do.

If you're really concerned about security or use your devices on public hotspots for work, then you should consider a VPN or Virtual Private Network. A VPN encrypts all the data you send and receive over a network. There are a few good ones to choose from, some have a free option with a limited amount of data and others you pay a subscription.

Take a look at www.tunnelbear.com, windscribe.com & speedify.com

**36**

# Setting up Email Accounts

You can add all your email accounts to the Mail app, so you keep all your mail in one place. To do this, tap the settings app icon on your home screen.

Scroll down the list of settings until you see 'accounts & passwords'.

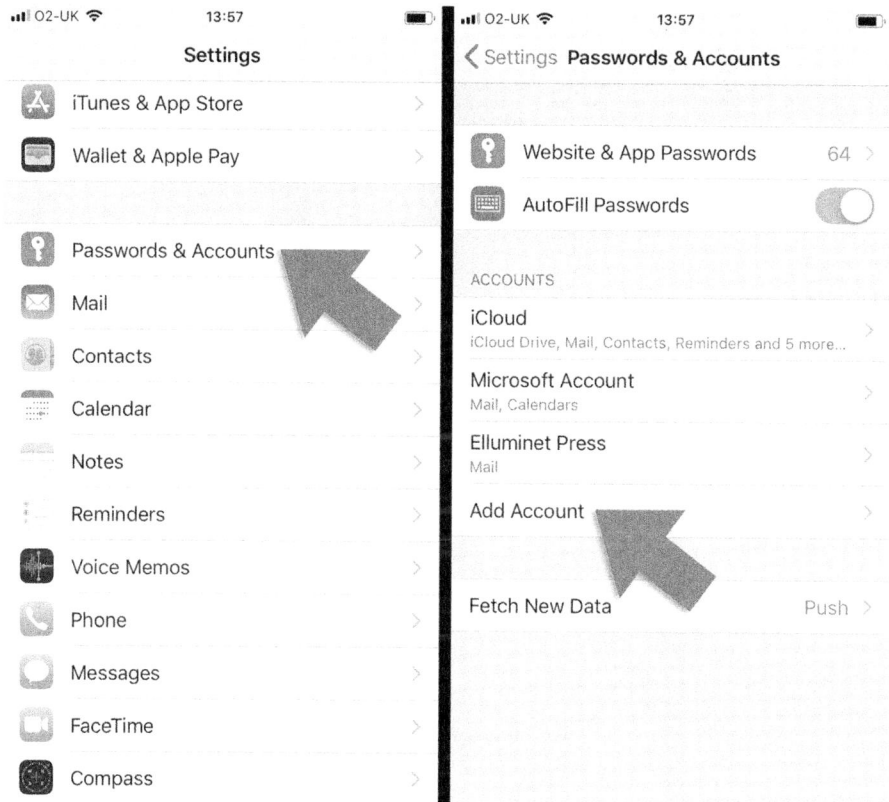

On the next screen tap 'add account'.

Select the type of account you want to add. If you have a Yahoo account, tap 'yahoo', if you have a Google/GMail account, tap 'google', or a Hotmail or Microsoft Account, tap 'outlook.com'.

In this example I am going to add a Microsoft Account. So I'd tap on 'outlook.com'.

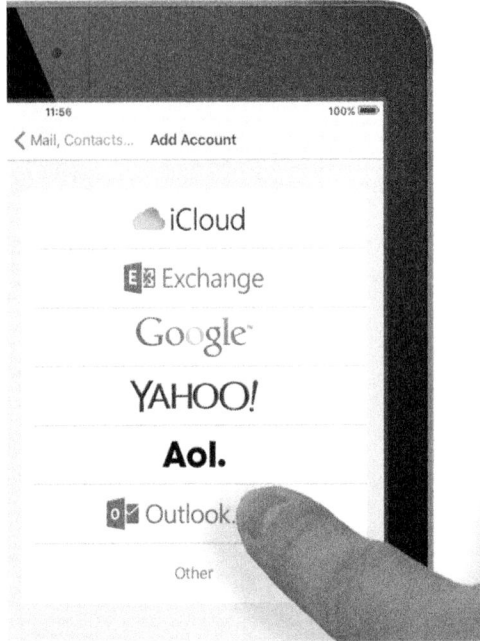

In the box that appears, enter your account email address, tap 'next', then your password.

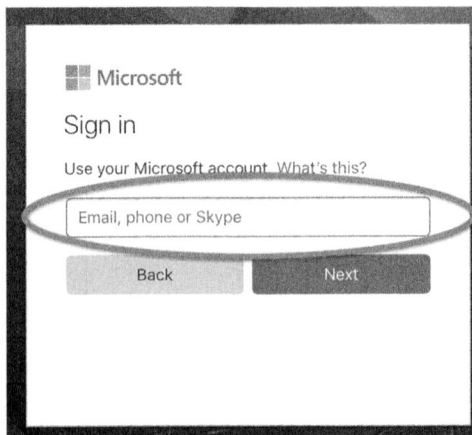

Tap 'next'.

Select 'yes' to the permission confirmation, to allow your iPhone to access your email account.

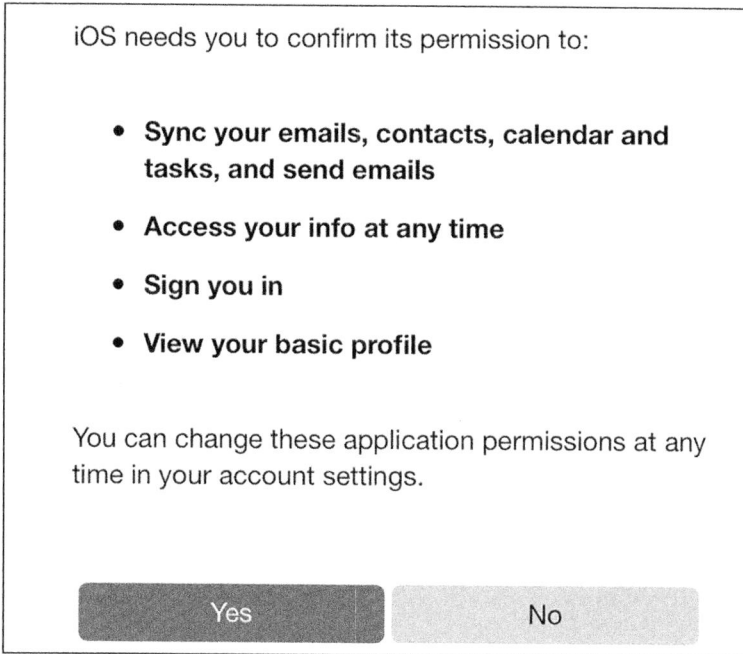

iOS needs you to confirm its permission to:

- **Sync your emails, contacts, calendar and tasks, and send emails**

- **Access your info at any time**

- **Sign you in**

- **View your basic profile**

You can change these application permissions at any time in your account settings.

Yes    No

Select what you want your iPhone to sync from the mail server. You can copy email, contacts, your calendar and any reminders onto your iPhone by turning all the toggle switches to green, as shown below.

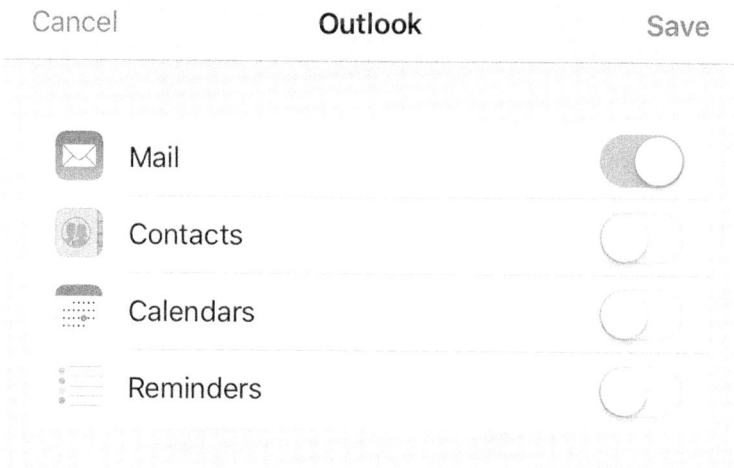

Cancel    **Outlook**    Save

Mail

Contacts

Calendars

Reminders

Tap 'Save'.

**39**

# Add Social Media Accounts

You can add your Facebook and Twitter accounts to your iPhone. The easiest way to do this is to go to the App Store and download the app for Facebook, Instagram, and the app for Twitter.

Tap on the App Store icon on your home screen and in the search field on the top right type 'facebook'.

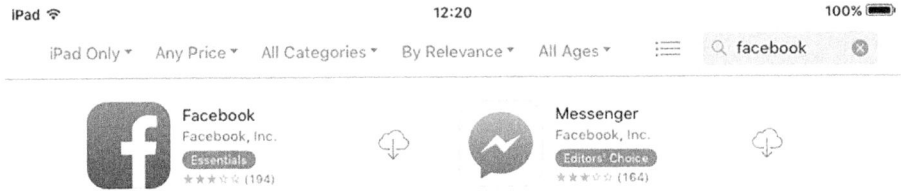

Tap 'get', next to the Facebook icon to download it. This icon might also look like a cloud if you have downloaded it before on another device, such as an iPod or iPhone.

Once it has download, hit your home button, then tap the Facebook icon on your home screen.

You can now sign in with your Facebook username and password.

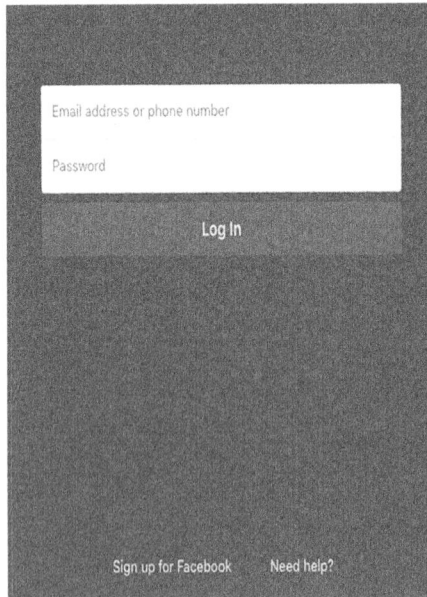

You can use the same procedure to setup Twitter, Instagram and any other social media account you have.

# Change your Wallpaper

You can set a photograph as a background on your lock screen and home screen.

You can do this from inside the Photos App.

Tap the photograph you want to set.

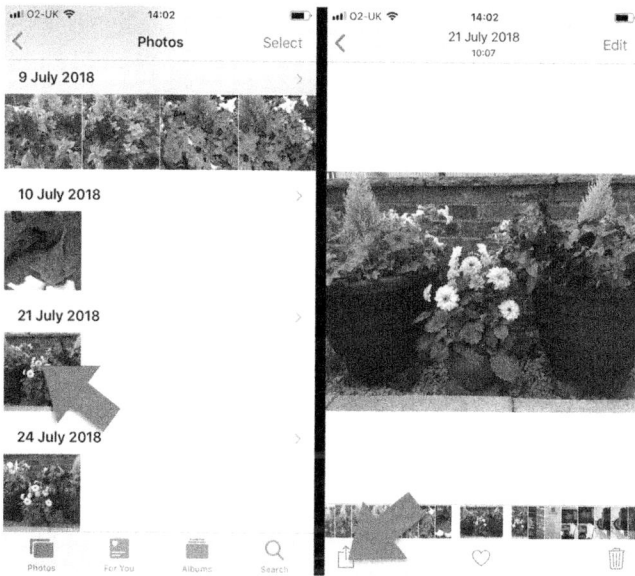

Tap the share icon on the top right of the screen. This will open up some sharing options along the bottom.

From the options that appear, select 'use as wallpaper'.

# Chapter 2: Setting up Your iPhone

Drag the photograph with your finger until it's in the desired position. You can also make the photograph smaller, by pinching the screen with your thumb and forefinger. Tap 'set' when you're done.

To set as both home and lock screen tap 'set both'. If you just want the photo on your home screen, tap 'set home screen'. Likewise for lock screen.

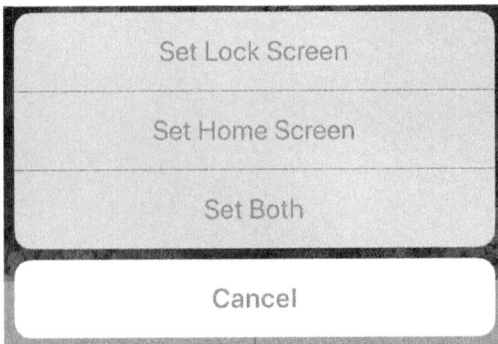

# Touch ID

Open your settings app, tap Touch ID & Passcode. Enter your passcode when prompted.

Tap 'add fingerprint'.

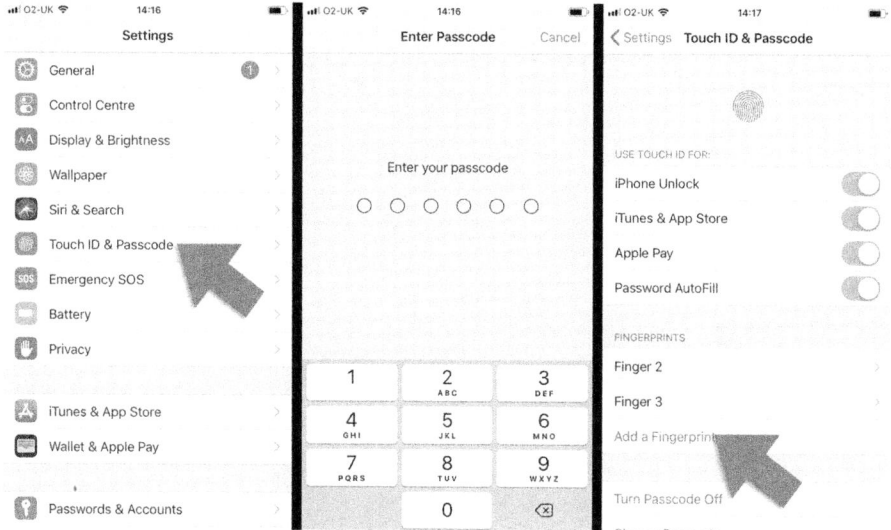

Scan the finger you are most likely to use to press the home button with. In most cases this is your thumb, so it makes sense to scan this finger. Follow the instructions on the screen.

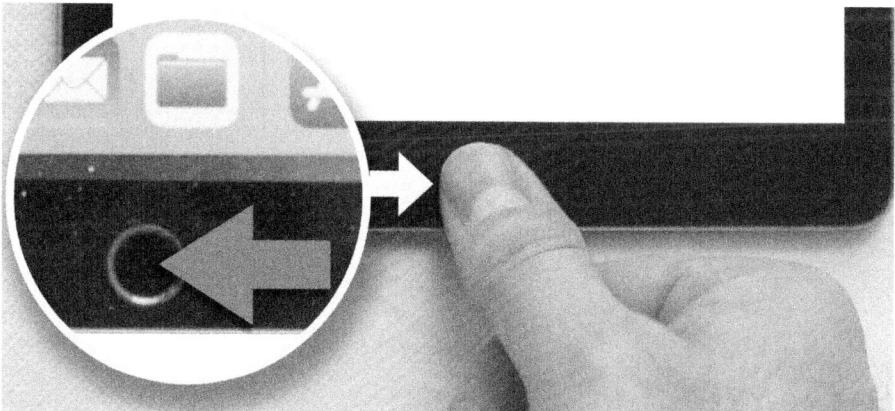

You'll need to scan your finger a few times, so the system can account for different variations, as you wont always put your thumb on the pad in exactly the same position every time. Do what it says on the screen. When you're done, tap 'next'.

**43**

# Find iPhone

This feature is quite useful if you have misplaced your iPhone or had it stolen.

## Setup

First you need to activate it on your phone. Tap the settings app, then select your account.

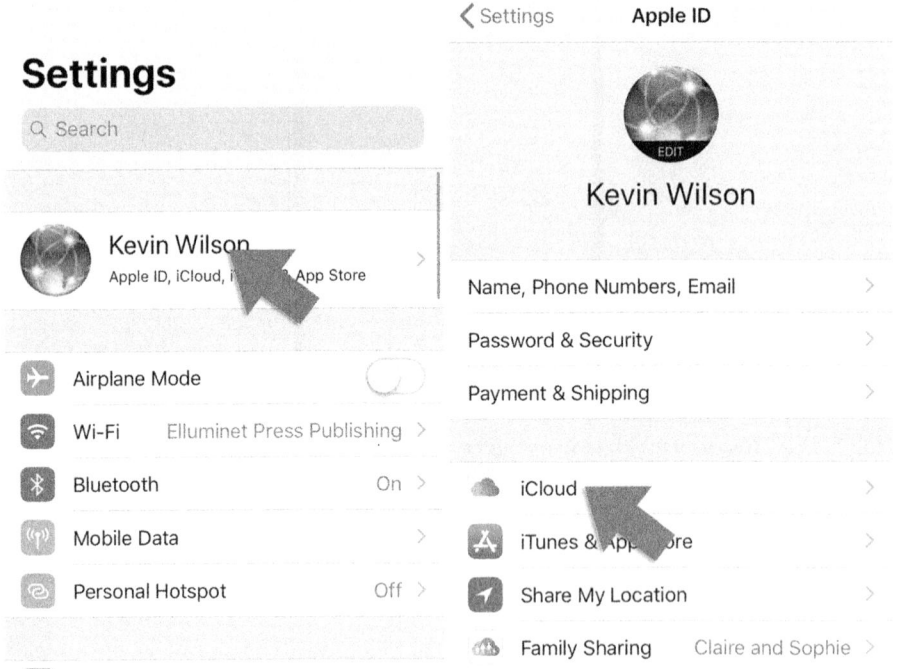

Scroll down to 'find my iPhone'

Switch the slider to 'on'.

Also make sure location services is turned on. To do this go back to the settings home page and select 'privacy'. Tap 'location services', and turn the slider to 'on'.

**44**

# Locating & Taking Action

On any device - iPad, Mac or PC, open your web browser and navigate to:

www.icloud.com

Sign in with your Apple ID. Select 'find iPhone' from the iCloud control panel.

You can locate your phone. Select the name of your device from the drop down menu in the top middle of the screen.

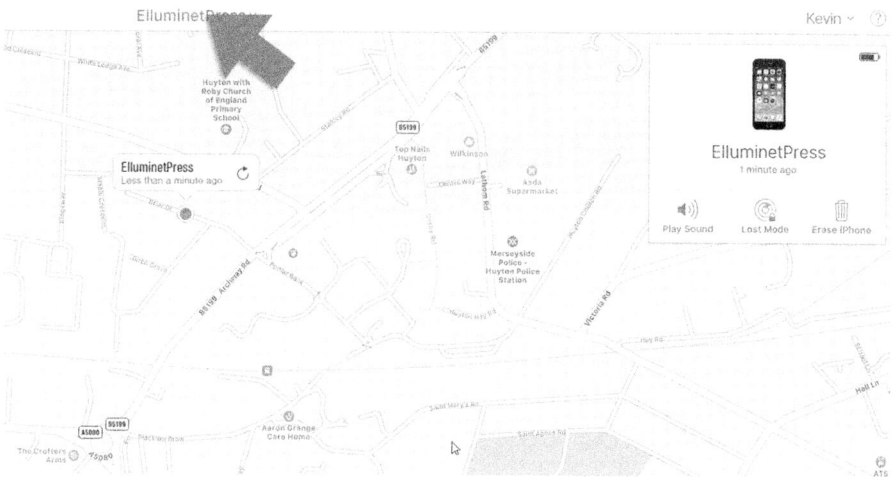

You'll see a green dot appear on the map. This is the current location of your device.

On the right hand side of the screen, you can take action. Here you can tap 'play sound' to play an annoying sound on your phone wherever it might be. This helps you to locate it, if you've lost it in your house somewhere, or annoy a thief if they have possession of it.

You can also put the phone into 'lost mode'. Lost mode allows you to remotely lock your device. You can also enter a message to display on the lock screen of the device.

Finally you can erase your phone completely. To remove any personal data that is stored on your phone.

# Pairing Bluetooth Devices

You can pair bluetooth keyboards, headphones, and bluetooth capable hardware in some cars.

To pair a device, first put the device into pairing mode. You'll need to refer to the device's instructions to find specific details on how to do this. On most devices, press and hold the pairing button until the status light starts flashing. This means the device is ready to be paired with your iPhone.

On your iPhone, open the settings app. From the settings app, select 'bluetooth'.

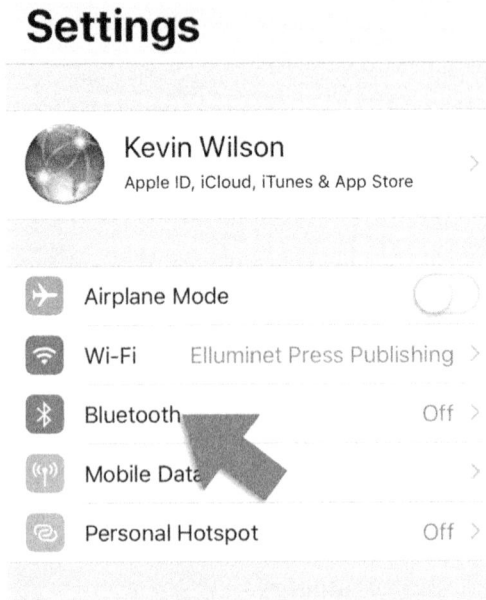

# Settings

Kevin Wilson
Apple ID, iCloud, iTunes & App Store >

Airplane Mode

Wi-Fi      Elluminet Press Publishing >

Bluetooth                          Off >

Mobile Data                          >

Personal Hotspot                 Off >

Turn it on, if it isn't already.

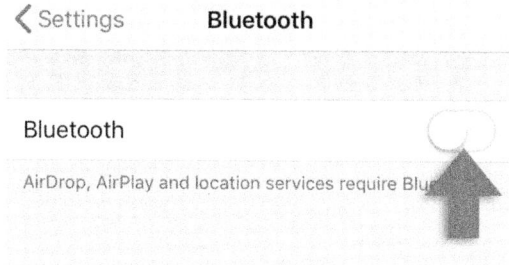

Your iPhone will scan for devices nearby. You'll need to give it a few seconds to work. Any devices found will be listed. Tap on the device in the list to pair it.

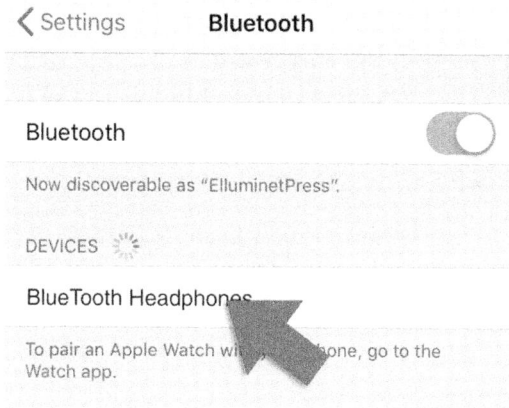

Some devices require a PIN code, enter it if prompted. Refer to the device's instructions to find out what the PIN code is. On most devices the default PIN is 0000, 1111 or 1234, but not always.

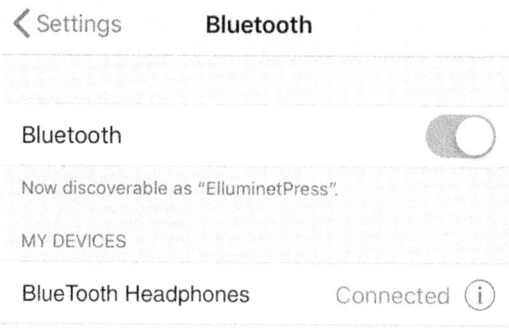

To remove a device, tap the 'i' info icon, then tap 'forget this device'.

# Getting Around Your iPhone

The iPhone runs Apple's own operating system called iOS. The latest version of iOS is currently version 12.

iPhones have touch screens allowing you to interact with the apps on the screen using touch gestures.

Your iPhone has a lot of features, we'll take a look at them in this chapter.

Lets begin by having a look at some of the iPhone models on the market and the new features of iPhone.

# Touch Gestures

Gestures, sometimes called multi-touch gestures, are what you'll use to interact with the touch screen on iPhone.

## Tap

Tap your index finger on an icon or to select something on the screen. For example, you can tap on an app icon, a link in safari, or even a song you want to download.

You can also tap and hold your finger on the screen to access other options that might be available (this is like right-clicking the mouse on your computer).

## Drag

Tap on the screen and without lifting your finger off the glass, slide your finger around the screen to drag up and down, left or right, and any other direction on the screen.

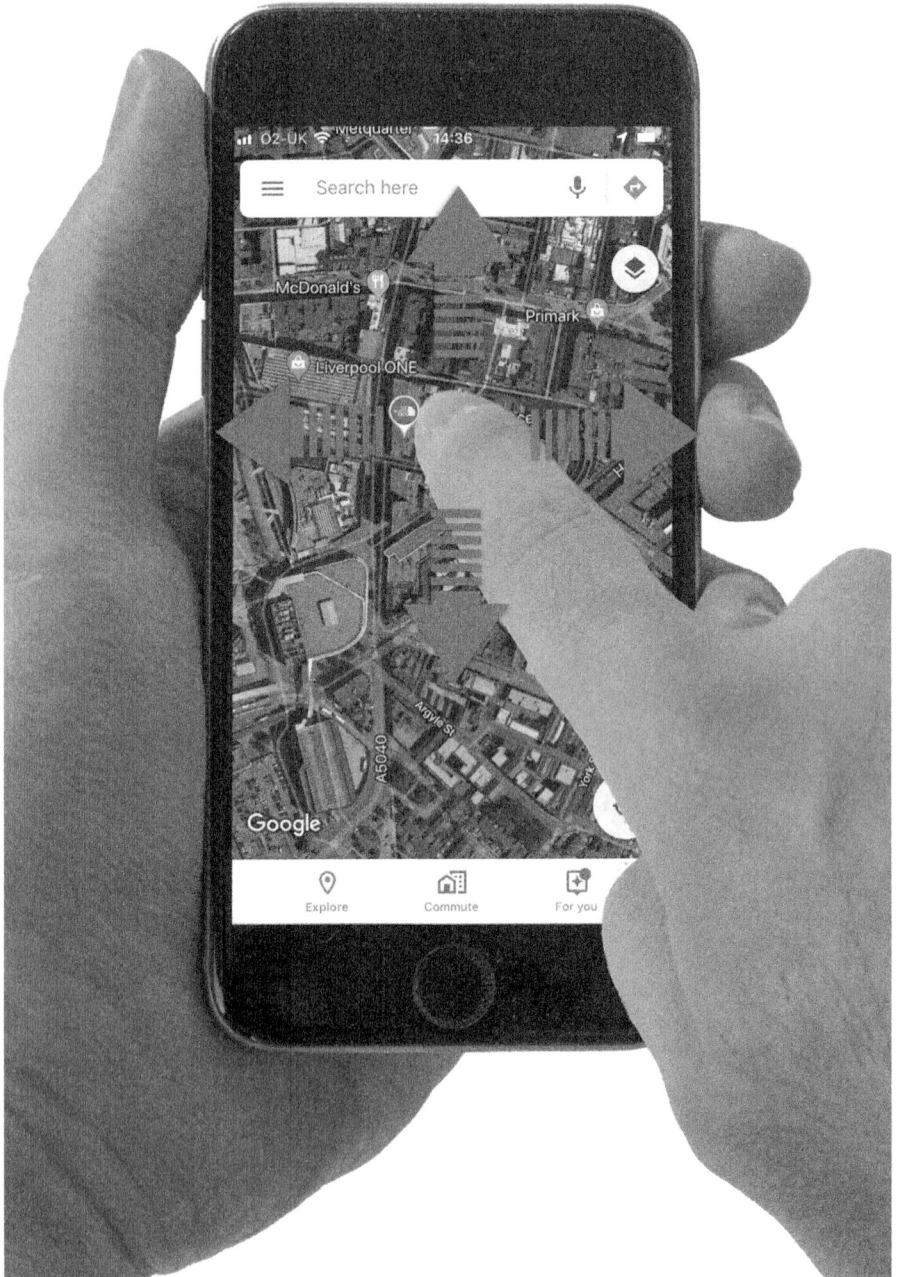

## Pinch & Spread

Hold your index finger and thumb on the area you want to zoom in or out on, then pinch the screen to zoom out and spread to zoom in.

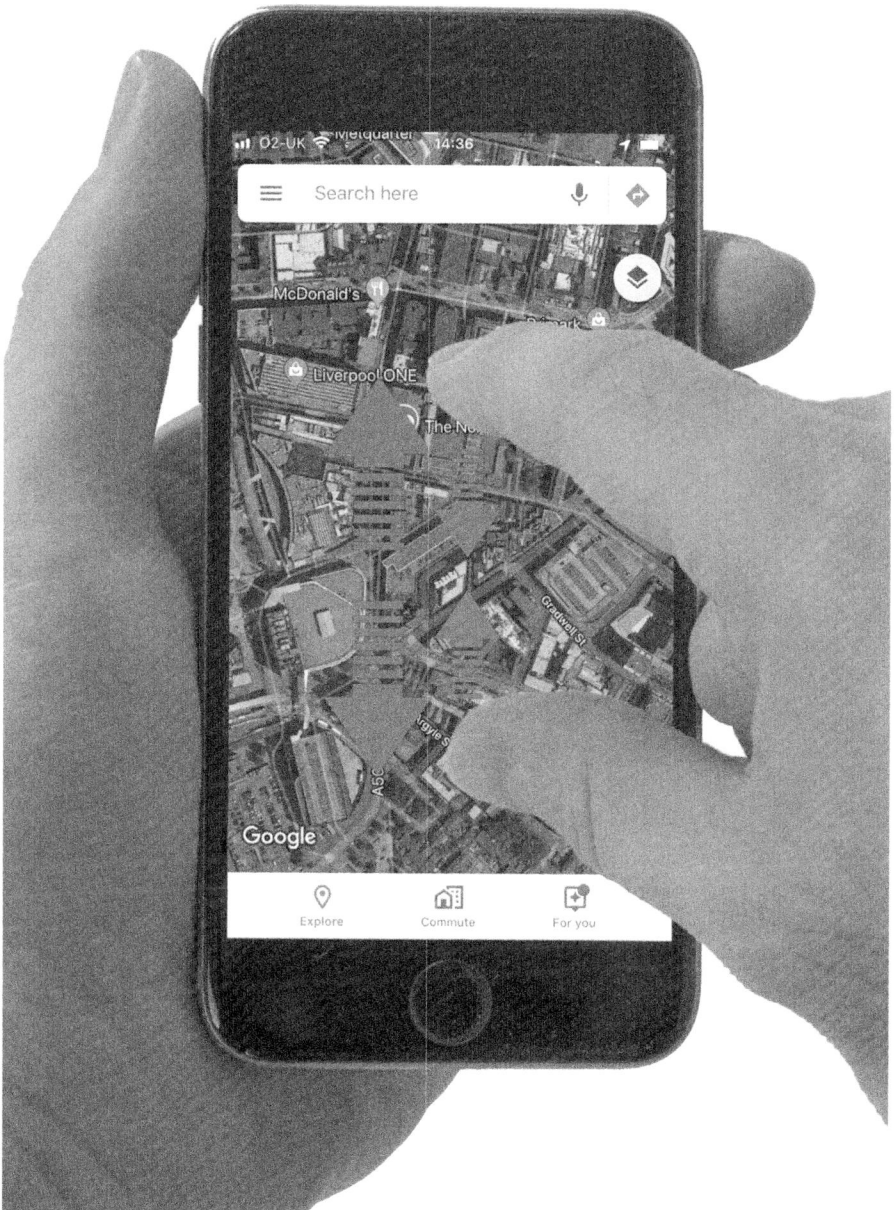

Spread is shown in the illustration above with the large red arrow, pinch is shown with the small red arrow.

## Swipe

This allows you to flip through photos, pages in an e-book, pages on the home screen. You swipe across the screen almost like striking a match. You can swipe up and down.

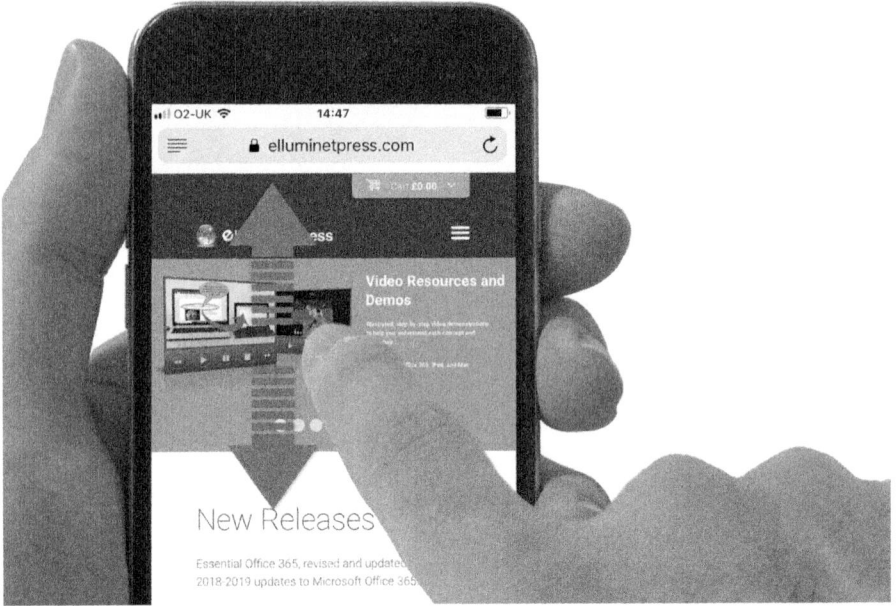

Or you can swipe left and right.

# Home Button

While using your iPhone, press the home button once to get back to your home screen, where you can select your icons to launch apps.

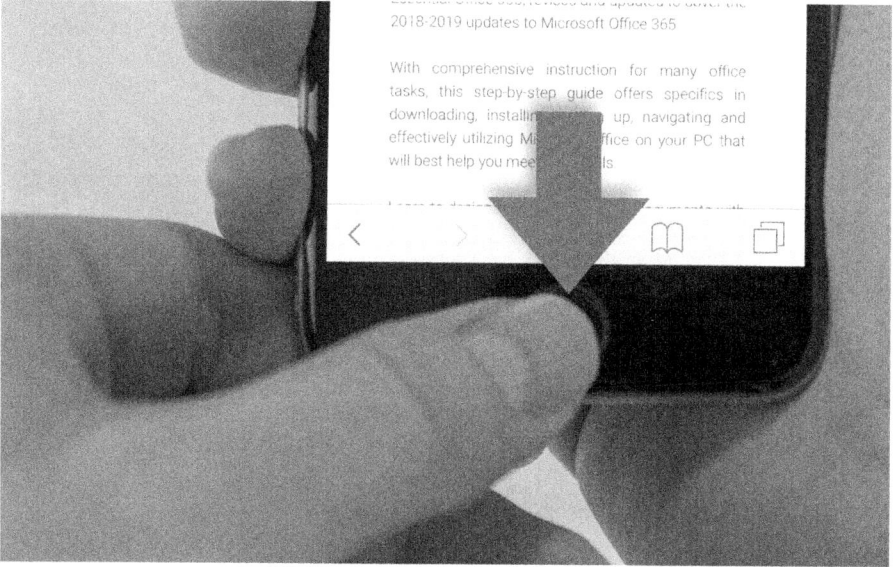

Double press your home button - that is pressing twice in quick succession - to bring up your multitasking app switcher, where you can view all your running apps, switch to a running app, or close apps.

## 3D Touch

3D touch is only included in the iPhone 6s and later. We're all used to tapping on icons to start different apps or to select options and so on. 3D touch adds a new method called a press. To press on an icon means to push it, applying a bit of pressure, as if you are pressing a button.

You can now press on the icons on your home screen to quickly access some basic features, without opening the app. For example, to take a quick selfie, press on the camera icon, and from the drop down, tap 'take selfie'.

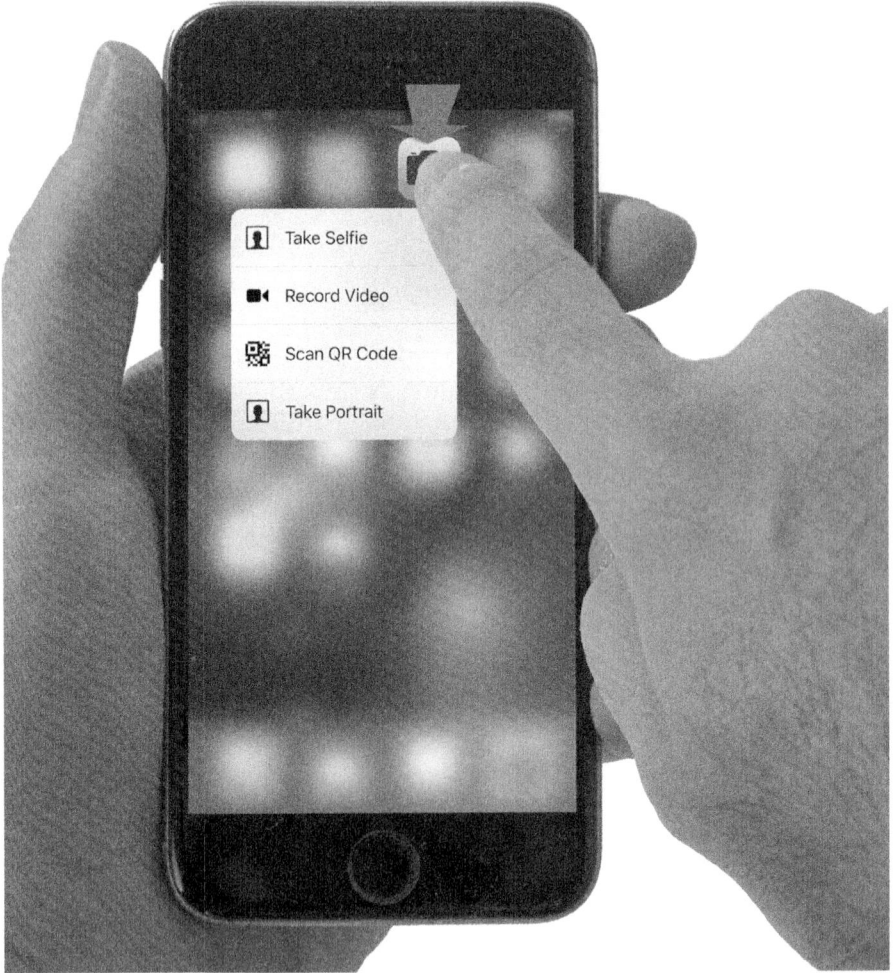

You can do this with any app on the home screen. These are called quick actions.

Another feature is called 'peek and pop'. If you are, for example, checking through your emails, you can press and hold on a message in your inbox to quickly preview the message.

A quick preview will open up. This is called 'peek'. From here, you can swipe up with your finger to reply without opening the email.

To open the email fully, press down again. This is called 'pop'. To dismiss the message, lift your finger off the screen.

You can use these features, on maps, photos, messages and so on. Give it a try and see what it does.

# Multitasking

iPhones run an operating system called iOS. iOS is a multitasking operating system. This means that you can run more than one app at the same time. Open apps that are not currently on your screen will be running in the background. To quickly see what apps are running, press your home button twice, the app thumbnail icons appear.

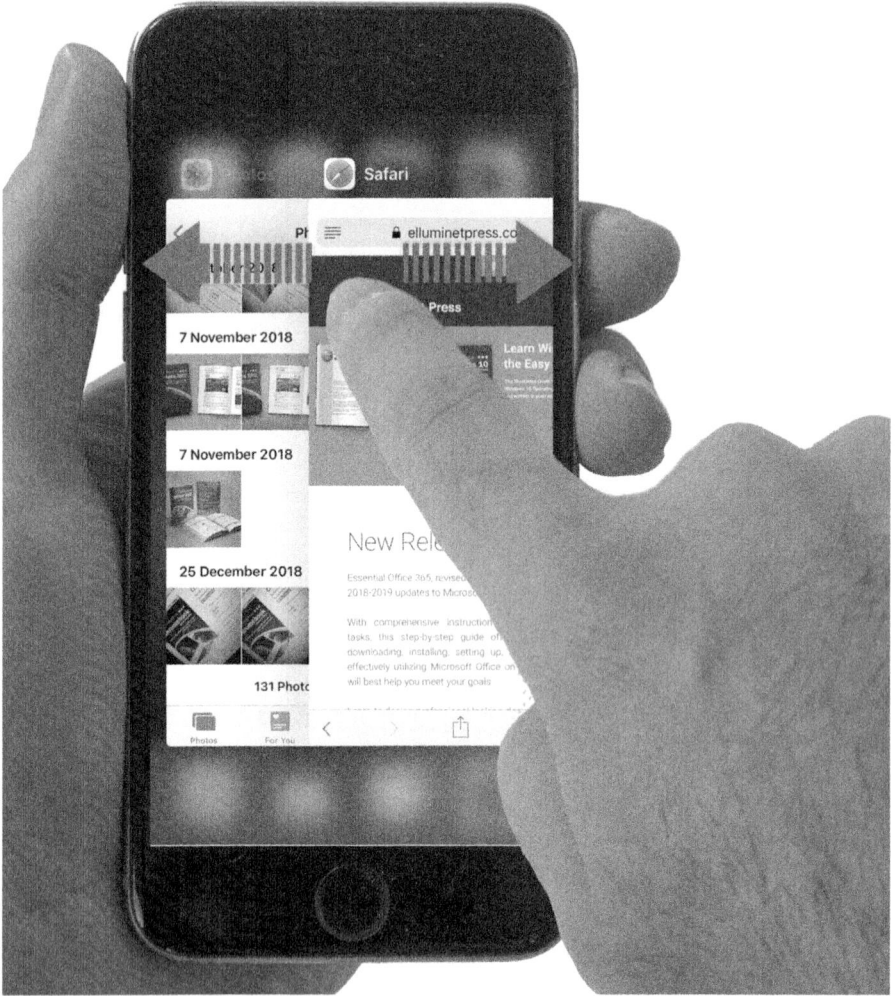

After using your iPhone, you will find that there are a lot of apps running, this can severely affect the performance of your iPhone and drain your battery more quickly.

Swipe left and right across the screen to browse through the apps that are currently running.

To close apps, press your home button twice, then swipe your finger upwards on the app you want to close, as illustrated below.

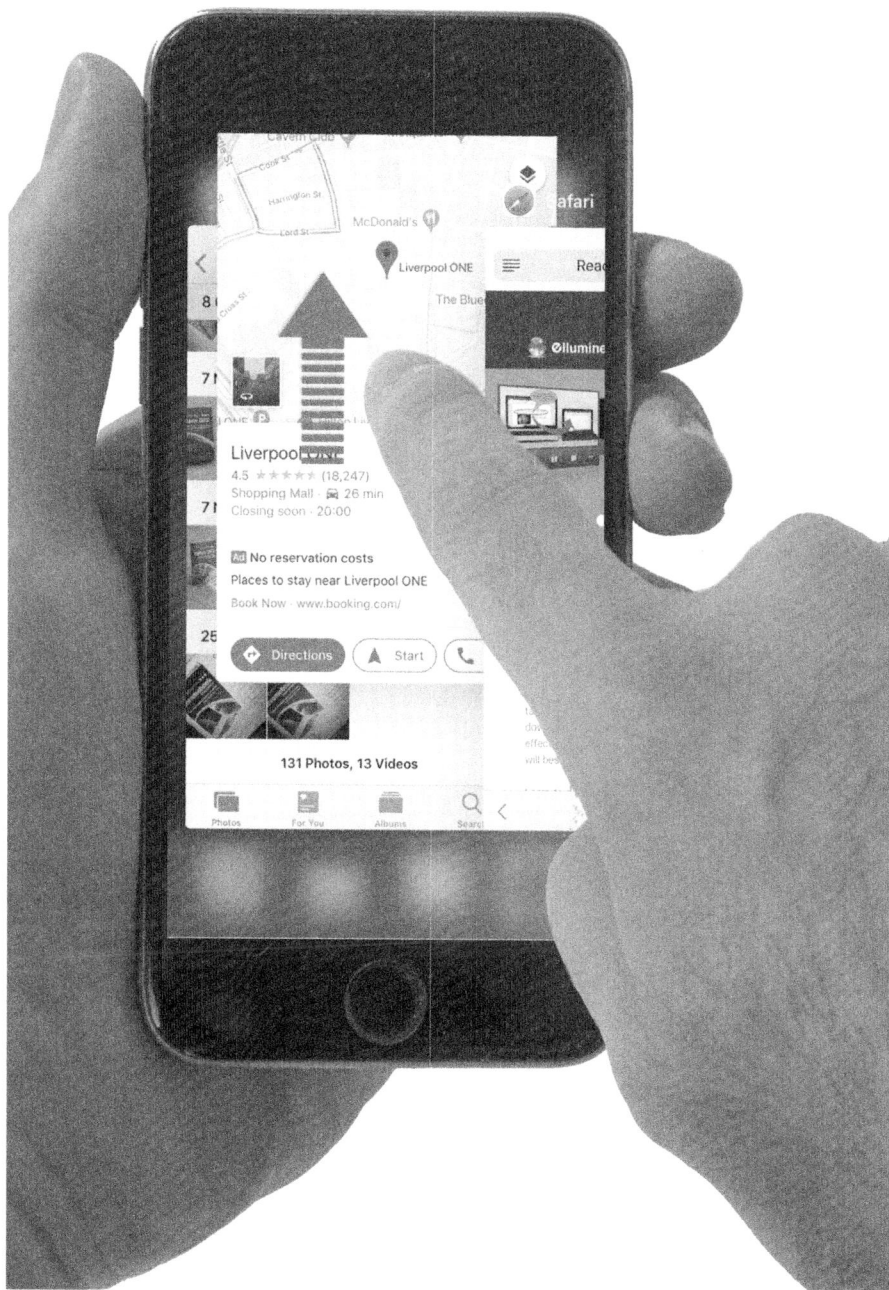

This will close the app. Do this on all the apps you want to close.

You can also use this technique to switch between apps. Press your home button twice, then swipe your finger left or right to browse through the apps.

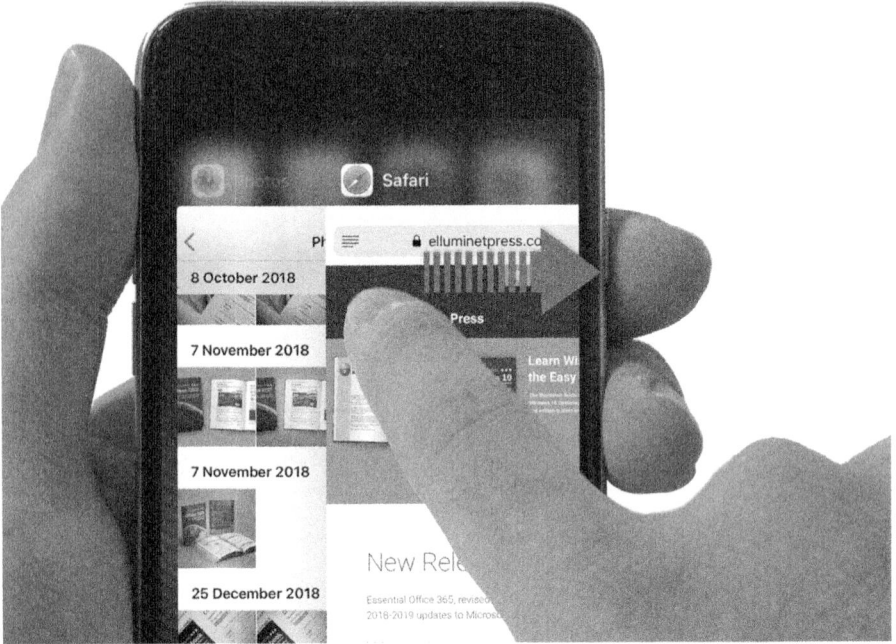

Tap on the app you want to switch to.

# Control Centre

The control centre is your control hub where you can adjust screen brightness, volume, access WiFi/bluetooth controls, access your camera, and other controls.

To open control centre, swipe upward from the bottom edge of your screen.

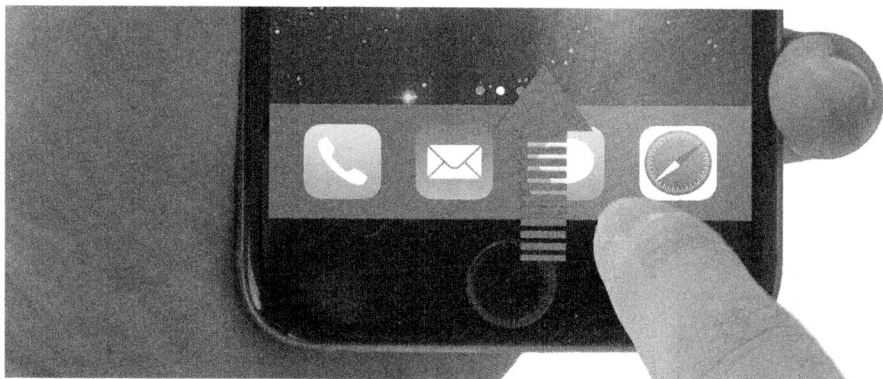

Here you can control the volume of playing music, turn on and off WiFi, blue-tooth, access your camera, set the orientation lock to stop the screen shifting - this can be useful if you are reading a book etc.

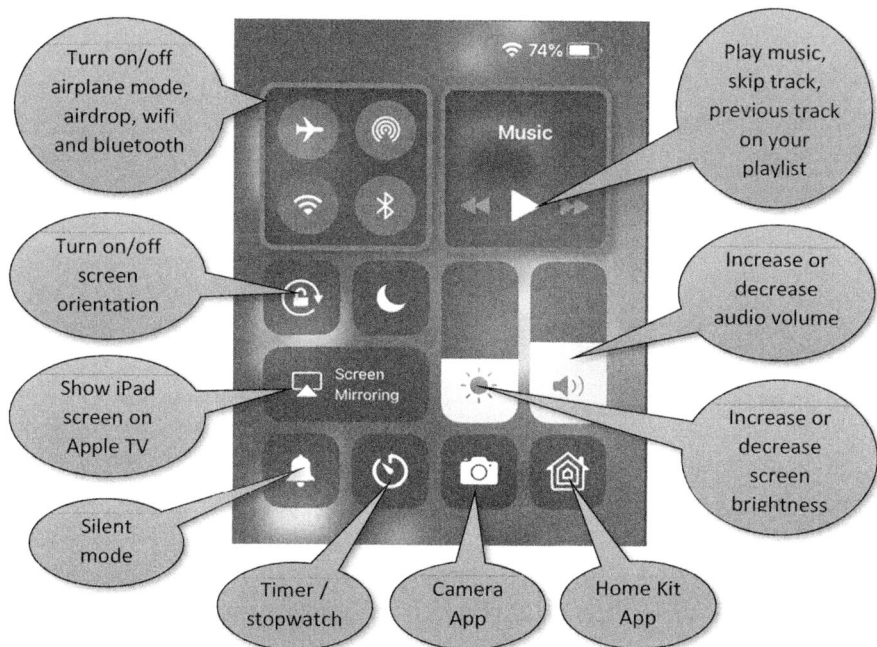

# Customising Control Centre

To customise the controls, first open your settings app. Tap 'Control Centre' then tap 'Customise Controls'.

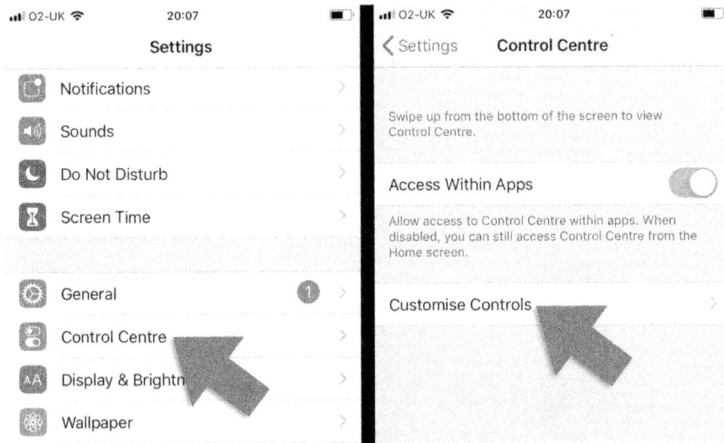

The settings for this are divided into two sections. The top section labelled 'include', shows apps and icons that will appear on the bottom row of the control centre. The bottom section labelled 'more controls', shows apps and features that are available but are not enabled.

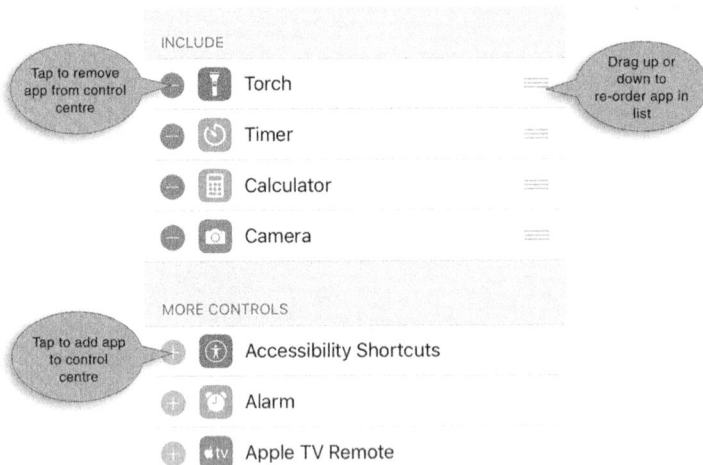

To remove apps or icons from control centre, tap the red '-' next to the app name in the top section.

To add apps or icons, tap the green '+'next to the app in the bottom section. The enabled app or icon will jump to the top section, meaning it is now enabled and will show up on the control centre.

# Notifications & Lock Screen

Swipe your finger downwards from the top edge of the screen, to invoke the lock screen & notifications.

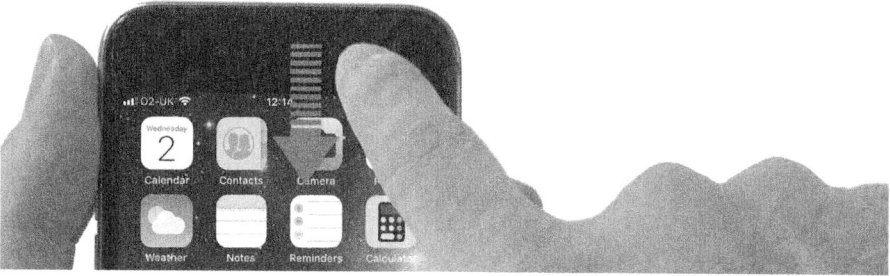

Notifications such as email, sms/text messages or reminders can also appear on the lock screen.

Tap on one of the notifications to see more information. Swipe left over the notification to reveal the message options.

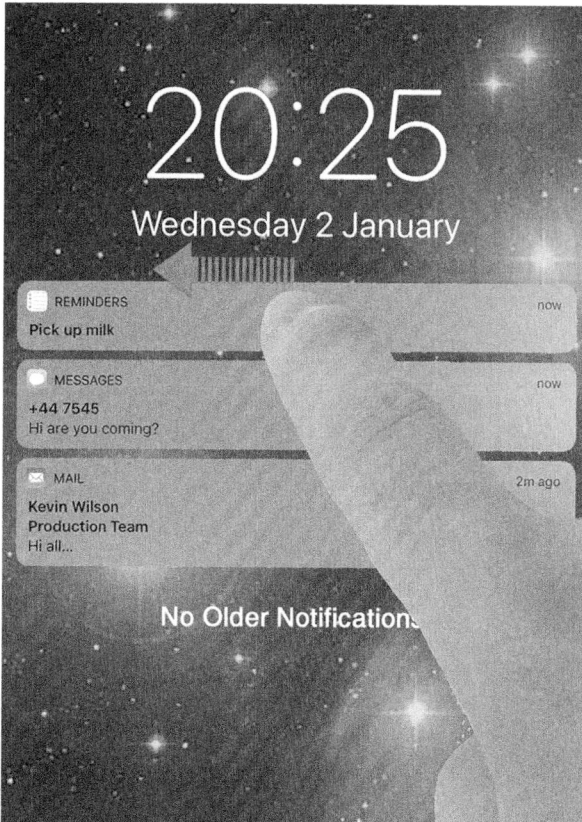

Tap 'view' to view the notification in full, tap 'clear' to remove the notification from your lock screen.

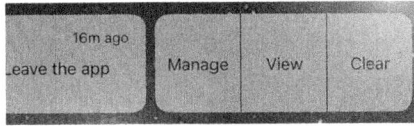

'Manage' allows you to change the notification settings for the app - eg you can turn off the notification for that particular app.

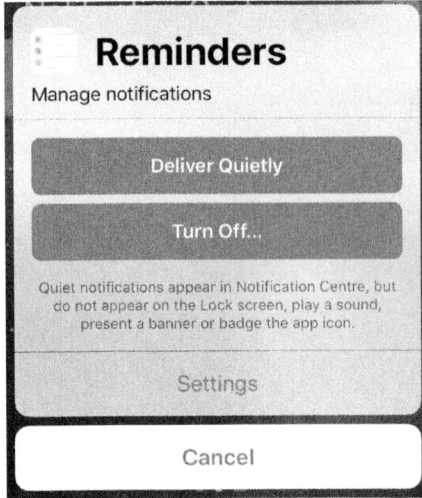

Tap settings and you can specify whether you want the notification to appear on lock screen & notification center, as well as what sound the notification makes when it pops up

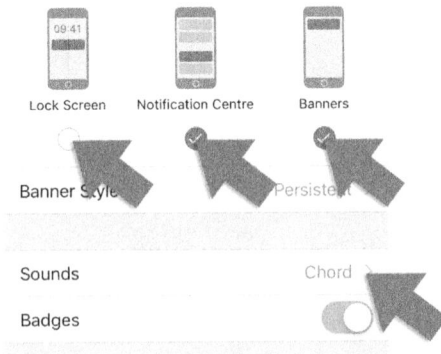

If you want the notifications to stay on your lock screen all the time, change 'banner style' to persistent. If you want the notification to popup, alert you, then disappear, change 'banner style' to temporary.

# Handoff

Handoff allows users to share documents, e-mails, and websites over WiFi to your other devices.

For example, if you're browsing the web with Safari on your Mac, you'll see a banner showing the app, along the bottom of your iPhone's app switcher. To open the app switcher, press the home button twice.

Your iPhone will allow you to pick up where you left off from the app you were using on your Mac. Tap the banner on the bottom of the screen to continue.

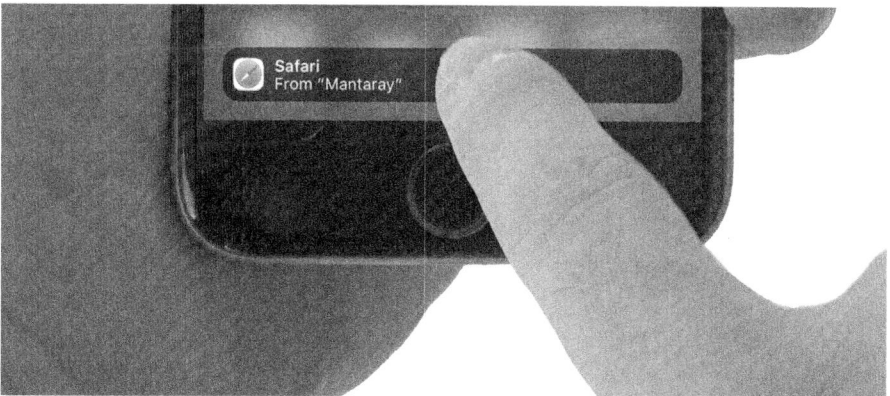

Sometimes the banner doesn't show up if your app switcher is empty - try opening an app if this happens.

# The On-screen Keyboard

Typing on an iPhone is easy, using the on-screen Multi-Touch keyboard. When you tap into any text field, email, or message, the on-screen keyboard will pop up on the bottom of the screen.

You can tap on the keys to type. Along the top you will see some predictive text suggestions that appear according to what you're typing in. If the correct word appears, you can quickly tap on the appropriate suggestion instead of typing in the whole word.

Predictive text suggestions – tap to use word

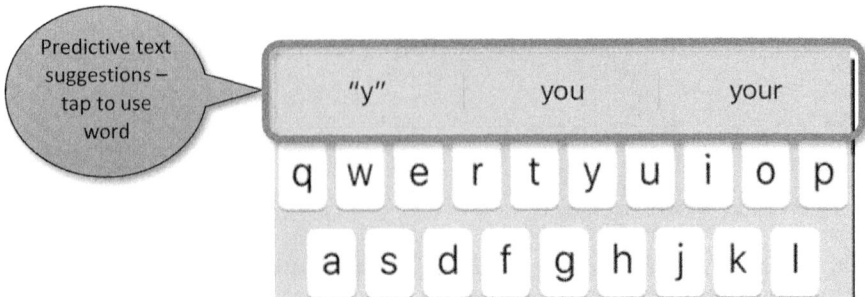

Some icons along the bottom worth noting are: the '123' key, this locks in numbers and symbols so you can quickly enter a series of numbers just by tapping the keys.

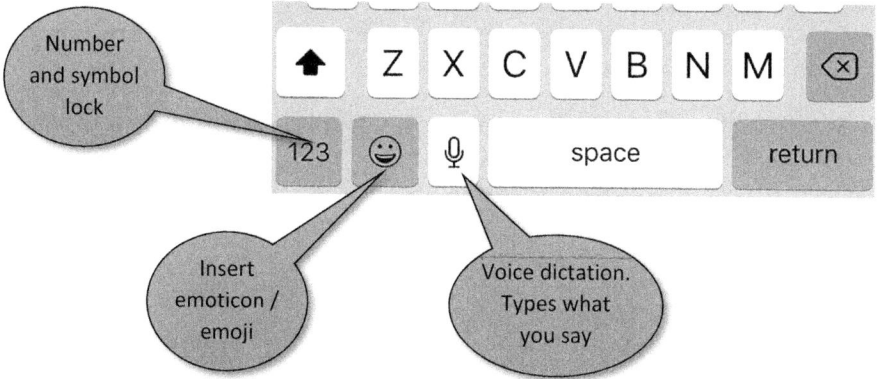

The 'smiley face' icon opens the emoji panel. These emojis or emoticons are small smiley faces, thumbs up, expressions, and small images that are intended to show how you're feeling in your messages. Just tap the smiley face icon and select an emoji from the options.

Tap on the categories along the bottom of the panel to find different types of emojis. Tap 'abc' on the bottom left to go back to the keyboard.

Finally, the 'microphone icon' is a dictation tool that transcribes or types out voice dictations. In other words, it types out what you say.

Useful, since typing on a small keyboard can be frustrating.

# Spotlight Search

Spotlight is integrated with a number of web services so that users can search using Wikipedia, Bing, or Google. Other services include: news, nearby places, suggested websites, movie show times, and content that is not already on the device from the iTunes Store

You can activate spotlight search by swiping your finger downwards from the centre of your home screen.

Once you have spotlight's search screen, you can type your search into the search field at the top of the screen.

Search also gives you some suggestions. These are listed below the search field and are the most commonly searched for entries for your search term.

In the example below, I am searching for anything relating to 'planet earth'.

Scroll down the list to see files, apps, websites, news articles, and suggested websites according to your search terms.

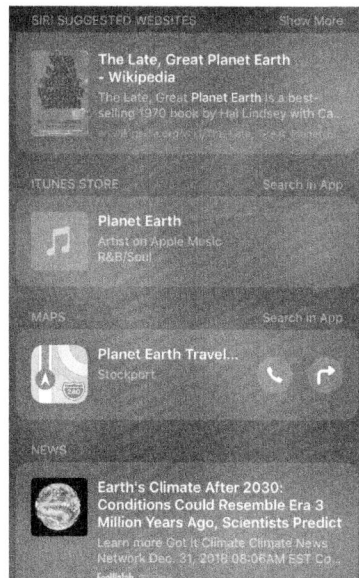

Tap on one of the items to open it up.

You can track flights. This is a useful feature, especially if you have arranged to pick up a friend or collect a colleague from the airport.

If you have the flight number, enter it into spotlight search. There might be more than one flight, so make sure you confirm the correct departure and arrival times.

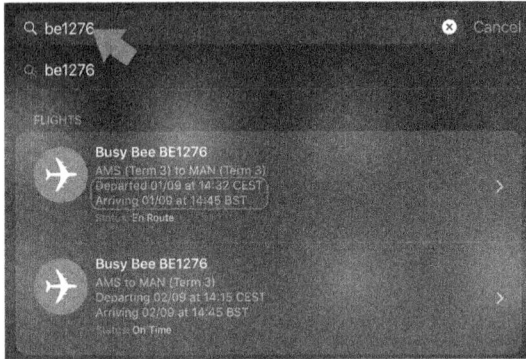

Tap on the flight to view tracking details. Here you'll see the current position of the aircraft on the map, which terminal the plane is arriving at and what time it is arriving - this plane is arriving at terminal 3 at 14:45.

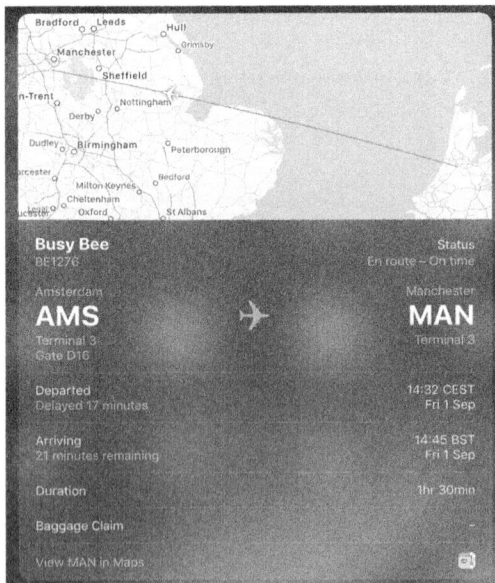

Underneath you'll also see baggage claim timings and how long passengers are expected to get through. At the bottom you can find driving directions to the airport using the maps app.

# Arranging Icons

To move an icon, tap and hold your finger on the icon - you'll notice a small x appear on each icon. Drag the icon across the screen.

The other icons on the screen will automatically move and rearrange themselves around the icon you're moving.

To move the icon onto another page, drag the icon to the right or left edge of the screen. Once the icon page turns, release your finger.

# Chapter 3: Getting around Your iPhone

You can get to the other pages by swiping your finger left and right to turn the page

The little dots, circled in the illustration above, show you what page you are on and how many pages of icons you have. This will vary depending on what apps you have installed.

You can identify what page you are on by looking at this icon, the one in bold is the page you are on.

# Removing Icons

This effectively deletes the app from your iPhone. To do this, tap and hold your finger on the app's icon you want to delete, until you see a small x appear on the top left of the icons.

Tap on the x on the top left of the icon to delete it. If you want to delete any other apps, tap the x on the icons. Press the home button when you're finished.

# Siri

Siri is an extremely useful feature. She allows you to talk to your iPhone, sometimes referred to as a virtual assistant; she can help you with all kinds of things. You can use Siri to send messages, schedule meetings, and search for nearby restaurants all without having to type a single letter.

## Using Siri

To use Siri, press and hold the Home button on your device until she appears. Then tell her what you need. You can also say 'Hey Siri'.

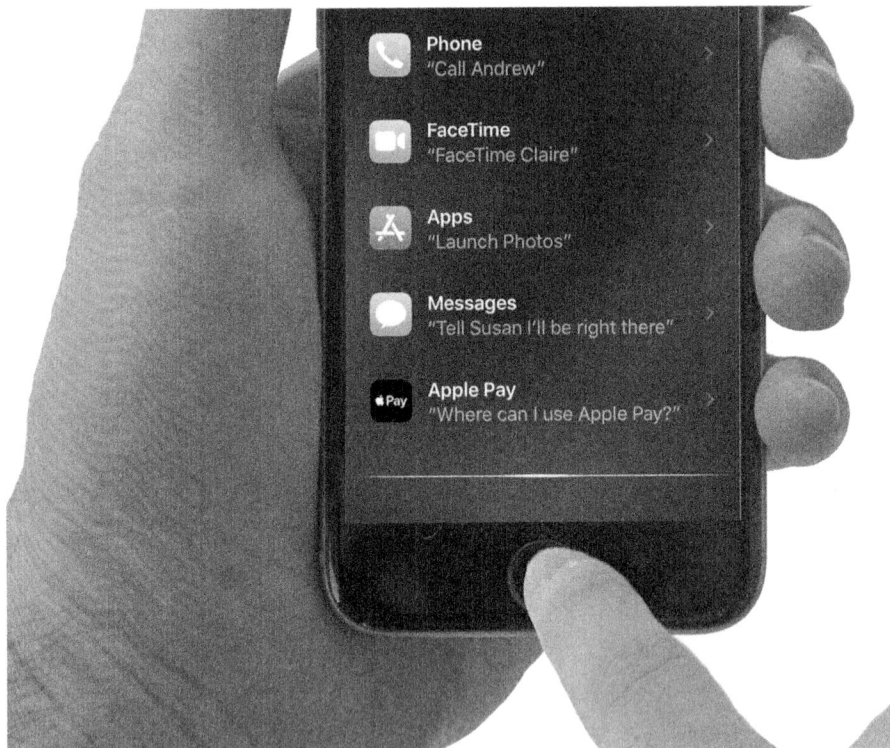

Try some of the following phrases...

*Try saying: "Hey Siri"*
*Try saying: "Send email to..." (pick a name from your contacts list)*
*Try saying: "What is the weather like tomorrow"*
*Try saying: "Find me a website on baking a cake"*
*Try saying: "Remind me to pick up milk on the way home"*
*Try saying: "Call..." (pick a name from your contacts list).*

# Siri Translate

Here's a good one for those who love to travel but don't speak the local language. At the time of writing, Siri can translate from US English to Arabic, French, German, Italian, Mandarin, Japanese, Portuguese, Russian, and Spanish.

To use the translator, hold down the home button until Siri appears and speak the word **"Translate"**.

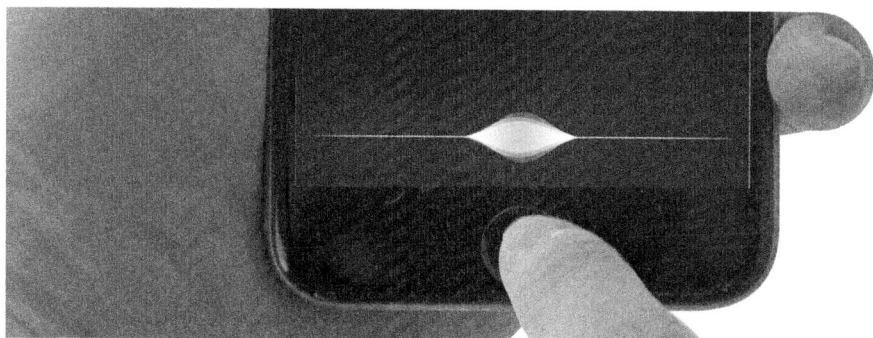

Siri will ask you which language you want to translate into. Say the language name or tap the option from the list. In this demonstration, I'm going to use Spanish.

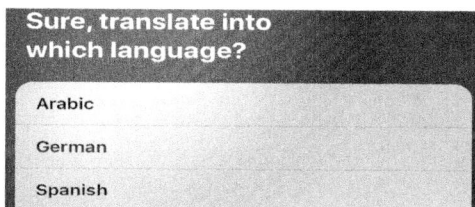

**Sure, translate into which language?**

Arabic

German

Spanish

Now speak the phrase you want to translate into the language you just selected.

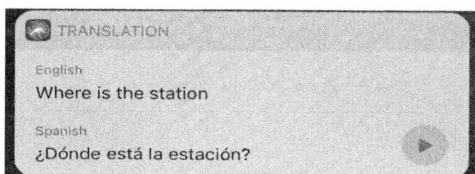

TRANSLATION

English
Where is the station

Spanish
¿Dónde está la estación?

To play the translation again, tap the play button next to the translation.

You can also say "How do I say <u>where is the train station</u> in <u>spanish</u>?"

Just replace the underlined bits of the phrase for the phrase and language you want to translate into.

# Voice Dictation

Another useful feature of Siri is voice dictation, which allows you to enter text without having to use the keyboard. You can search the web, take notes, post an update to Facebook, and more just by speaking.

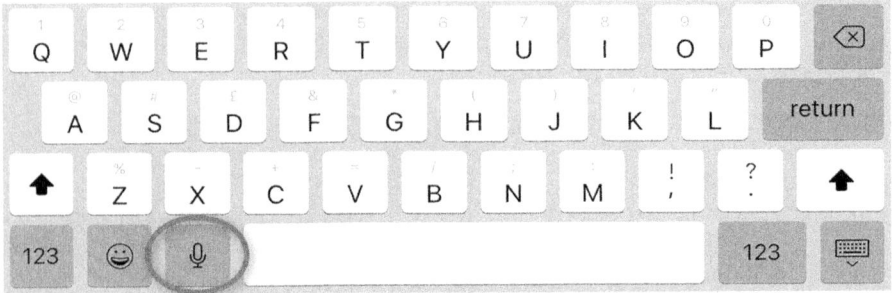

To use voice dictation, tap the microphone icon on your on screen keyboard.

*If the icon isn't there go to your settings app, tap 'general', then 'keyboard'. Go down to 'enable dictation' and switch the slider to on.*

Then start dictating the text you want Siri to type. She listens to what you say, and types it. The more you use it, the better Siri gets at understanding you.

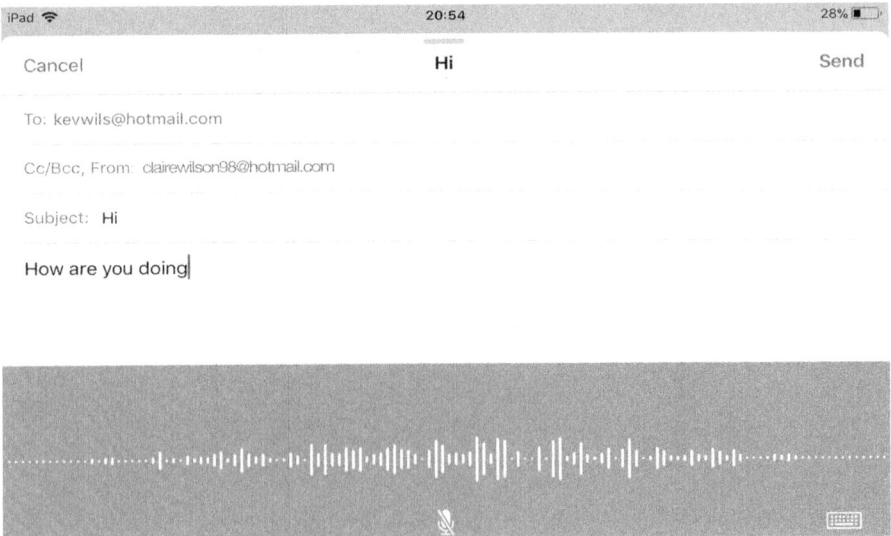

You can even add punctuation by saying words like "period" or 2 "question mark" when you reach the end of a sentence. Tap the keyboard icon on the bottom right to close dictation mode.

# Settings Search

Tap on the settings app. On the main screen at the top left, swipe your finger down under the word 'settings' This will reveal the settings search field.

In the search field, type in the setting you want to change. I'm adding my email accounts so I'll type 'mail' in this example.

Tap on 'mail' in the search results. Try searching for a different setting and see what happens.

# Family Sharing

You can now add six others users as family members. You can share iTunes and Apps, Apple Music, iCloud Storage, your location and authorize your kid's spending on the app store.

To set this up, go to settings and select your ID. Tap 'Set Up Family Sharing'. Then tap 'get started'.

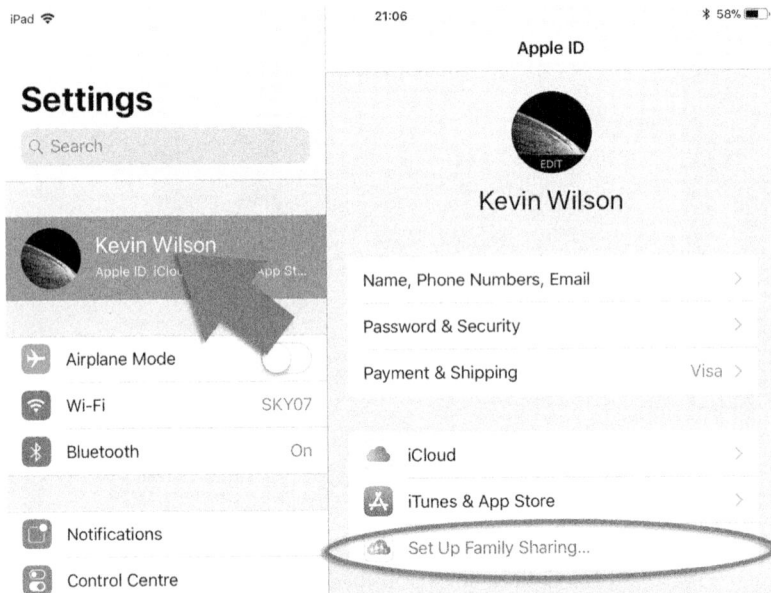

You'll see a screen with four options. You can share any of these options later on but this screen is asking which one you want to begin with. If you want to share books, apps, films and music; select the first option.

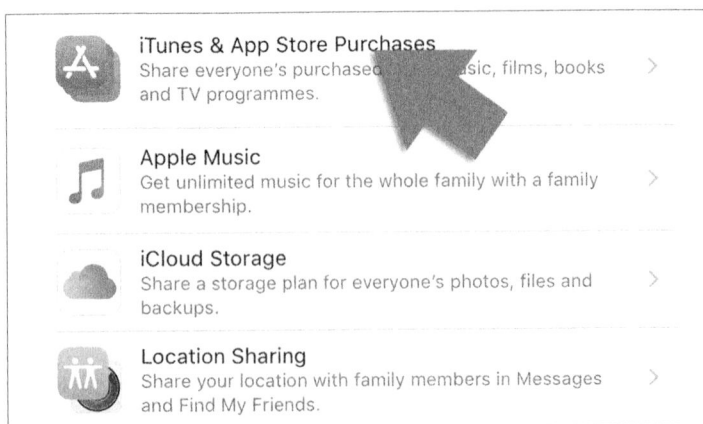

Tap 'continue' to confirm you want to use your Apple ID to share your purchases.

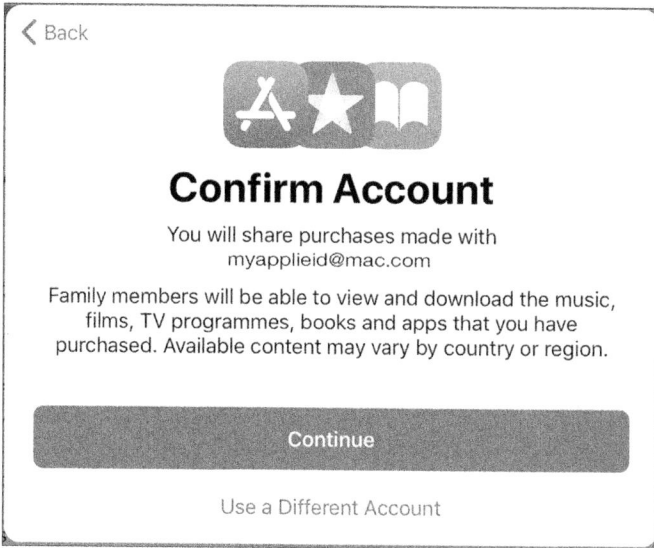

**Confirm Account**

You will share purchases made with
myapplieid@mac.com

Family members will be able to view and download the music, films, TV programmes, books and apps that you have purchased. Available content may vary by country or region.

Continue

Use a Different Account

Confirm the payment details you want to share. Any member of your family that requests an app will be charged to this payment method on your approval. If you want to use another one tap 'use different payment method' and enter the card details.

**Shared Payment**

As the family organiser, your payment method
(Visa •••••••• 0000) will be shared with your family members.

You agree to pay for iTunes, iBooks and App Store purchases initiated by family members using this payment method and will be responsible for all charges.

Managing Family Purchases

Continue

Use Different Payment Method

Tap 'continue' if you want to use your default Apple ID payment method.

## Chapter 3: Getting around Your iPhone

Tap 'invite family members'. Select 'invite in person' and enter their Apple ID email address. If they don't have an email address or too young, tap 'create a child account'.

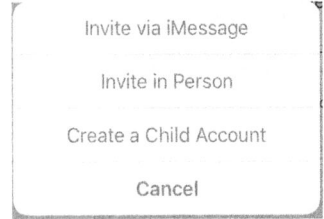

## Add a Family Member

Go to settings, select your ID. Tap 'family sharing then tap 'add family member'.

Now select how you want to invite them. You can invite then 'in person', ie enter their Apple ID email address, send an invitation via iMessage or 'create a new child account'.

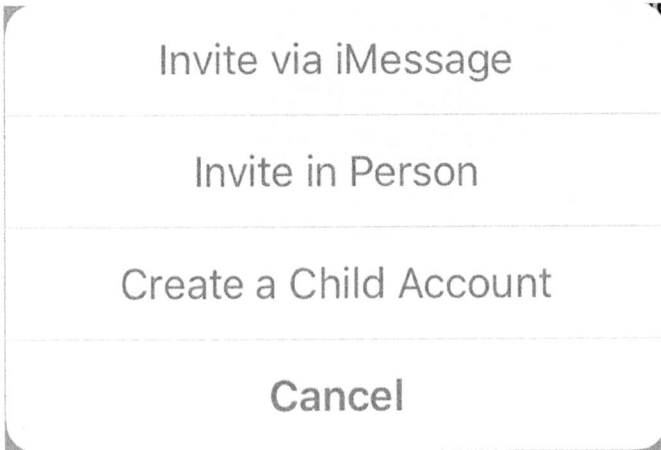

## Invite in Person

Select 'invite in person' from the popup. Enter the person's Apple ID email address and password. If their details are in your address book, you'll see a suggestion underneath. Tap on the name if it's correct.

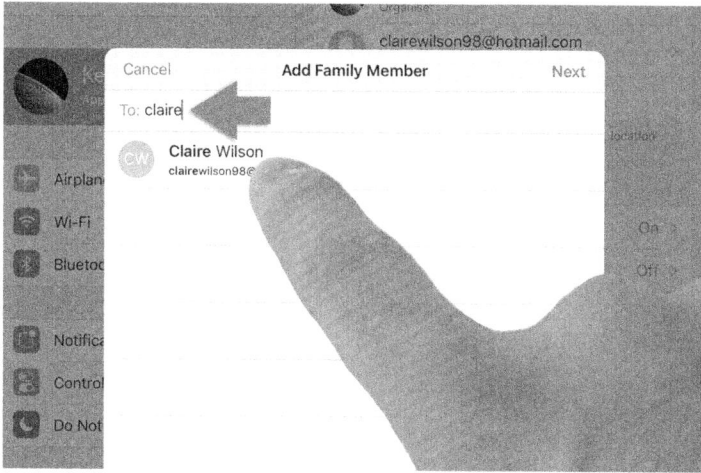

When the person signs into their iPhone and checks their email, they'll see an invitation to join the family.

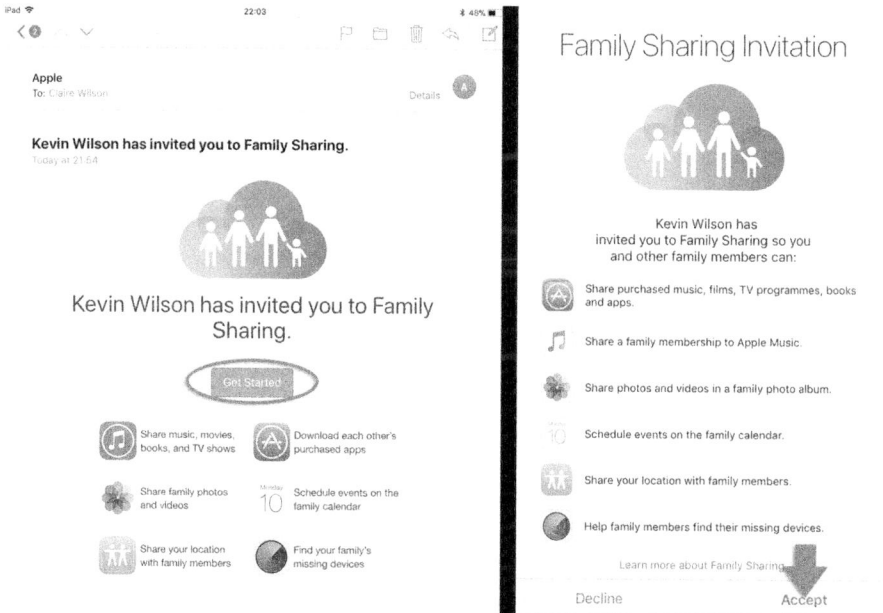

Click 'get started', then click 'accept' on the confirmation.

## Child Accounts

If you have young children it makes sense to create separate accounts for them rather than allowing them to use yours. This helps to protect them and to help you monitor what your child is up to.

To create a child account, go to settings, select your ID. Tap 'family sharing' then tap 'add family member'. From the popup select 'create child account'.

Now follow the instructions on screen. Tap 'next' on the top right of the screen.

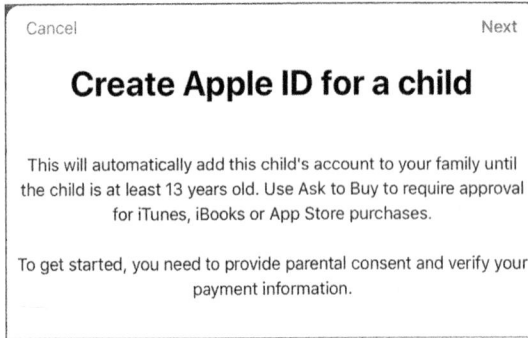

Cancel                                                        Next

### Create Apple ID for a child

This will automatically add this child's account to your family until the child is at least 13 years old. Use Ask to Buy to require approval for iTunes, iBooks or App Store purchases.

To get started, you need to provide parental consent and verify your payment information.

Enter your child's birthday using the rollers on the bottom of the screen, then tap next.

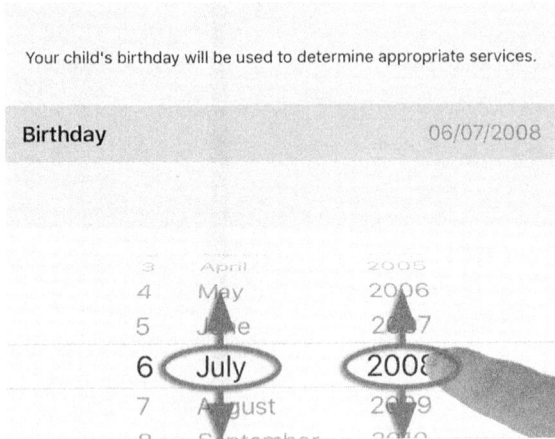

Your child's birthday will be used to determine appropriate services.

**Birthday**                                      06/07/2008

| 3 | April | 2005 |
| 4 | May | 2006 |
| 5 | June | 2007 |
| 6 | July | 2008 |
| 7 | August | 2009 |

Agree to the disclosure, tap 'agree'.

Enter your CVV code from the credit card you have registered with your Apple ID. Tap 'next'.

Enter your child's first and last name using the on-screen keyboard, then tap 'next'.

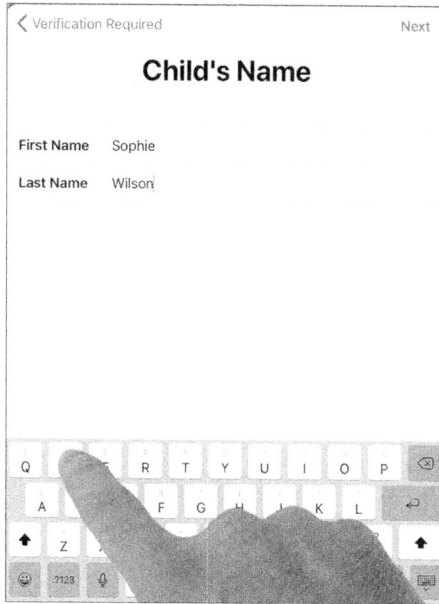

Enter an Apple ID email them. Tap 'next'.

Enter a password for them and tap 'next'.

This will create a new account for your child to use.

Now, select some security questions that you will remember the answers to. This is a security step that will be used to identify you when you need to change a password or recover a forgotten password.

Select a question from the 'question' field and type in an answer in the 'answer' field. Tap 'agree' to accept the terms and conditions

❮ Apple ID Password                                    Next

## Security Questions

Choose answers memorable to you so you can easily verify your identity when you make changes to your child's account.

**Question**    choose a question...                        ❯

**Answer**      Enter answer to question 1

**Question**    choose a question...                        ❯

**Answer**      Enter answer to question 2

**Question**    choose a question...                        ❯

**Answer**      Enter answer to question 3

Enable 'ask to buy'. This means that if your child tries to buy an app from the app store, a music track, tv show or film, you will receive an authorisation request where you can approve the purchase or deny it. Tap 'next'.

❮ Security Questions                                   Next

## Ask to Buy

**Ask to Buy**                                            ⬤

Require approval for all iTunes, iBooks and App Store purchases initiated by Sophie. You will be responsible for all charges to your account.

Now allow your child to sign into their iPhone with the Apple ID email address and password you just created. In this example it would be sophie20077@icloud.com

## Managing your Family

Family members can share purchased apps, music, and books using the same credit card. iPhone can also automatically set up photo streams for all family members. Calendars may be synced between all members.

Kids can also send iTunes and App Store download requests for apps, music, movies, and more to their parents provided this service is set up correctly.

On your device, tap 'review' from the prompt to see details of the request.

# Screen Time

Screen Time collects usage statistics on the various apps you use on your iPhone. It records how much time you've spent using a particular app, can generate activity reports, allows you to set app time limits, and can be useful for monitoring your kid's activity.

You can find screen time on your settings app. Scroll down and select 'screen time'.

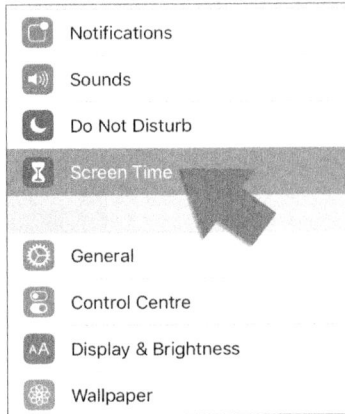

Turn on screen time if it isn't already enabled. Follow the on screen prompts. Set up as 'this is my iPhone'.

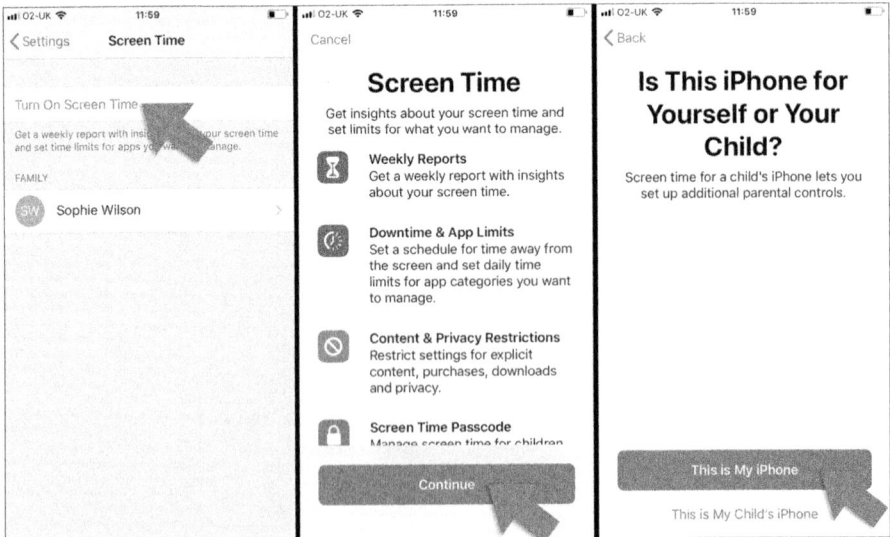

Repeat the procedure on your child's phone, except, set it up as 'this is my child's iPhone' when prompted.

Lets take a look at the main screen. Scroll down the screen to see all the details.

SCREEN TIME                    Today at 09:45

iPad                                          >

## 25m

| Other | Creativity | Entertainment |
| 6m | 4m | 4m |

Breakdown of usage stats of apps used on your iPad

**Downtime**
Schedule time away from the screen.

Set a period of time when your apps will be unavailable

**App Limits**
Set time limits for apps.

Add time limits to specific genres of apps. Eg 1 hour for games

**Always Allowed**
Choose apps you want at all times.

**Content & Privacy Restrictions**
Block inappropriate content.

Add apps that are allowed to run regardless of set limits

FAMILY

SW    Sophie Wilson                           >

Allow or block certain content or apps. Eg age appropriate films

Use Screen Time Passcode

Use a passcode to secure Screen Time settings and to allow for more time when limits expire.

Share Across Devices

You can enable this on any device signed in to iCloud to report your combined screen time.

Set a passcode to prevent users from changing screen time restrictions

Turn Off Screen Time

Here you'll be able to monitor your activity, and the activity of your children's phones if you have them set up.

You'll also see any family members you have added. From here, you can monitor their activity from your iPhone.

## Downtime

With downtime, you can set a period of time, say a couple of hours, that your iPhone apps are unavailable.

Select 'downtime' from the main screen, and turn it on using the switch at the top.

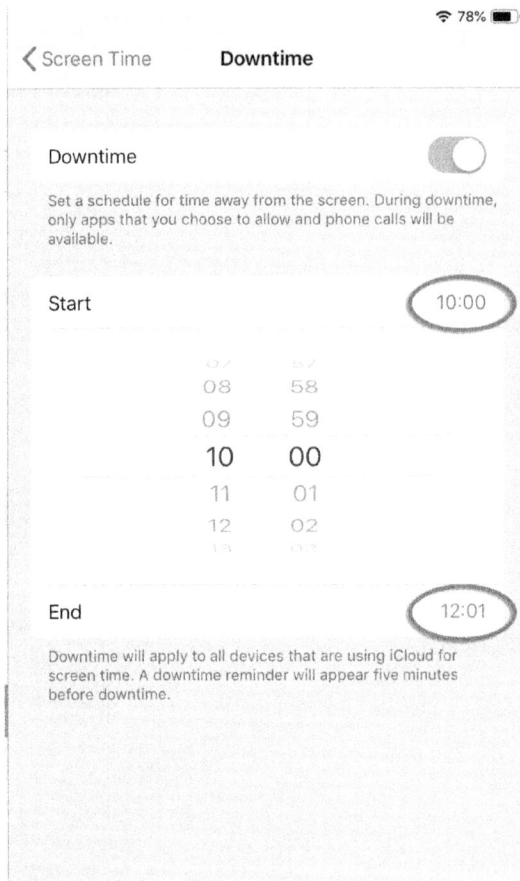

Below, you'll see two options appear. Use this to set the start and end times you want apps to be unavailable. Tap on the times to change them.

For example, you could set it from 9pm to 7am. This would mean, from 9pm, your iPhone apps will turn off until 7am the next morning - preventing you from using your iPhone late at night.

You could also set a limit so if your children use the iPhone, they can't use it until a certain time - perhaps after they've done their homework.

# App Limits

You can set the length of time you want a particular app to be available. To do this, select 'app limits' from the main screen, then tap 'add limit'.

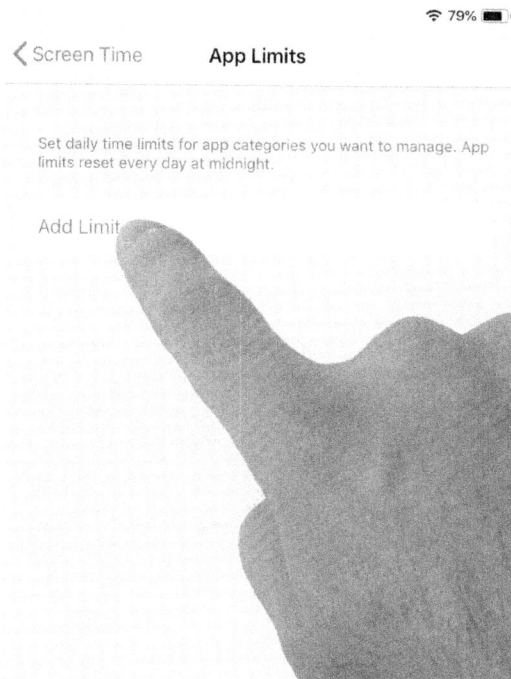

Choose the genre of apps you want to add the limit to. In this example I'm adding a limit to all social networking apps such as facebook, instagram and so on, then tap 'add'.

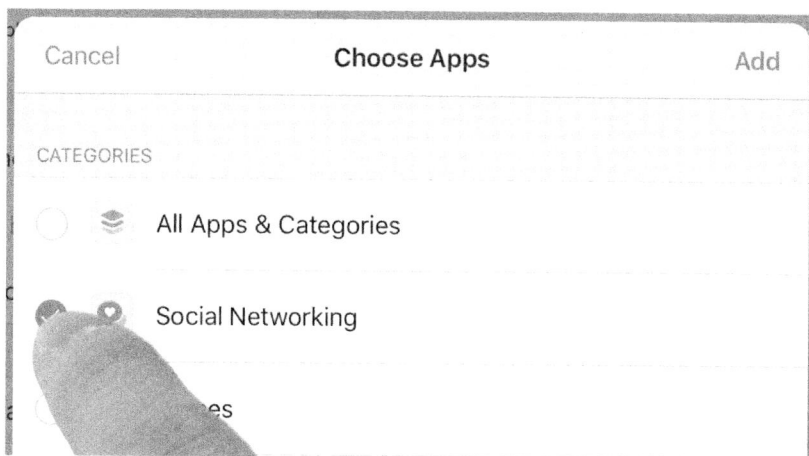

Set the length of time using the sliders indicated with the red arrow.

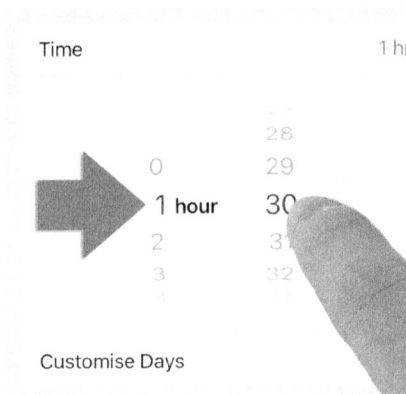

Time                                          1 hr,

```
                    28
         0          29
    1 hour          30
         2          31
         3          32
```

Customise Days

If you want different times on different days, select 'customise days'. This will allow you to input different time limits on different days. Eg, you might want to allow more time at the weekends. Tap on the time limits to change them.

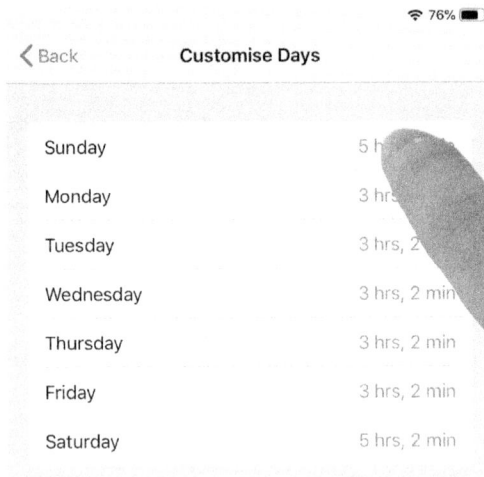

⏶ 76% 🔋

⟨ Back          **Customise Days**

| | |
|---|---|
| Sunday | 5 h |
| Monday | 3 hr |
| Tuesday | 3 hrs, 2 |
| Wednesday | 3 hrs, 2 min |
| Thursday | 3 hrs, 2 min |
| Friday | 3 hrs, 2 min |
| Saturday | 5 hrs, 2 min |

Tap 'back' to return to the previous screen.

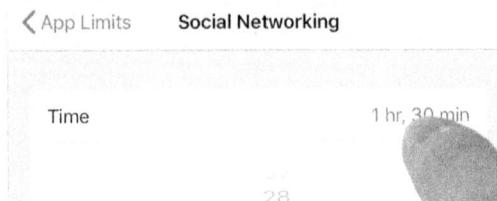

⟨ App Limits     **Social Networking**

Time                          1 hr, 30 min

28

Tap the set time on the top right to confirm.

# Always Allowed

This allows you to choose the apps you want to be available regardless of any content restrictions or time restrictions that are set. Tap the green + to add an app from the list, or tap the red - to remove an app.

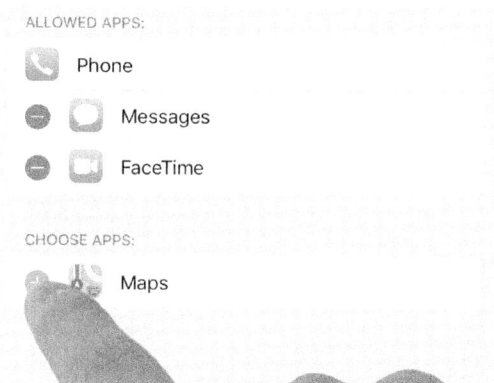

# Content & Privacy Restrictions

Content & Privacy allows you to set restrictions on certain content such as age appropriate films and television programs, or songs, websites, and books with adult themes. This is useful if your kids are using the iPhone.

To set content & privacy restrictions, from the settings app, on the screen time page, select 'content & privacy restrictions'.

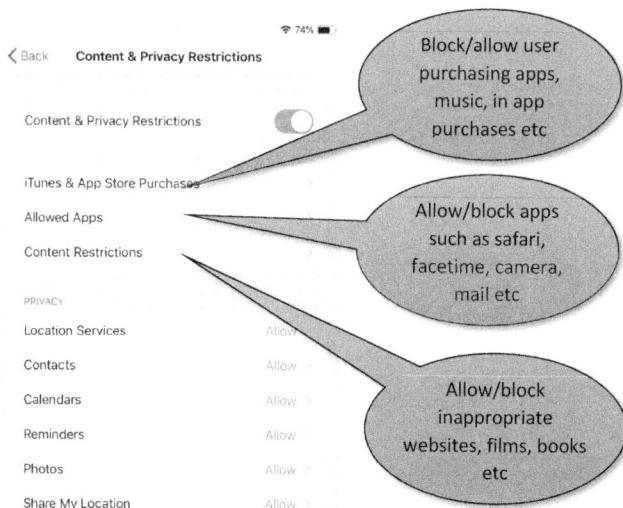

# Allowing and Blocking Content

Go to the 'content & privacy restrictions' section of screen time. From here you can add restrictions on content, apps and websites.

Tap the options to make your selections about what content to allow and what content to block.

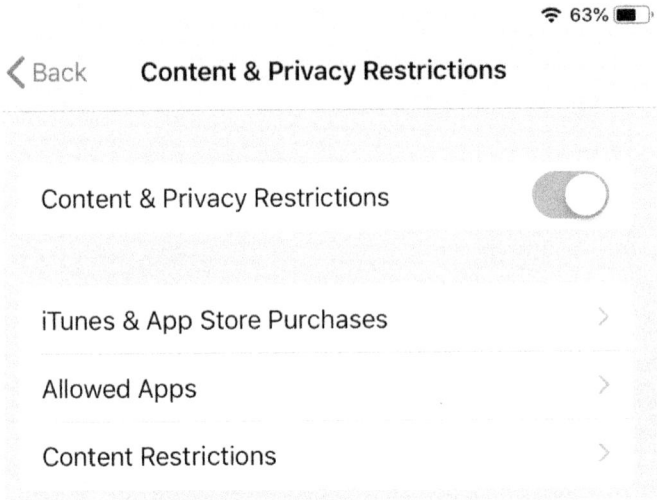

🛜 63% 🔋

❮ Back      **Content & Privacy Restrictions**

Content & Privacy Restrictions

iTunes & App Store Purchases ❯

Allowed Apps ❯

Content Restrictions ❯

For example, to allow or block app store purchases, tap 'iTunes & App Store Purchases'

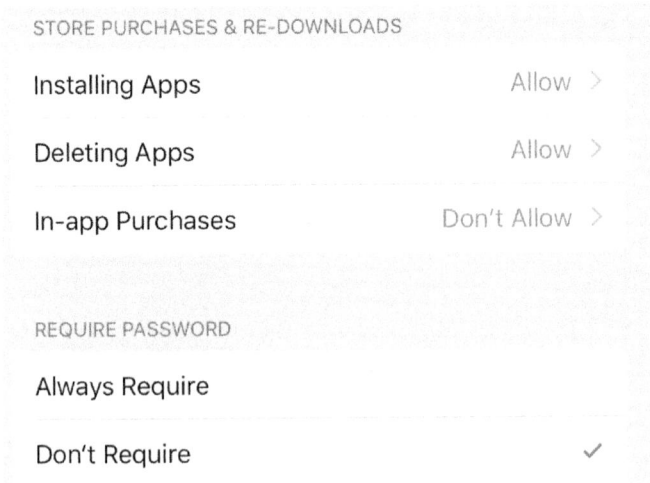

STORE PURCHASES & RE-DOWNLOADS

Installing Apps                          Allow ❯

Deleting Apps                            Allow ❯

In-app Purchases                    Don't Allow ❯

REQUIRE PASSWORD

Always Require

Don't Require                                    ✓

Change the setting to 'allow' to allow the feature, change it to 'don't allow' to deny the feature.

You can do the same for content restrictions such as age appropriate apps, films and websites.

To change these settings, tap 'content restrictions'

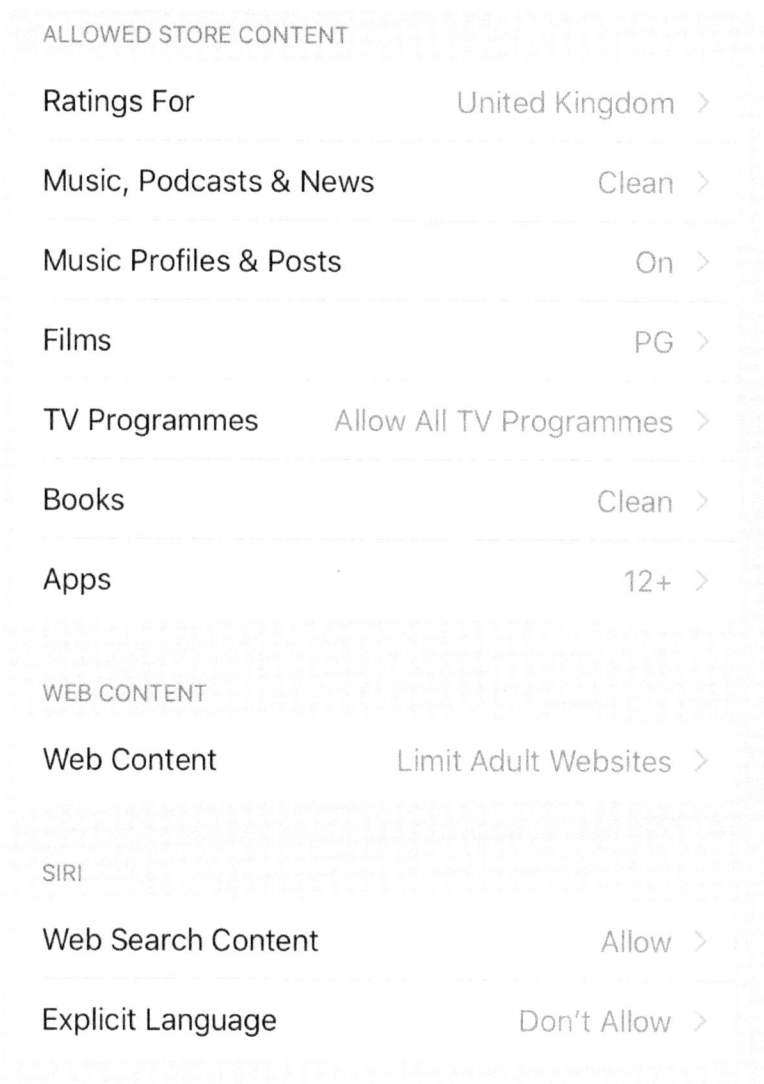

ALLOWED STORE CONTENT

Ratings For                                            United Kingdom >

Music, Podcasts & News                                         Clean >

Music Profiles & Posts                                            On >

Films                                                             PG >

TV Programmes                       Allow All TV Programmes >

Books                                                          Clean >

Apps                                                           12+ >

WEB CONTENT

Web Content                              Limit Adult Websites >

SIRI

Web Search Content                                      Allow >

Explicit Language                               Don't Allow >

Tap on and change the settings appropriately. For example, to only allow PG rated films, tap 'films' and select 'PG'

Do the same for websites, web search content and language. Tap and set these to the appropriate settings, as shown in the example above.

# Internet, Email, Communication

Your iPhone has a lot of features that allow you to connect to the internet, browse the web, send and receive emails, share pictures with friends, store addresses and contacts, have video chat conversations with friends and family, as well as make phone calls and send text/sms messages.

To do this, Apple have provided some built in apps; Safari for web browsing, Mail for email and Face Time for video chat.

You also have apps for social media, and an address book to keep track of contacts addresses and details.

Lets start by taking a look at Safari web browser.

# Using Safari

Safari is your go to app for browsing the internet. To launch Safari, tap on the Safari icon located on your dock.

This will launch Safari. Lets take a look at the main screen.

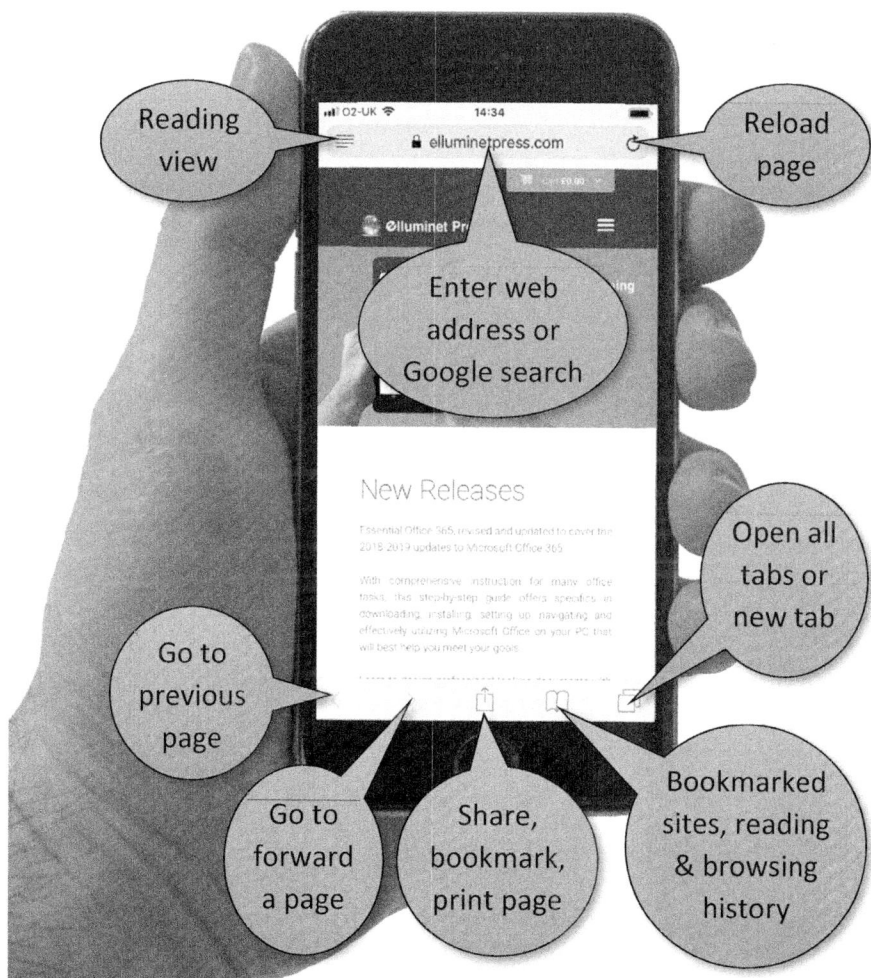

**93**

# Chapter 4: Internet, Email & Communication

In Safari's main screen, tap in the website address field to enter the website's address, or Google search keyword.

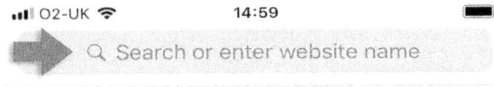

Two menus to take note of. The first menu allows to share, bookmark or print a web page. The second menu opens your list of bookmarked websites, reading list, and browsing history.

The final icon on the right hand side or the bar, allows you to see all the tabs you currently have open.

From the open tabs, tap the one you want to switch to. Swipe right to left over the tab to close it.

Hit the + sign to add a new tab where you can open another website or Google search. Tap 'private' to browse the web without Safari recording your browsing history

## Bookmark a Site

Bookmarking sites makes it easier to find websites that you visit most often, without having to search for them or remember the web address. To bookmark the site you're on, tap the sharing icon on the bottom toolbar.

From the popup menu, tap 'add bookmark'.

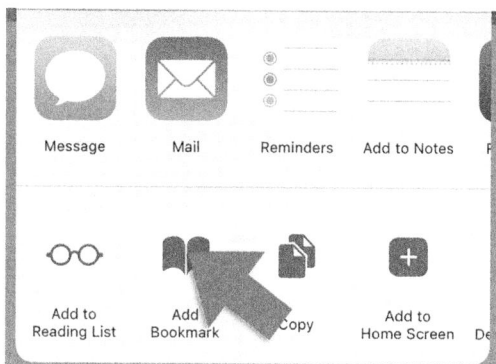

Enter a meaningful name if required, then tap 'save'.

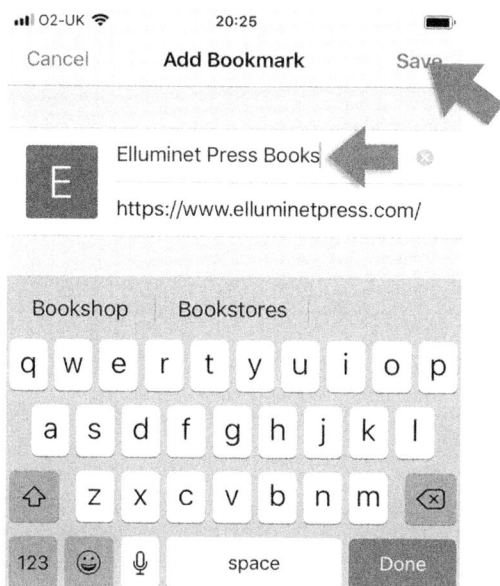

You'll find all your bookmarked sites on the reading menu. To access this menu, tap the icon on the toolbar along the bottom of the screen.

From the popup menu, select the bookmarks icon.

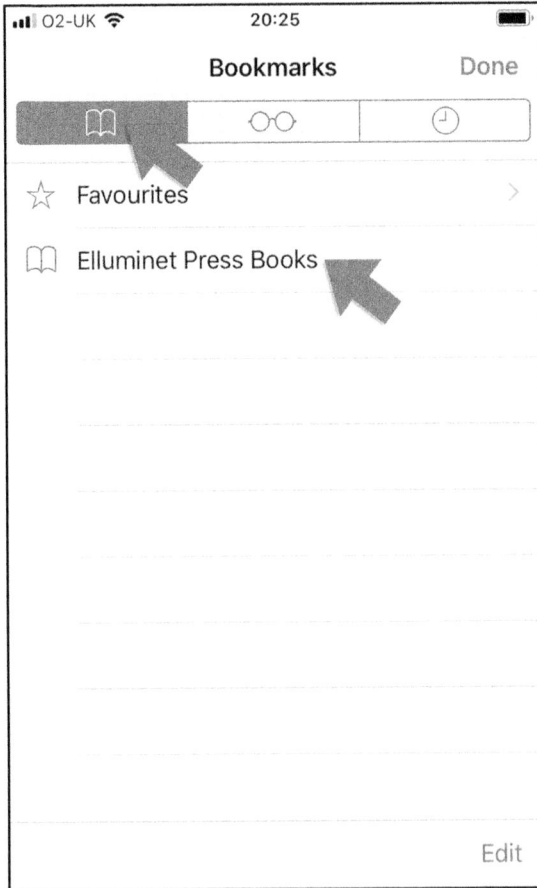

Tap on a bookmark in the list to return to the site.

**To Delete:** Swipe right to left across the bookmark, and tap delete, to remove a bookmark.

**To edit a bookmark**, tap 'edit' on the bottom right corner, then tap on the bookmark in the list you want to edit. You can enter a new name, or change the web address.

# Browsing History

Safari keeps a list of all the websites you have visited in the browser history. To view the history, tap the reading menu icon on the toolbar at the bottom of the screen.

Tap the history icon from the selection at the top of the screen.

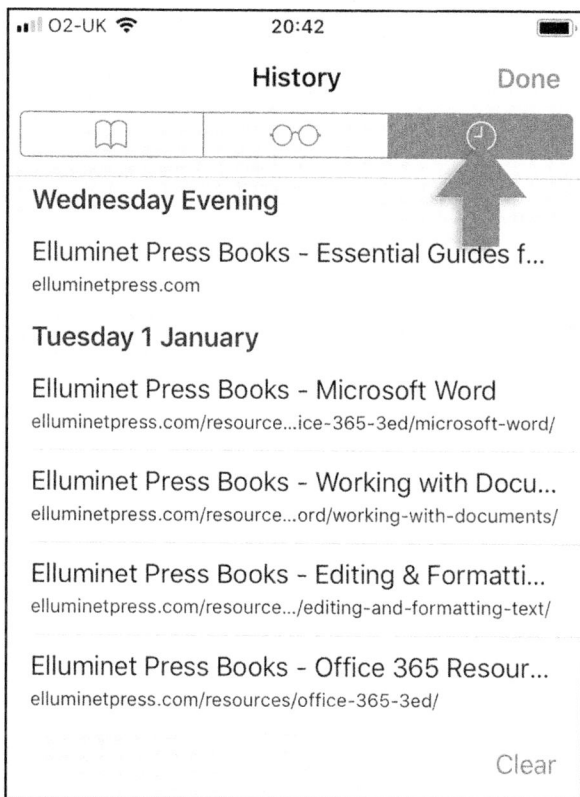

**History**  Done

**Wednesday Evening**

Elluminet Press Books - Essential Guides f...
elluminetpress.com

**Tuesday 1 January**

Elluminet Press Books - Microsoft Word
elluminetpress.com/resource...ice-365-3ed/microsoft-word/

Elluminet Press Books - Working with Docu...
elluminetpress.com/resource...ord/working-with-documents/

Elluminet Press Books - Editing & Formatti...
elluminetpress.com/resource.../editing-and-formatting-text/

Elluminet Press Books - Office 365 Resour...
elluminetpress.com/resources/office-365-3ed/

Clear

Scroll down the list, tap on a site to revisit.

Swipe right to left over the site in the list and tap delete, to remove the site from the history.

Tap 'clear all' on the bottom right to clear the entire history.

Tap 'done' on the top right when you're finished.

## Reader View

Reader view makes it easier to read web pages without all the unnecessary background clutter that usually comes with a website.

Reader view is not available on all web pages but is on most. To enable reader view, tap the reader icon on the left hand side of the web address search field.

Here you can see on the left, the normal view and on the right you can see the reader view.

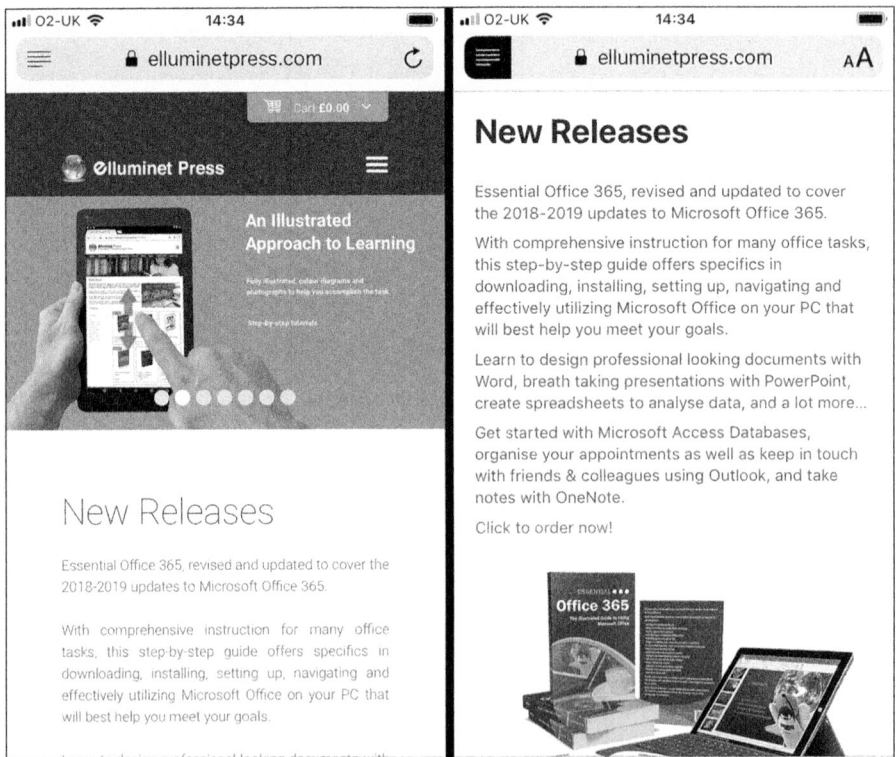

The reader view is designed to improve readability on screen and often removes a lot of graphics, photos and other media, so it's worth keeping this in mind if you are visiting media rich websites.

Tap the same icon to go back to normal view.

# Using Email

To start the mail app, tap Mail on the bottom of the screen.

Once your email is setup it will open on the main screen. In the main window, you'll see a list of all your emails. Just tap on one to view.

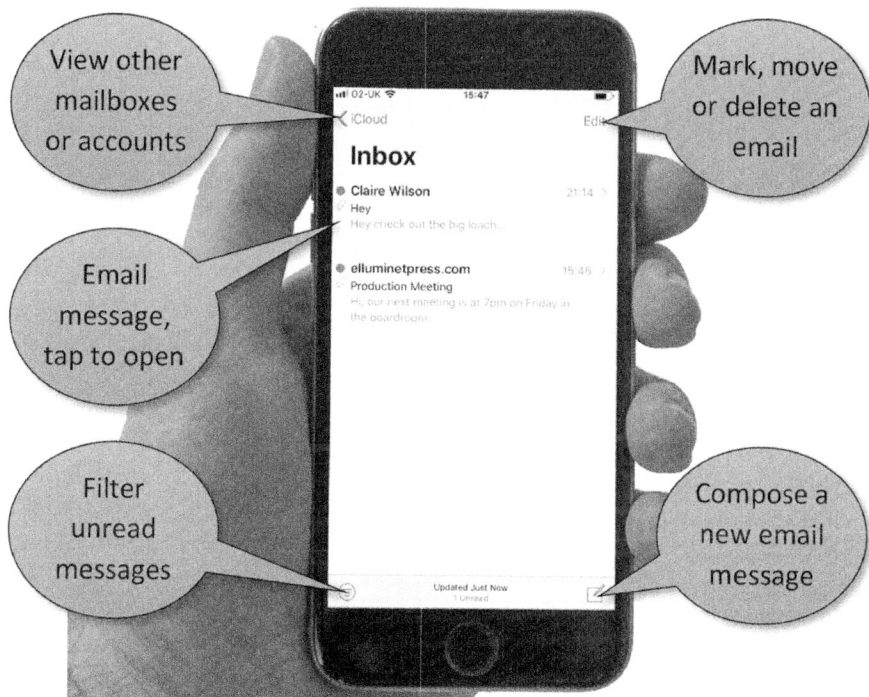

View other mailboxes or accounts

Mark, move or delete an email

Email message, tap to open

Filter unread messages

Compose a new email message

**Inbox**

Claire Wilson — 21:14
Hey
Hey check out the big lunch

elluminetpress.com — 15:46
Production Meeting
Hi, our next meeting is at 7pm on Friday in the boardroom

Updated Just Now
1 Unread

If you have multiple email accounts, you can view your other mail boxes using the link on the top left of the screen.

You can swipe right to left across the email message to view options such as mark, move, flag, or delete.

Tap the filter icon on the bottom left to show all unread messages in your inbox.

# Chapter 4: Internet, Email & Communication

To reply to an email, select the email you want from your inbox. Tap the reply icon from the toolbar on the bottom of the screen.

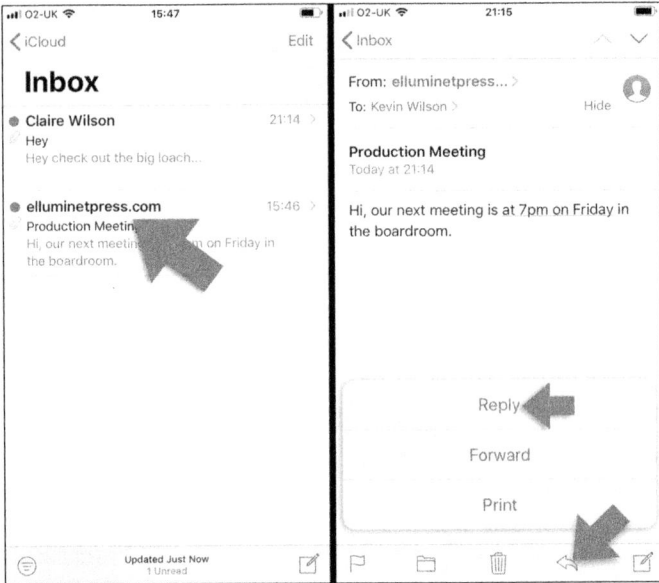

From the popup menu, tap 'reply'. *To forward or print an email, tap on the reply icon, and select 'forward' to forward the email to someone else. Tap 'print' to print the email.*

Type in your message using the on screen keyboard at the bottom of the screen, then tap 'send' when you're done.

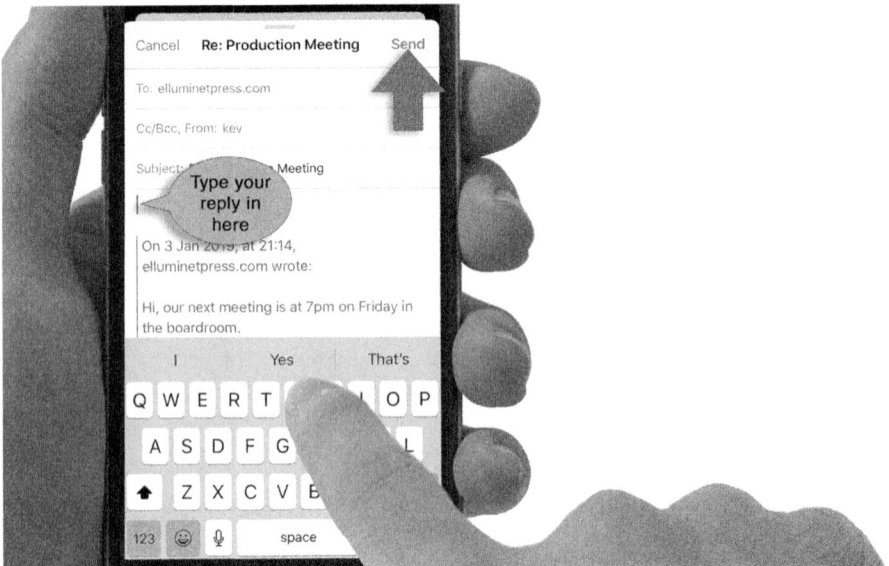

To send a new message, click the 'compose new email' icon on the bottom right.

This will bring up a new email. Tap in the 'To:' field to enter an email address. As you type, Mail will search your contacts for matching names and addresses, tap on the one you want.

Tap in the subject field and add some text.

Tap in the message body underneath and type your message using the pop up on screen keyboard.

If you look on the top of the on screen keyboard you'll see some icons. At the top you have some text predictions - this shows up words you're most likely to type while writing your email - tap word to insert into message.

When you have finished, tap 'send' on the top right of the screen.

# Chapter 4: Internet, Email & Communication

To save time, if you have 3D touch enabled, you can press and hold on a message in your inbox to quickly preview the message.

A quick preview will open up. This is called 'peek'. From here, you can swipe up with your finger to reply without opening the email.

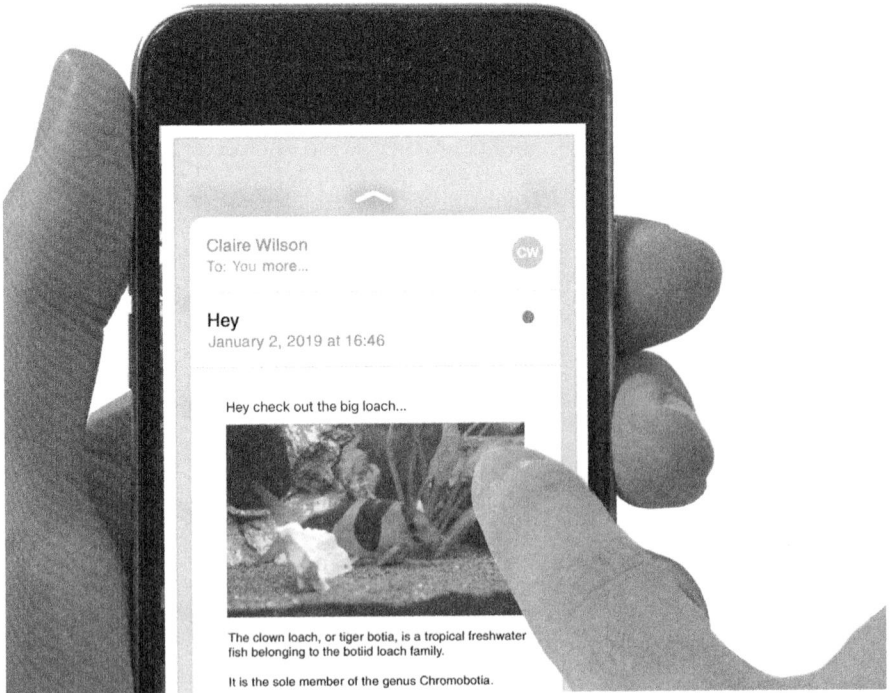

To open the email fully, press down again. This is called 'pop'. To dismiss the message, lift your finger off.

# Contacts

The Contacts App is your address book. It contains all the names, email addresses, phone numbers and addresses of the people you correspond with.

To launch contacts, tap on the app icon on your home screen.

This is the main screen. You can browse contacts, or add new ones.

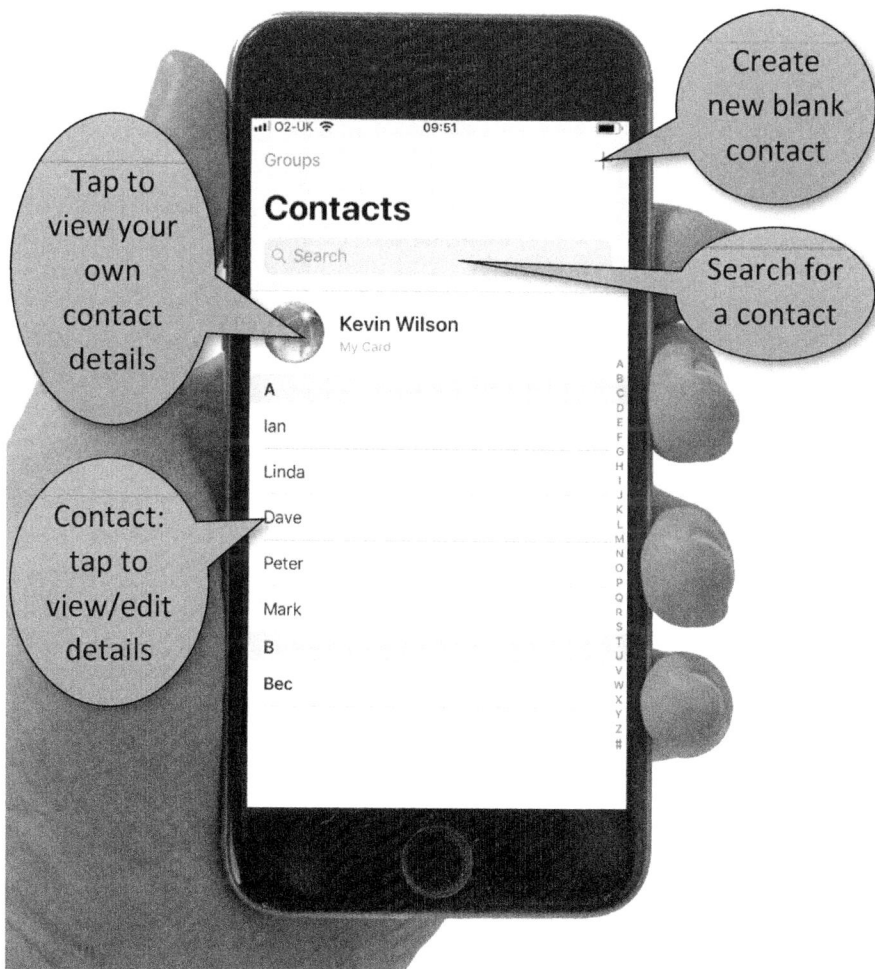

## View Contact Details

To view a contact's details, tap on the name in the contacts list.

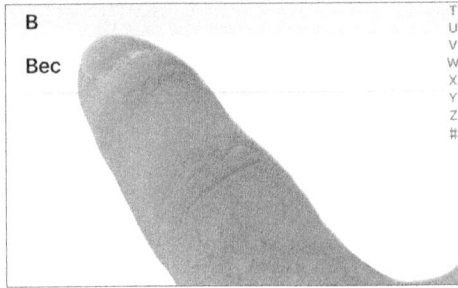

From here you can edit their details, send a message, email, FaceTime them if they have an iPhone, or give them a call.

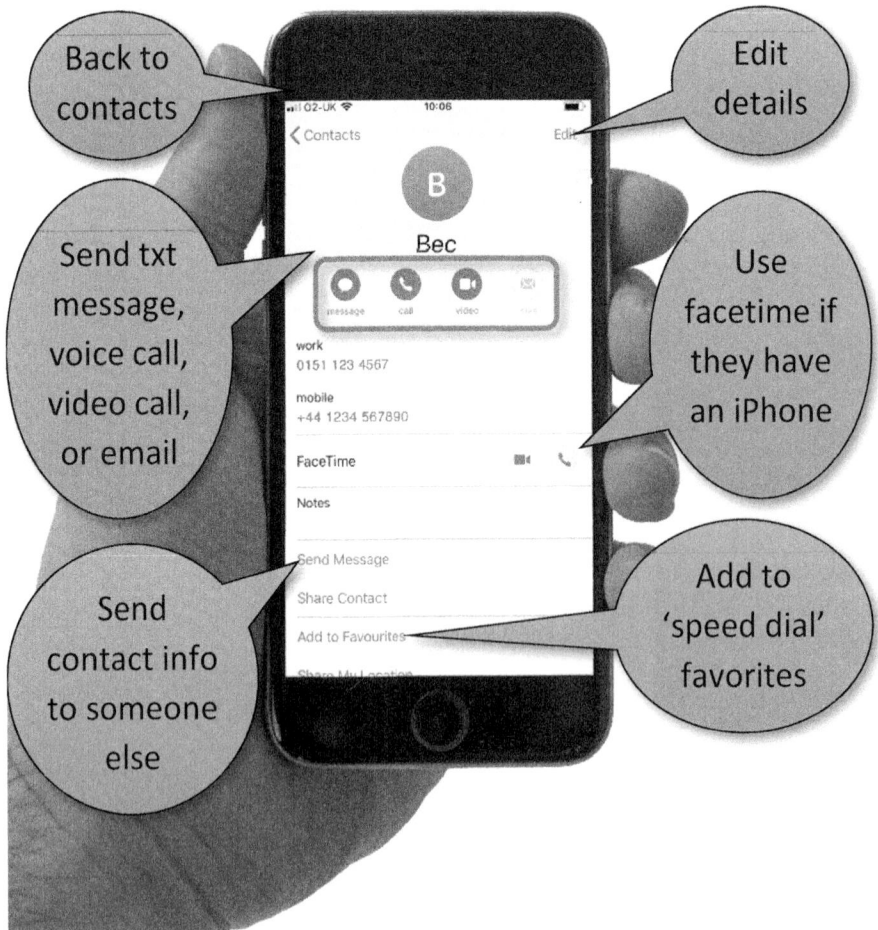

Back to contacts

Edit details

Send txt message, voice call, video call, or email

Use facetime if they have an iPhone

Send contact info to someone else

Add to 'speed dial' favorites

# New Contact

Tap on the + sign on the top right of the main page to add a new contact.

On the screen that appears, enter the person's name and contact details in the fields.

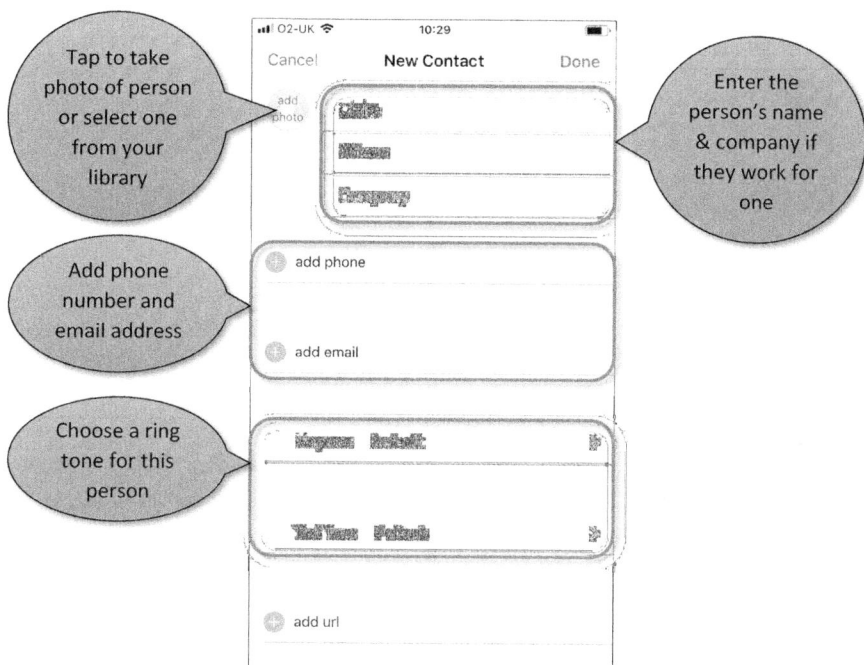

Add a profile photo. This photo appears on your phone screen when the person calls. To take a photo tap 'take photo', you can either take one with your camera or select one from your photo library.

Add their phone number, and email addresses in the relevant fields.

Choose a specific ring and text tone for this person. This is the sound you'll hear when this person sends you a message or calls you.

Tap 'done' on the top right when you're finished.

# New Contact from a Message

You can also add a contact from an email message. Open the email message in the Mail App and tap on their name at the top of the email.

Tap 'create new contact'. iPhone will automatically add the names and email address the message was sent from.

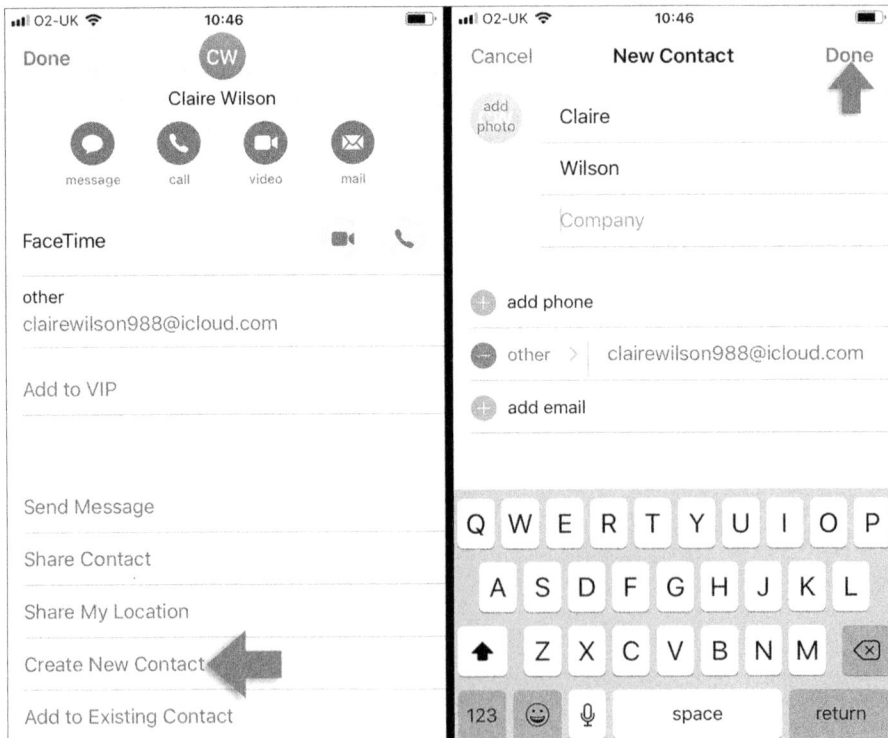

Tap done when you're finished.

*You can do the same with text messages in iMessage. Tap on the message, then tap 'details', tap the 'i' icon (top right), tap 'create new contact'. Enter their name and details in the screen that appears.*

# Calendar (iCal)

To start calendar app, tap the icon on the main screen

This will bring up the calendar main screen. Lets take a look...

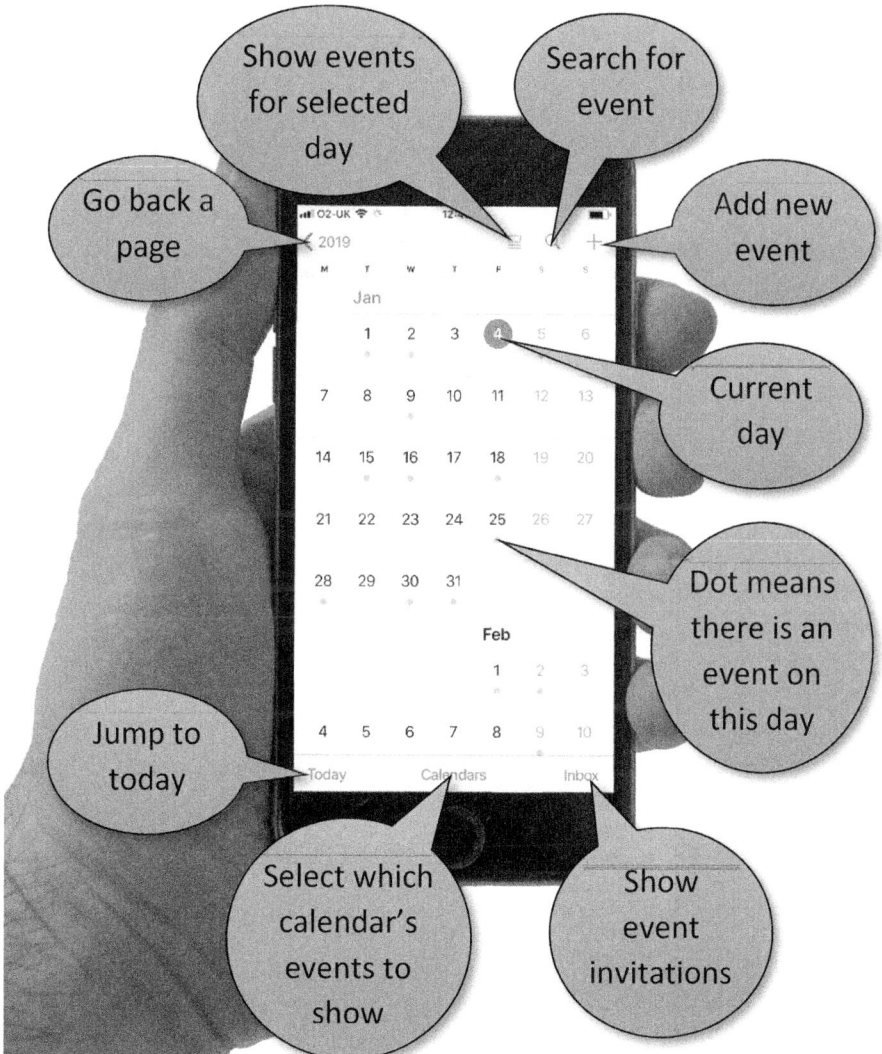

Show events for selected day

Search for event

Go back a page

Add new event

Current day

Dot means there is an event on this day

Jump to today

Select which calendar's events to show

Show event invitations

## Adding an Appointment

To add an event to the calendar, tap on the + sign on the top right of the screen.

In the popup that appears. Tap 'title', then type a title (what the event or appointment is).

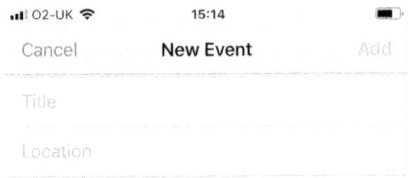

Turn off 'add-day' unless the event is an all day event. Tap on 'starts', then slide the dates and time until they show the date and time the event is due to start. Do the same for 'ends', enter the time the event is scheduled to finish.

Add an alert, this is a reminder, you can set this to remind you a week before, the day before, or 5 minutes to an hour before.

Once you are finished tap 'add' on the top right of the screen.

# Add a Recurring Appointment

Sometimes the same event happens daily, weekly or monthly - this is called a recurring event. To add a recurring event to the calendar, tap on the + sign on the top right of the screen.

In the popup that appears. Tap 'title', then type a title (what the event or appointment is).

Turn off 'add-day' unless the event is an all day event. Tap on 'starts', then slide the dates and time until they show the date and time the event is due to start. Do the same for 'ends', enter the time the event is scheduled to finish.

Now to create a recurring event, tap 'repeat'

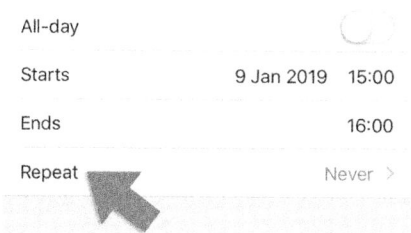

# Chapter 4: Internet, Email & Communication

Here you can set the event to recur once a week, once a month, every two weeks and so on. All you have to do is tap on the one you want.

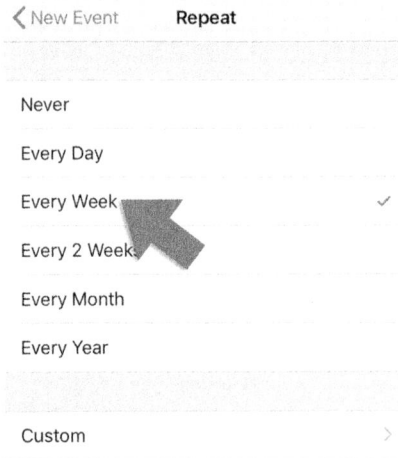

<New Event  **Repeat**

Never

Every Day

Every Week                                      ✓

Every 2 Weeks

Every Month

Every Year

Custom                                          >

You can also set a custom option, tap 'custom'. Say the event occurs every three weeks. Set the frequency to 'weekly'. Then tap 'every' and select the number of weeks. In this example, three weeks, so slide the number to '3'.

<Repeat  **Custom**

Frequency                                    Weekly

Every                                        1 week

1                              week
2
3

Event will occur every week.

Sunday

Monday

Tuesday

Wednesday                                       ✓

Once you are finished, tap 'repeat' on the top left of the repeat window to go back. Tap 'add' to add the event to your calendar.

# Adding an Appointment from a Message

Apple Mail, iMessage and FaceTime will scan your message for phrases that look like dates and times and will create an underlined link in the email for you. To add the event from the email or text message, tap on this link.

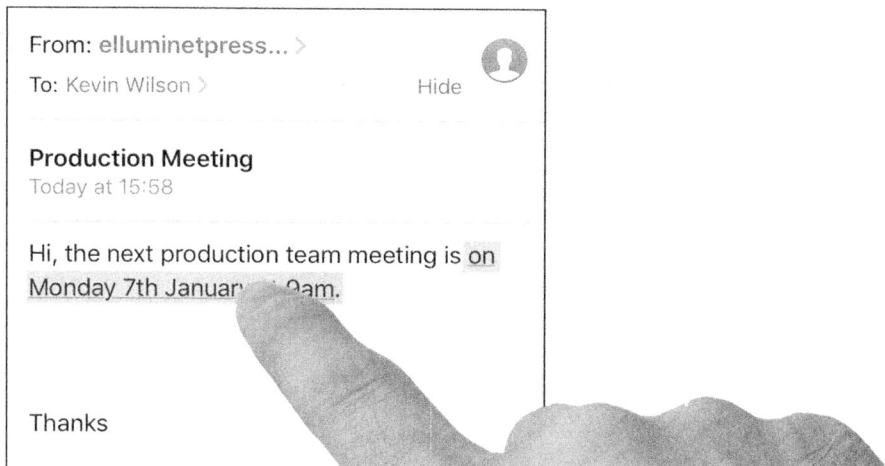

From: elluminetpress... >
To: Kevin Wilson >                    Hide

**Production Meeting**
Today at 15:58

Hi, the next production team meeting is on
Monday 7th January  9am.

Thanks

From the popup box tap 'create event'.

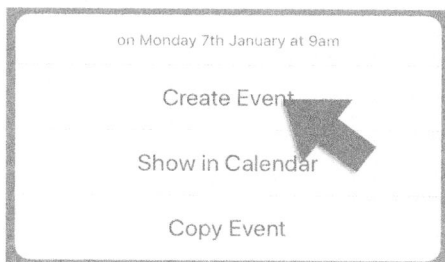

on Monday 7th January at 9am

Create Event

Show in Calendar

Copy Event

Enter a title and location if calendar didn't pick one up from the email. You can also tweak the information and add additional information if required.

.ıl O2-UK 🤎          15:59          ■)

Cancel          **New Event**          Add

Production Meeting

Location

Once you have done that, tap 'add' to enter the appointment into your calendar.

# Phone App

Making phone calls on the iPhone is quite straight forward. To open the phone, tap the phone icon on the dock along the bottom of the screen

Lets take a look at the phone app...

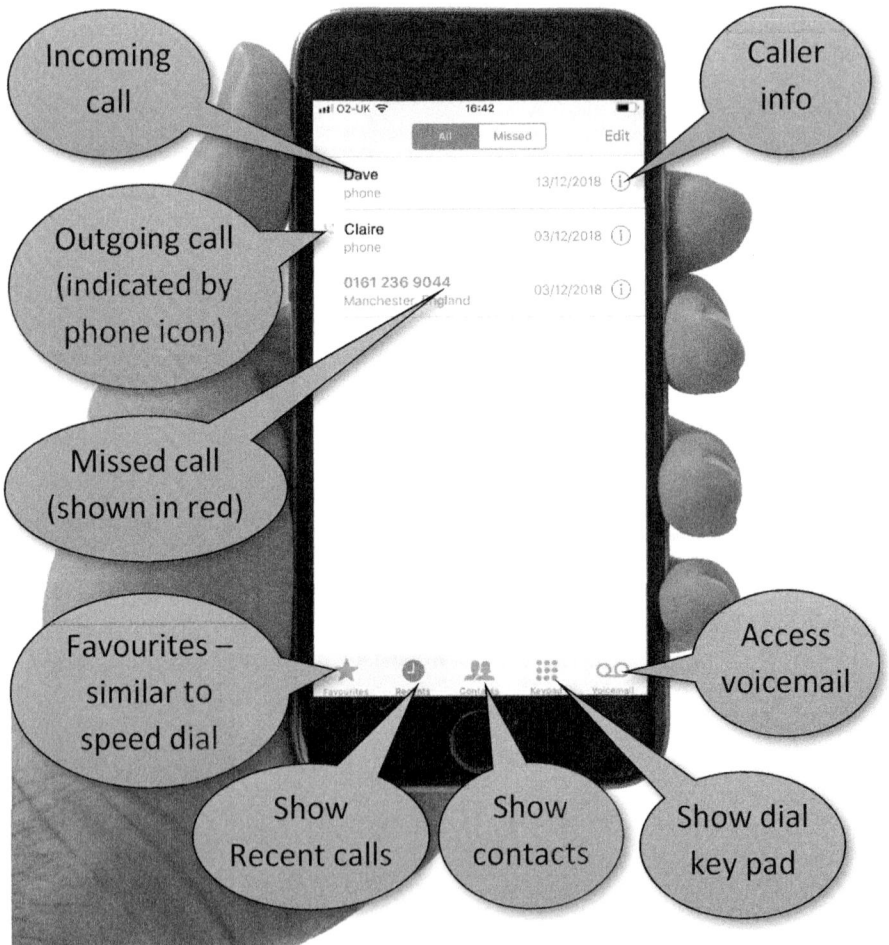

Incoming call

Caller info

Outgoing call (indicated by phone icon)

Missed call (shown in red)

Favourites – similar to speed dial

Access voicemail

Show Recent calls

Show contacts

Show dial key pad

Along the bottom of the screen, you'll see a toolbar with some icons. Use these to navigate between the different sections.

## Answering Calls

Incoming calls will be displayed on your screen, your phone will also play a ringtone and/or vibrate.

Along the top, you'll see the caller's name if their number is in your contacts list, and where they're calling from. You'll just see a number if the caller isn't in your contacts list.

You'll be able to

- Tap 'accept' to answer the call
- Tap 'decline' to refuse call the call
- Tap 'message' to send a quick call decline message
- Tap 'remind me' to set a reminder to call them back

You can set custom quick messages in the settings app, which will appear in this list. These are called 'call decline messages'.

## Dialling Numbers

If you have a phone number for a friend, colleague, or a company, you can key it in using the keypad. To do this tap the keypad icon on the tool bar along the bottom of the screen

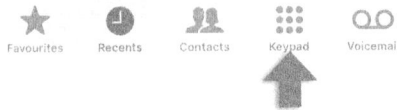

Tap in the number using the keypad. Tap the green icon to place the call.

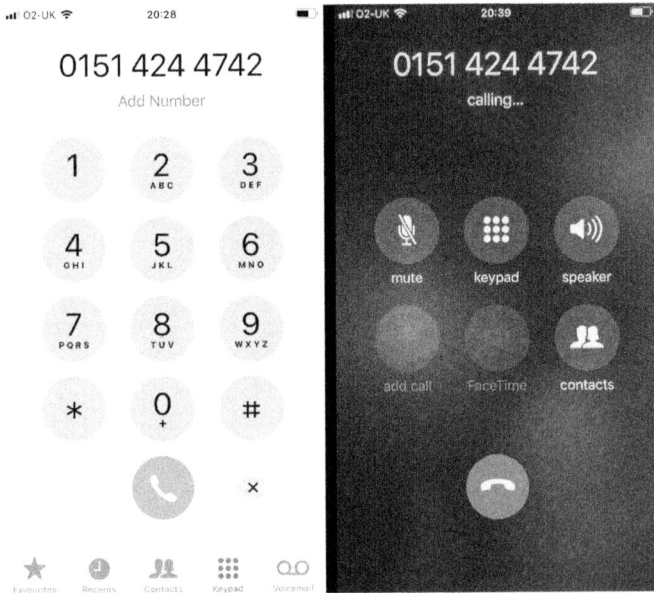

Wait for the other person to answer. When the other person answers, the call will be established. While in call...

- Tap **'mute'** to temporarily mute your microphone, so the other person can't hear you.
- Tap **'keypad'** to open up the keypad - useful if you need to make menu choices when calling some numbers.
- Tap **'speaker'** to put the call on speaker phone.
- Tap **'add call'** to add someone else to the call if the other person's phone supports this.
- Tap **'facetime'** to transfer the call to facetime video chat, if the other person has an iPhone.
- Tap **'contacts'** to view your contacts list.
- Tap the red icon at the bottom to end the call.

# Call Someone from Contacts List

Open the phone app, tap the 'show contacts' icon on the toolbar along the bottom of the screen.

Tap on the person you want to call.

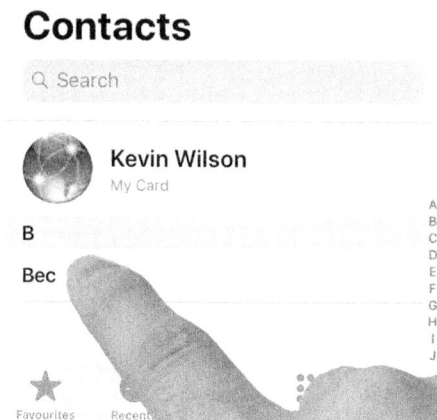

## Contacts

From the person's profile, tap 'call' to call them. If they have more than one phone number, tap on the number you want to call them on underneath.

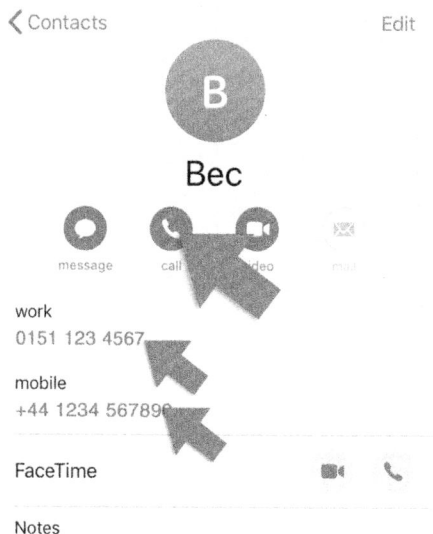

## Call Someone from Recent Calls List

Open the phone app, tap the 'recents' icon on the toolbar along the bottom of the screen.

Tap on the person you want to call.

All missed calls show up in red. Calls you have placed, are indicated with a small phone icon.

All incoming calls you have answered show up in black text.

To see all calls you have placed & received, tap 'all' along the top of the screen. To only see missed calls, tap 'missed'.

Swipe right to left over the call in the list, and tap delete to remove it.

# Add Someone to Favourites

The favourites list is similar to speed dial. The idea is to put all your most used contacts on the favourites list, so you can access them easily.

To do this 'Favorites' on the toolbar along the bottom of the screen.

Tap the "+" sign in the top right of your screen.

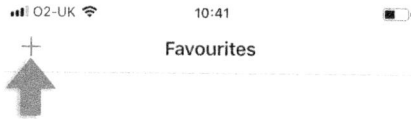

Select a contact from your contacts list

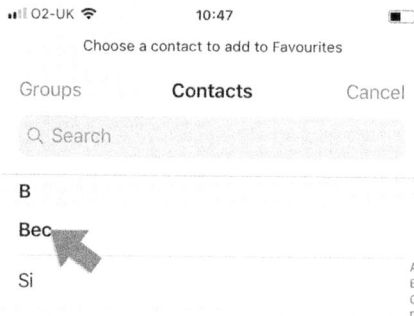

Now select the method you want to contact them with. This could be a phone call, text message, or facetime. Select the method you most likely use to contact this person. In this example, I'm going to call them

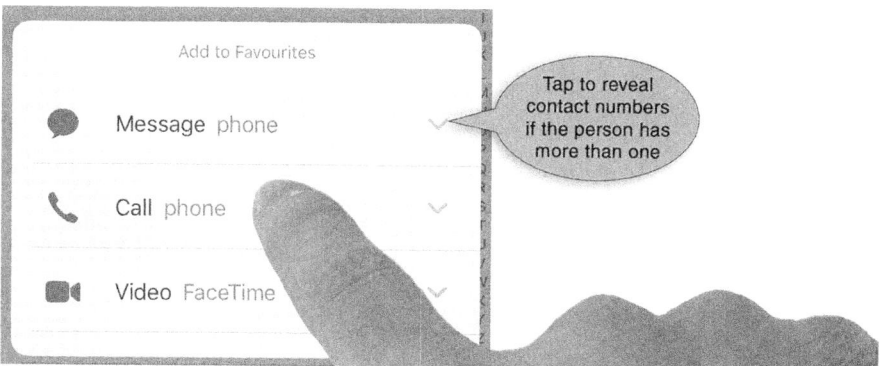

# Chapter 4: Internet, Email & Communication

If the person has more than one contact number, eg home, work, or mobile, tap the small down arrow next to the method of contact to reveal all the person's contact numbers

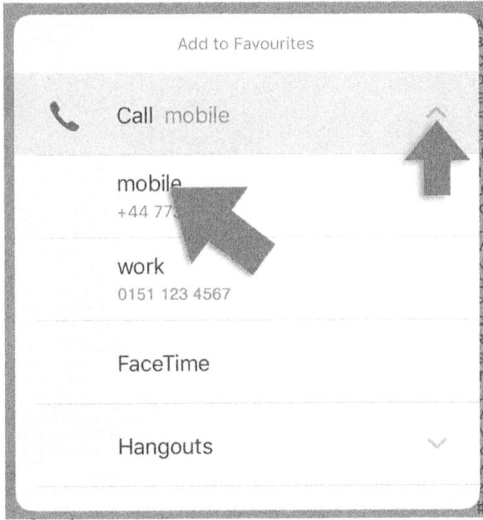

The numbers will appear on your favourites section. Tap on one to call the person.

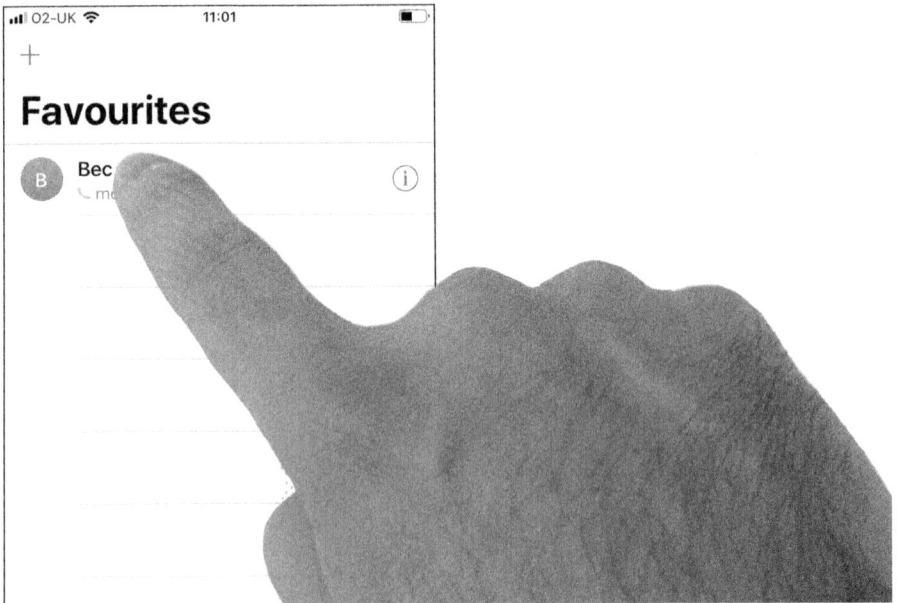

To delete a favourite, swipe right to left over the name in the list, then tap 'delete'.

**118**

## Voice Mail

If someone has left you a voice message, you can check those here. To check, tap 'voice mail' on toolbar along the bottom of the screen

You'll see a list of phone numbers or names of people who have left you a voice message. Tap on one of these.

From the voice message screen, tap play icon to listen to message, tap 'call back' to return call.

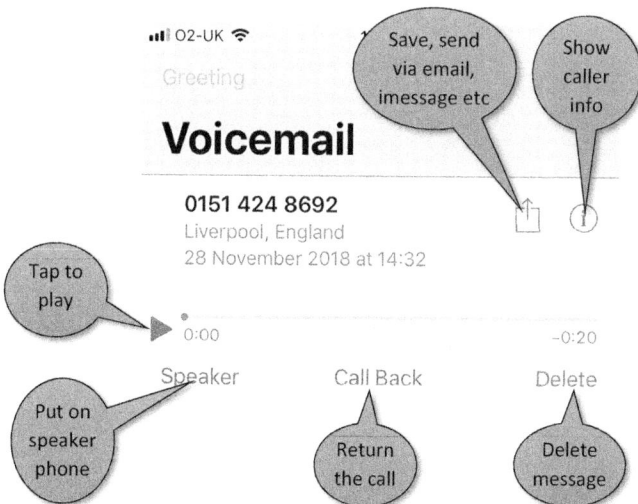

You can also put the message on speaker phone, or send the message to someone else using the share icon on the top right. You can send the message via email, iMessage, etc

# Custom Call Decline Messages

Open the Settings app from your home screen, scroll down the list and tap 'phone'.

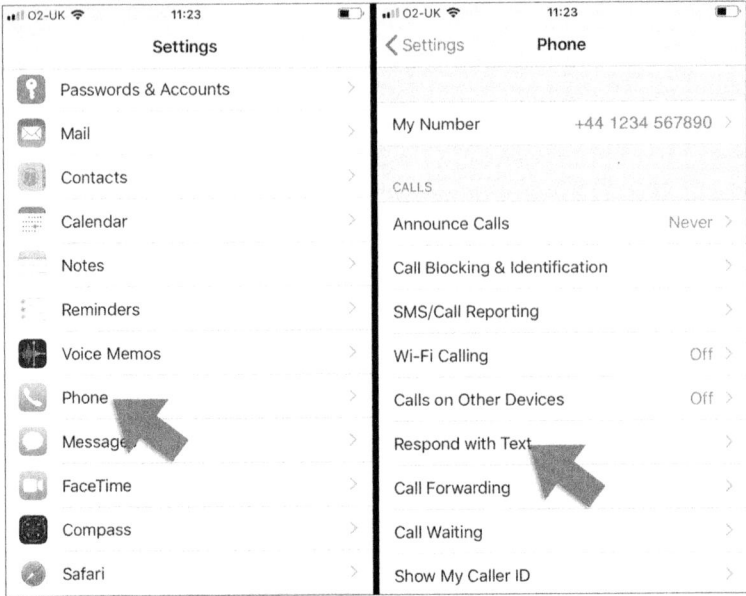

Tap 'Respond with Text'.

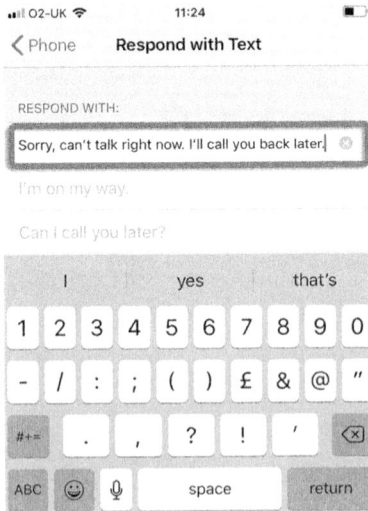

Tap any field you want to replace or customize and type your message. Your message will automatically appear as an option from now on when you tap the message button to decline a call.

## Ringtones and Text Tones

You can set individual ring tones for different people - this helps you identify people when they call. You can assign a different ring tone to each of your friends.

To do this, open the contacts app on your home screen, and tap on the person's name. In their contact details, tap 'edit' on the top right of the screen.

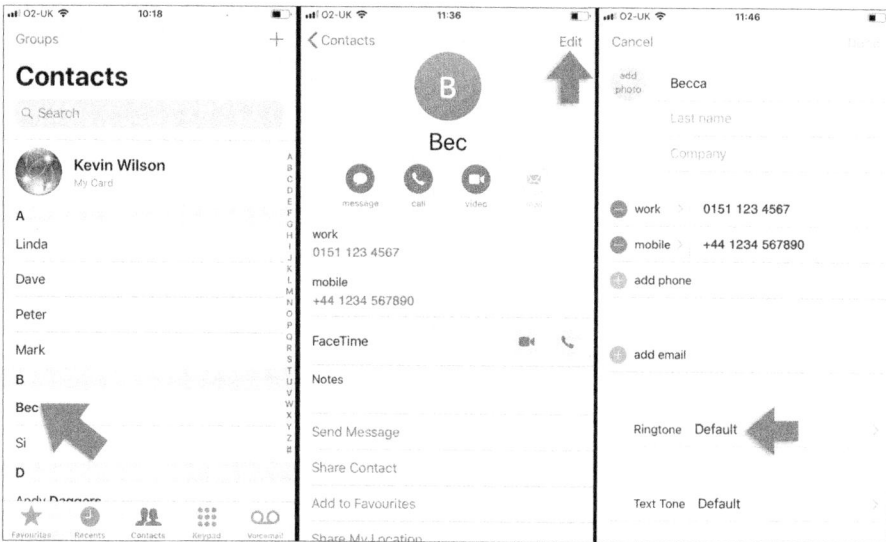

Scroll down and select 'ringtone'.

Select a ringtone from the list.

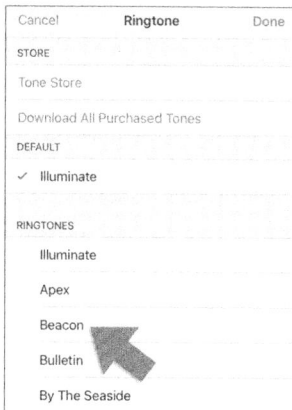

You can also purchase more ringtones from the tone store. To do this ta' tone store'.

# FaceTime

To use FaceTime, tap the icon on the home screen. You will need your Apple ID and a wifi/data connection to the internet.

When you open FaceTime, you will be prompted to sign in if you haven't already done so.

## Making a Call

In this demonstration, Claire is going to FaceTime Sophie from her iPhone. Tap the '+' on the top right of the screen.

Start typing the person's name or phone number you want to FaceTime, into the search field on the top of the screen. If the name is in your contacts, then it will appear underneath.

Tap 'video'.

In the background of your screen, you'll see a preview of your camera - so make sure you're squarely in the frame so when the call is answered, the other person can see you clearly.

Along the top of your screen, you'll see the name or phone number of the person you're calling.

Along the bottom, you'll see three icons. The icon on the left mutes the call, the red icon in the centre hangs up, and the three dots icon on the right opens more options such as flip to rear camera, send message, speaker phone, and the ability to turn on and off your camera.

Wait for the other person to answer...

Once the other person answers, you can now have a video conversation. The onboard microphone on your iPhone/iPhone will pick up your voice, so just talk naturally.

You'll see an image of the person calling in the centre of your screen with a thumbnail view of your own camera on the top right. Here's the view of Claire's call from her iPhone.

Along the bottom, you'll see three icons. If these icons disappear, tap the screen once and they'll re-appear. The icon on the left mutes the call, the red icon in the centre hangs up, and the three dots icon on the right opens more options such as effects, flip to rear camera, send message, speaker phone, and the ability to turn on and off your camera.

During your call, tap on the screen to reveal the in call icons. Tap on the three dots icon on the right to reveal the full panel.

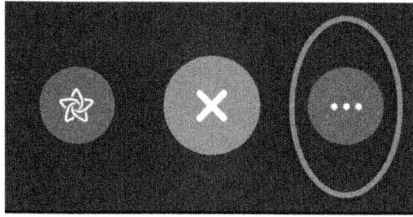

On the top row of icons you have a button for adding effects, ending the call, and switching between front and rear camera on your iPhone.

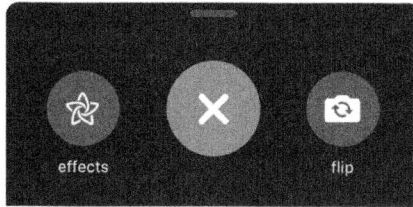

On the second row you have buttons to mute your microphone, mute iPhone speaker, and blank your camera.

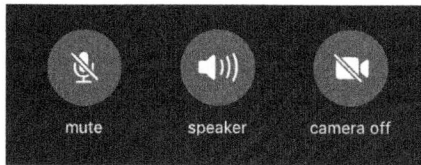

Under these icons you can open an iMessage conversation and see contact details of the person you're face-timing with.

## Adding Effects

During a call, you can add all sorts of effects to your image. To do this, tap the effects icon on the bottom left of the in call window.

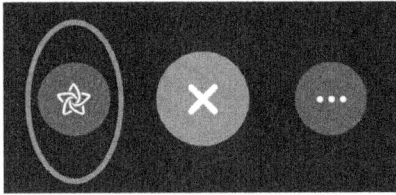

Select the type of effect you want to add. You can add filters, text, shapes, and icons. In this example we're going to add a text effect.

Tap the text icon, select an effect,

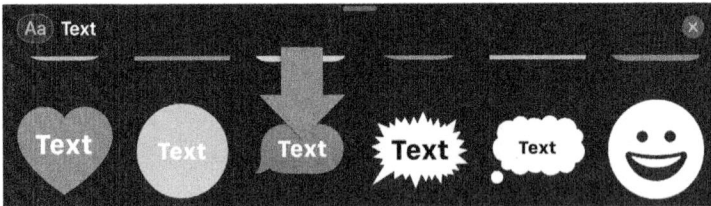

Then type in some text and drag the effect into place.

Lets have a look at what the effect will look like. This is what the other person you're talking to will see.

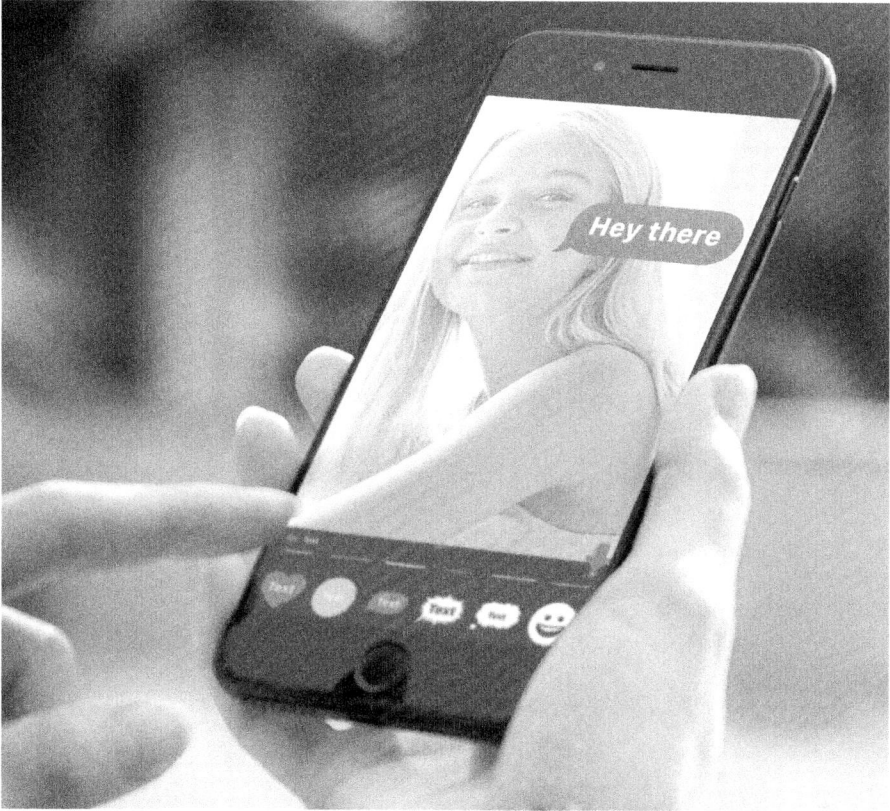

Tap the small x on the top right of the effects panel to close. Tap the effects icon to close the panel.

Try some of the other effects and filters on the panel. Try adding a shape or an icon and see what happens.

## Group FaceTime

Group FaceTime allows you to set up groups and chat to up to 32 people at a time. To use Group FaceTime, all participants must have iOS 12 installed, otherwise you won't be able to add them to the group.

To place a group call, on the left hand panel tap on the + icon on the upper corner.

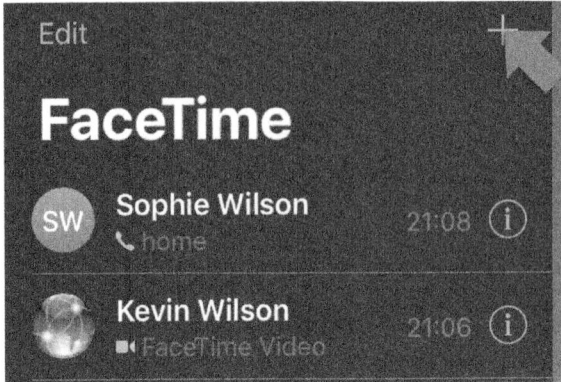

Type the names of the people you want to place a group call to in the 'to' field, or tap the + icon and add them from your contacts list.

If they all have iOS 12 installed on their devices, you'll see two green buttons appear along the bottom of the side panel.

Tap on 'video' to place a group video call.

When your contacts answer, you'll see a thumbnail of each of them on your main display.

In this demo, the girls are having a group FaceTime with grand dad.

You'll see a thumbnail of your own camera in the bottom right of the screen. The other contacts in your group will show up in a thumbnail window in the main area of the screen.

The clever bit is, when one of your contacts starts talking, their thumbnail window will temporarily enlarge.

FaceTime is useful for keeping in touch with family and friends who don't live near by, or live in another country.

# iMessage

You can send photos and videos and also voice messages to anyone
with an Apple device. To start iMessage, tap the icon on the dock on
your home screen.

When you open iMessage, you will see a list of all your received
messages. Tap on a message to read and reply.

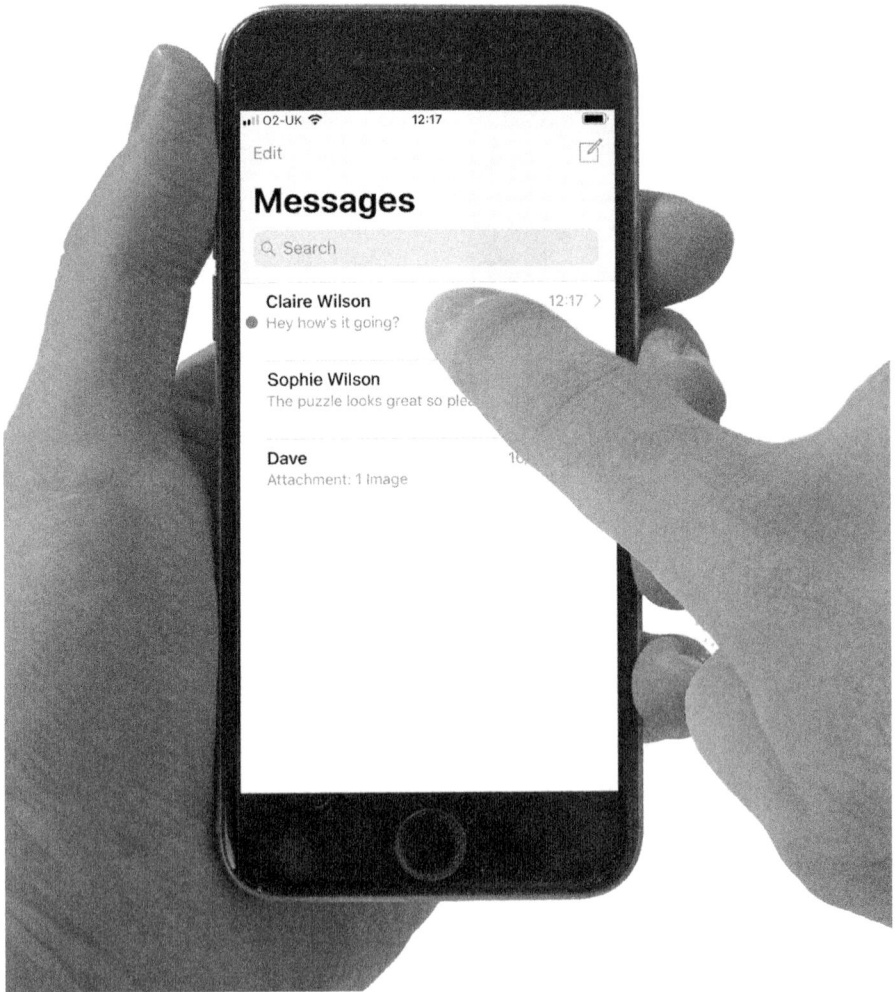

Tap the new message icon on the top right of the screen.

## New Message

Tap the + sign to add an address or phone number from your contacts. Or start typing the person's name or phone number into the 'to' field.

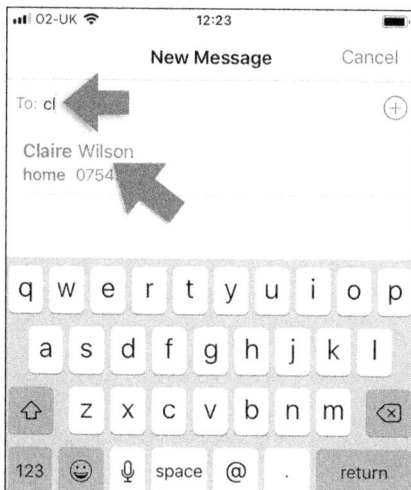

Type your message in the box indicated with the red arrow.

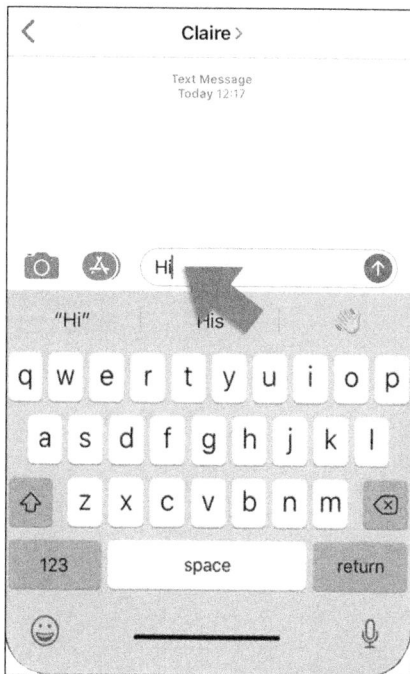

Tap the blue arrow on the right hand side to send the message

## Send Voice Message

You can send a voice message by tapping and holding your finger on the mic icon. Record your message, then release your finger to stop.

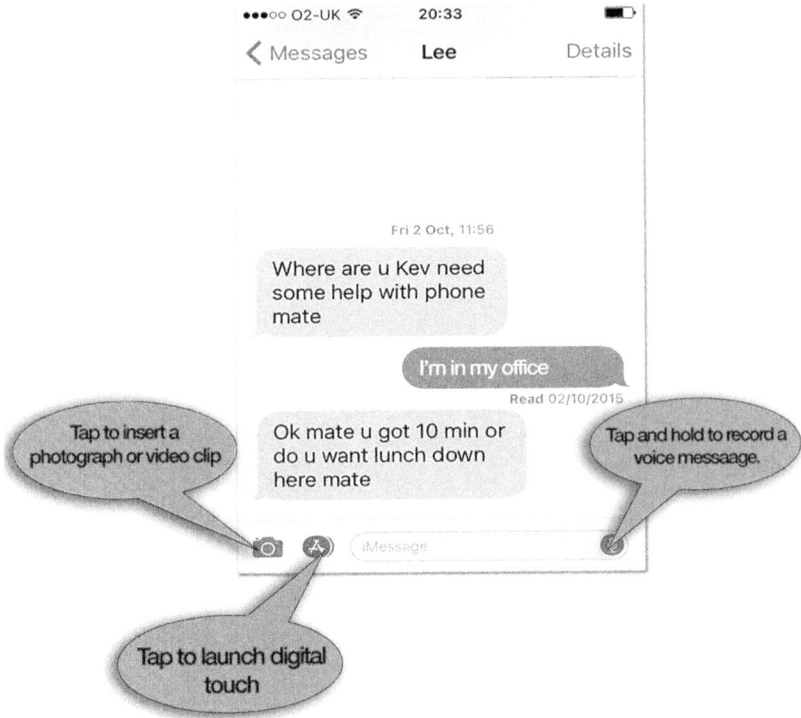

From the options that appear, select from the icons below.

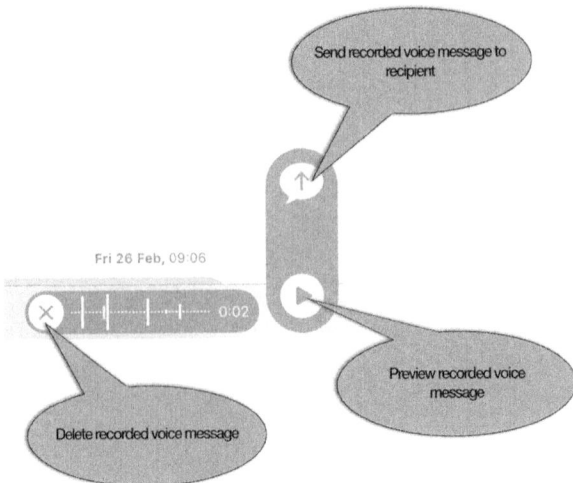

## Send a Photo

To send a photograph or video, tap the small camera icon on the bottom left of your message window.

Your camera app will open up. Select 'photo' from the list on the bottom right, then tap on the white circle to take the picture.

Once you've taken your photo, you can add effects and annotate the image before you send it. Just tap the markup icon on the right hand side of the screen.

Draw directly onto the photo with your finger or pencil.

Tap 'save' on the top right, then tap the blue arrow to send.

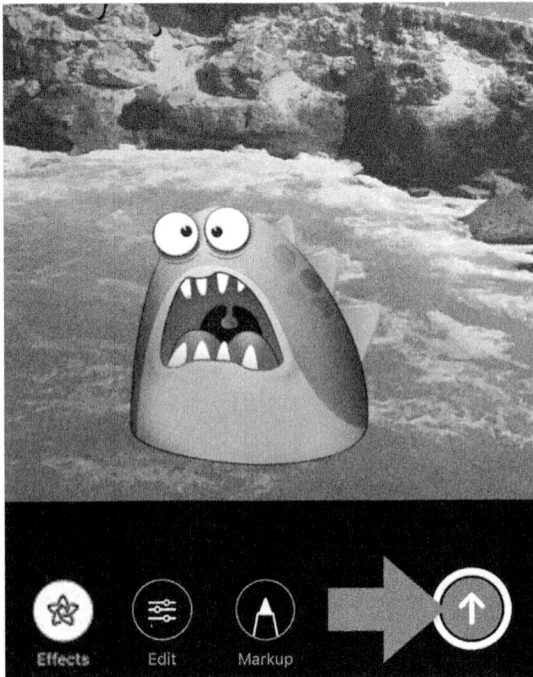

# Effects

You can also add effects to a photo or video. To do this, select 'photo' from the list on the bottom right, then tap on the white/red circle to take the picture.

Once you've taken your picture, select the effects icon from the panel on the bottom of the screen. Then select an effect from the panel that appears.

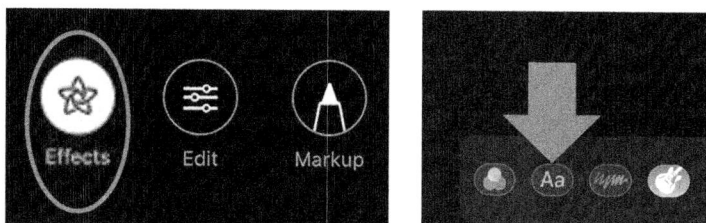

Add some text and effects to your image. Tap and drag the effect into place.

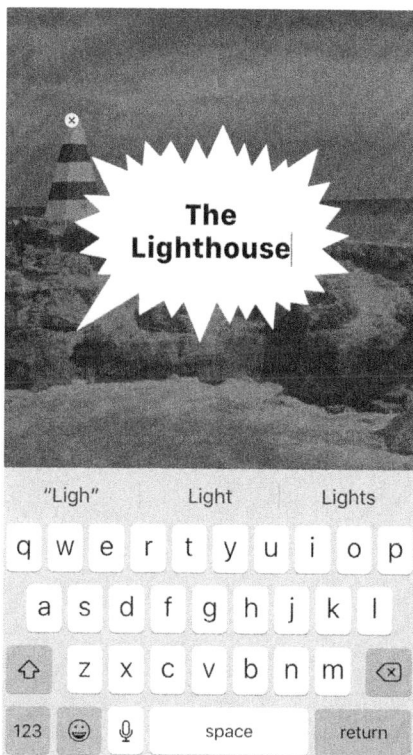

Try a few of the other effects.

Tap the blue arrow on the right hand side to send immediately, or tap 'done' on the top right of the screen to return to the message window.

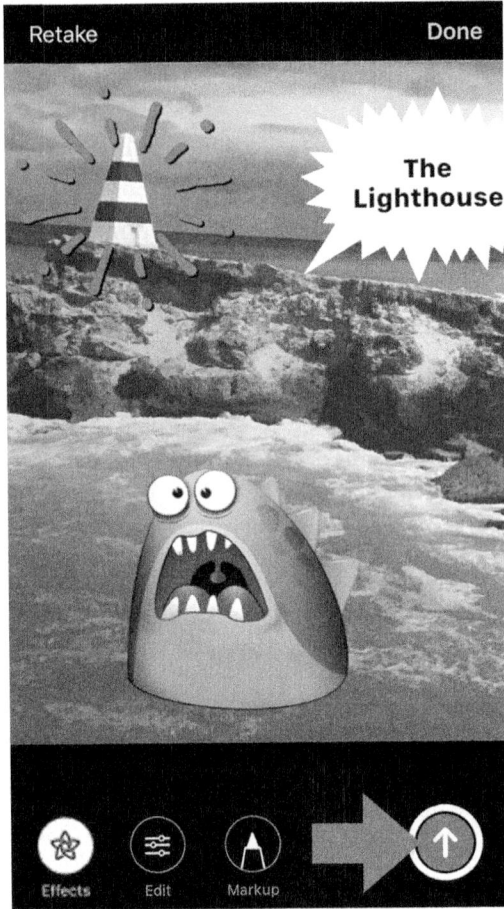

If you returned to the message window, enter a message in the text field, tap the blue arrow to the right of the text field to send.

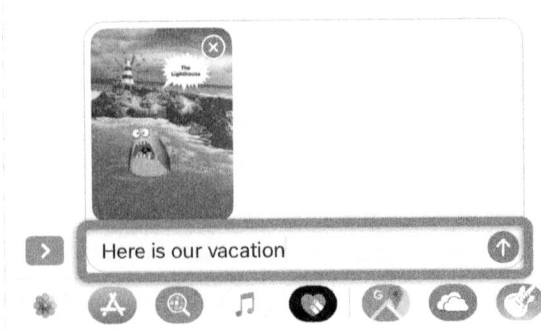

# Digital Touch in iMessage

In digital touch mode, you can draw with your finger and send animations.

Tap the store icon to the left side of the text field to reveal additional options.

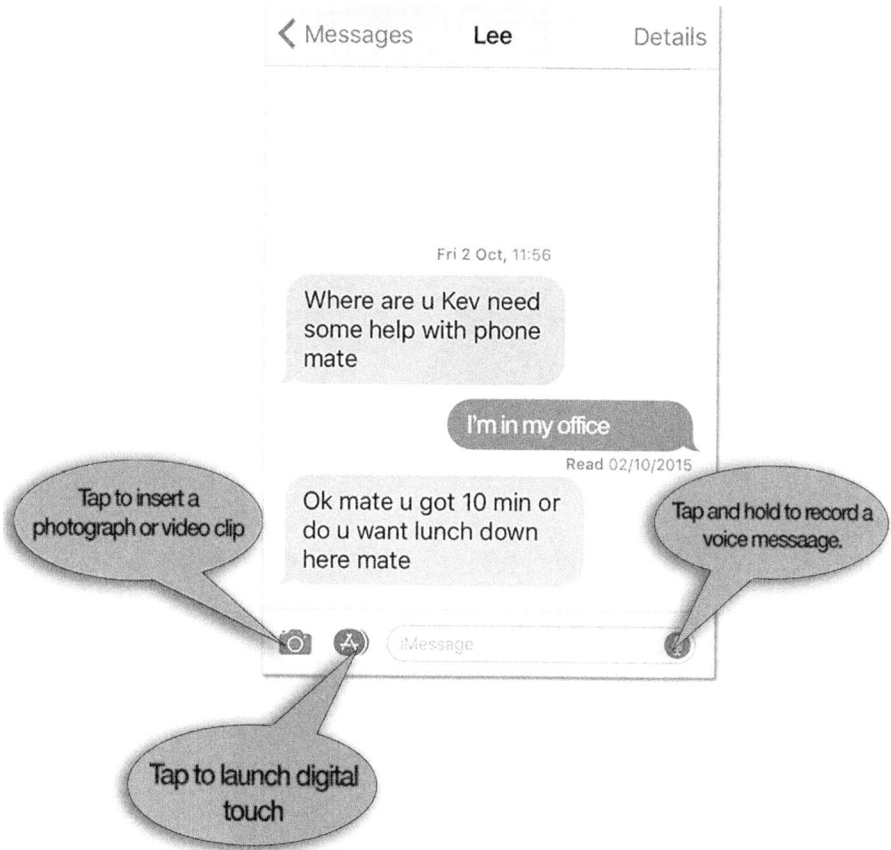

Then tap the digital touch icon. This opens up the digital touch interface.

Tap the blue circle on the left hand side. This will open up the digital touch panel

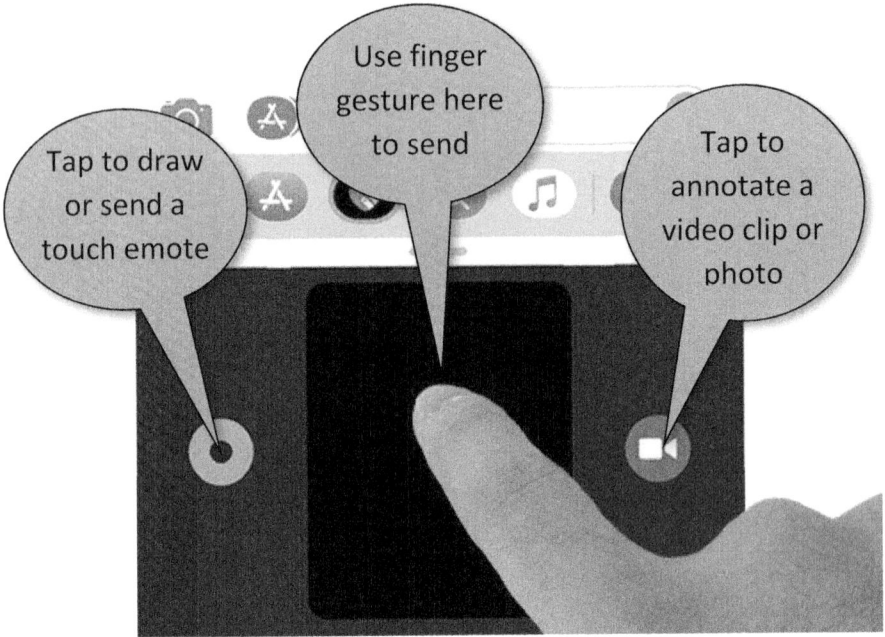

You can use certain finger gestures to send different emotes. For example, you can use one finger to draw or write something, press with one finger to send a fireball effect, tap with two fingers to send a kiss and so on. Here's a list of a few of the good ones...

You can also draw using your finger. Tap on the dot on the left hand side to open up the colours.

Tap on a colour along the left hand side, then draw a diagram on the black screen in the centre.

Tap on the blue arrow to the right to send.

You can also annotate a video or photograph using digital touch. To do this, from digital touch interface, tap the camera icon.

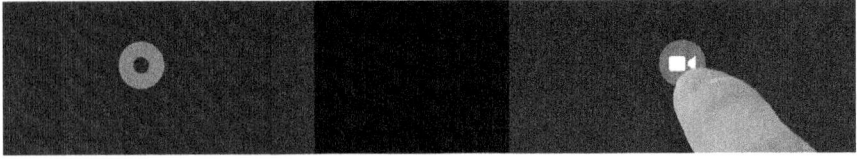

Tap the red button to start recording. While the video is recording, use the digital touch tools to draw on it. Tap a colour, then draw or write on the image with your finger.

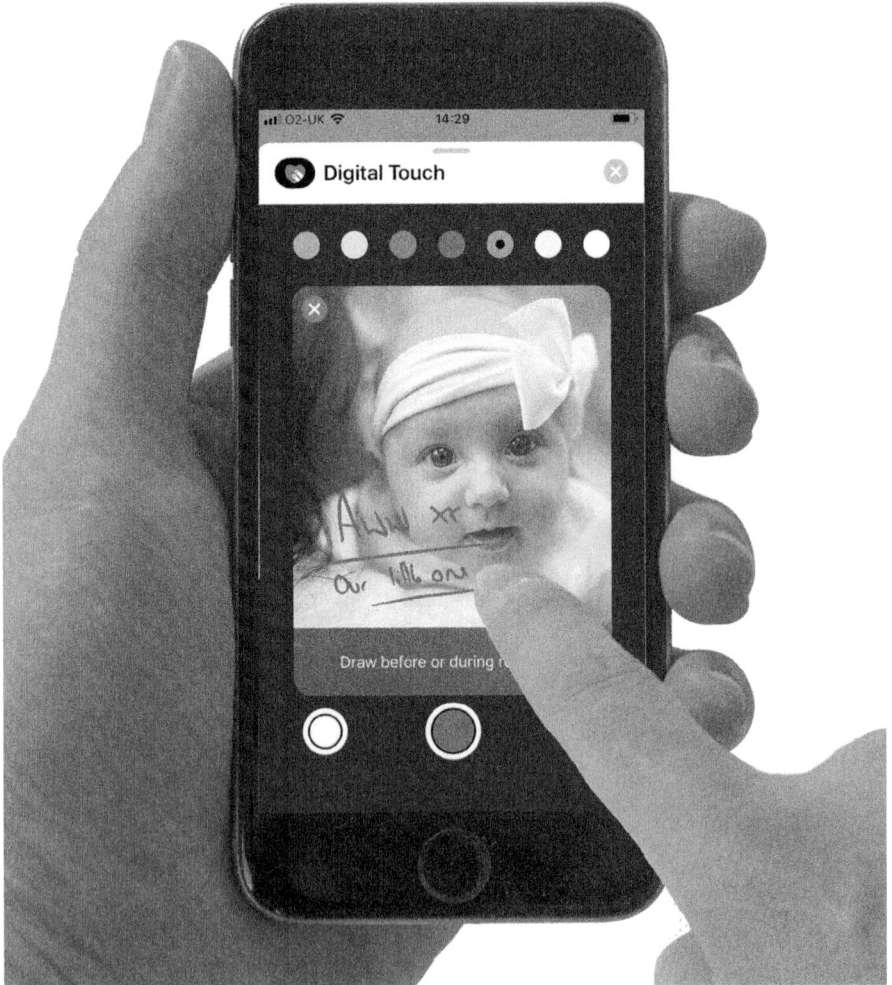

*The white button at the bottom left takes a photo, while the red button in the centre records a video.*

Try a few 'tap and holds' with two fingers to add a few hearts. Or tap with two fingers to send a kiss.

Tap the record button again to stop recording.

Tap the blue arrow at the bottom right to send your finished piece.

You can also share gifs which are short animations. Select the digital touch icon circled below. Then along the bottom of the screen, select the 'search gif' icon. Tap on a gif to add it to your message or type in to the 'find images' field to search for something specific.

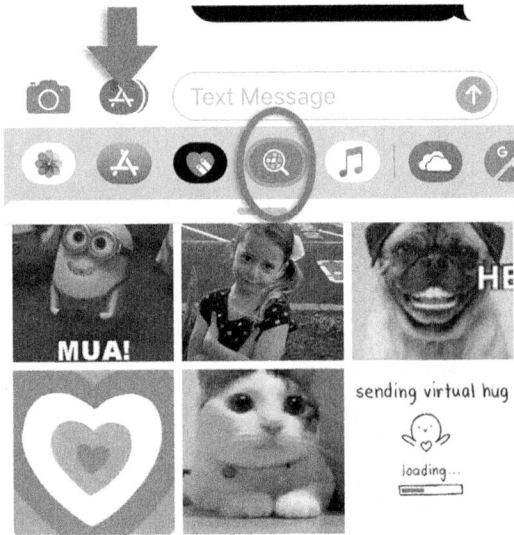

You can also share what music you are listening to on iTunes. Select the digital touch icon circled below. Then along the bottom of the screen, select the 'iTunes' icon.

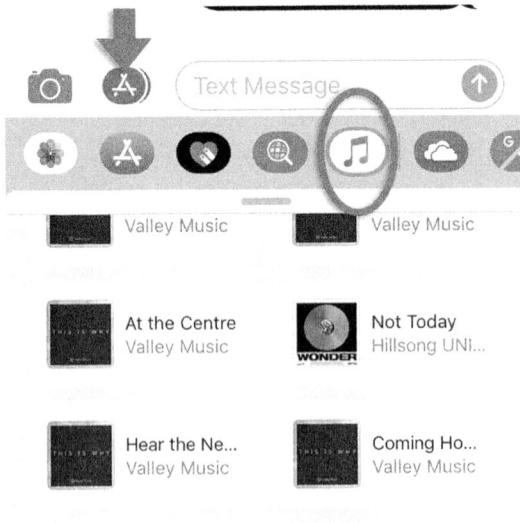

You'll see all the music you have been listening to or currently listening to on your iPhone. Tap on a track to share.

# Sending Payments with iMessage

You can send payments to contacts on iMessage using Apple Pay. This only work between Apple devices at the moment, so you can't send payments to users of other phones or tablets. This feature is not available in some countries yet.

Tap the store icon to the left side of the text field to reveal additional options. Then tap the Apple Pay icon.

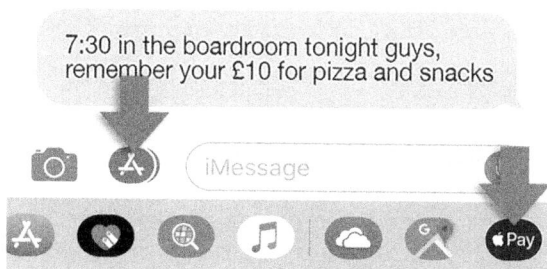

Enter the amount. Either use the + and - buttons to increase/decrease the amount, or tap 'show keypad' and tap in the amount. Once you're done hit 'pay'.

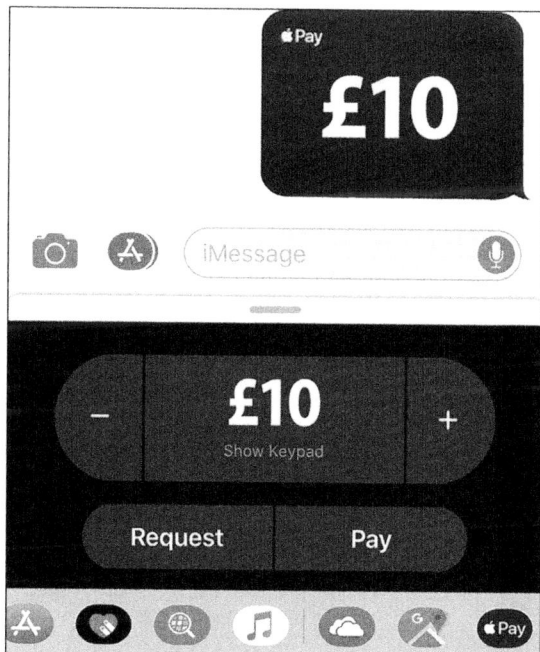

If people are owing you money, you can enter the amount as above and tap 'request' to send them an invite to pay you the amount.

# AirDrop

AirDrop allows you to transfer files from one device to another using bluetooth wireless technology.

To use AirDrop you will need a compatible device, such as the iPhone 5 or later, fourth-generation iPhone, iPhone mini, and fifth-generation iPod touch, and have both Bluetooth and Wi-Fi enabled.

Swipe your finger downwards from the top right edge of your screen to open control center. Tap the icons to yurn on Wi-Fi and Bluetooth.

To enable AirDrop open Control Centre and press the AirDrop icon. Make yourself discoverable to just those in your contacts.

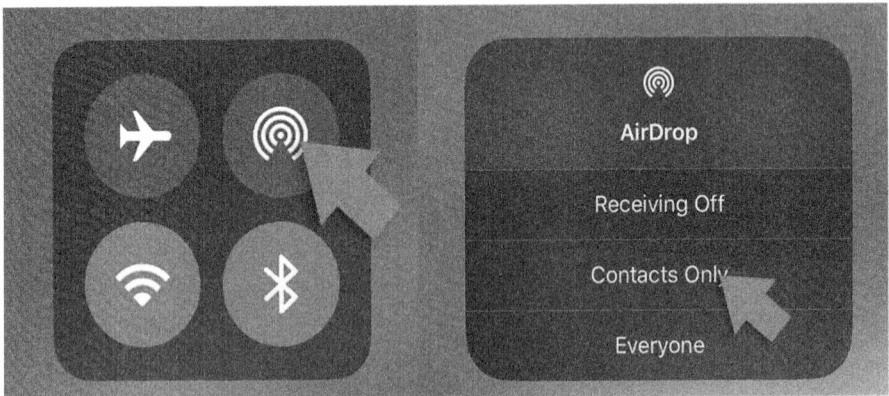

Be careful if you select 'everyone' as this means anyone in your vicinity that has an airdrop enabled device can connect to and send files to your device, which could be a possible security risk.

**144**

## To Send a file to Someone using AirDrop

You can send a file or photo from your iPhone to another iPhone, Mac, or iPad.

In this example, I am going to send a photo. So launch Photos app.

Tap the image or video you want to share from your albums, tap next.

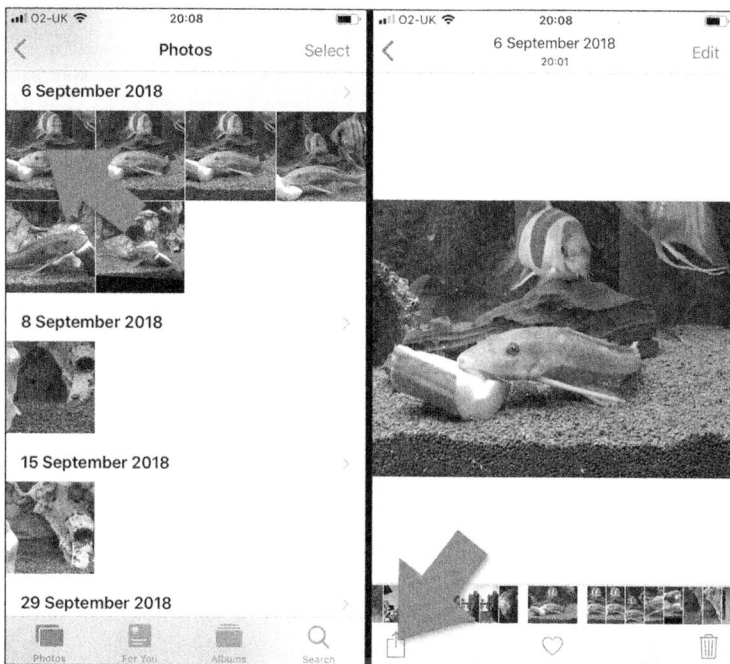

Tap on the Share icon. AirDrop will detect other devices in the vicinity. In this example, AirDrop has detected my iPhone. This is the one I want to share with.

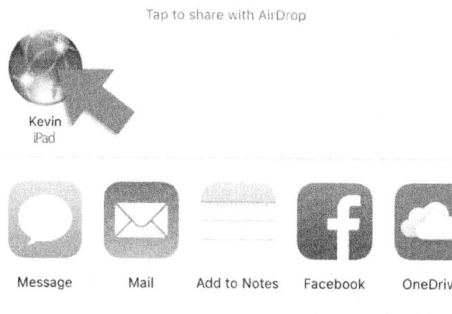

Tap the icon of the person/device you want to send to.

Now when you send the photo, the other person will get a prompt to download the image. Accept the confirmation and your image will download.

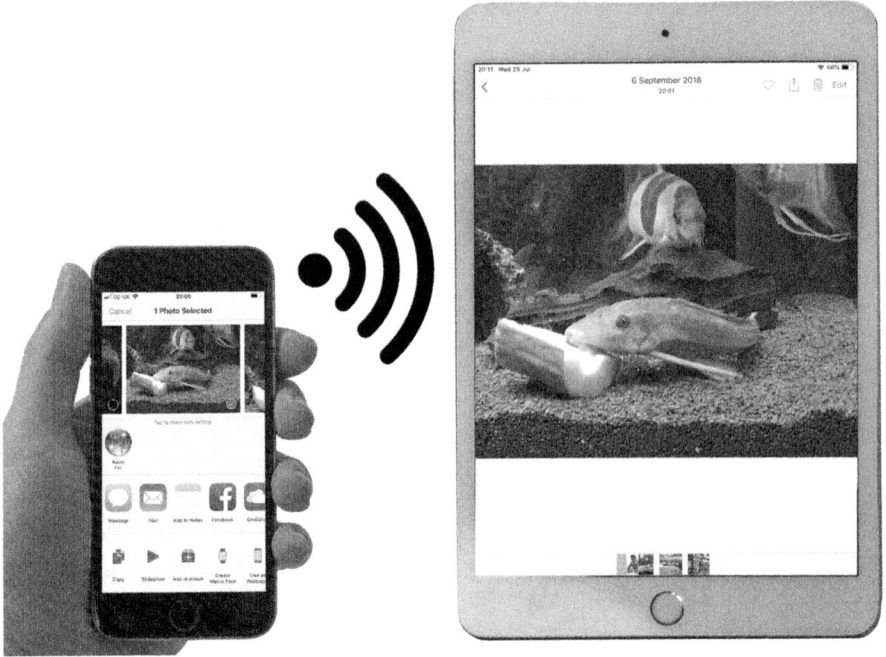

The image/video will be added to your photo library. The photo sent has appeared in photos app on the iPhone.

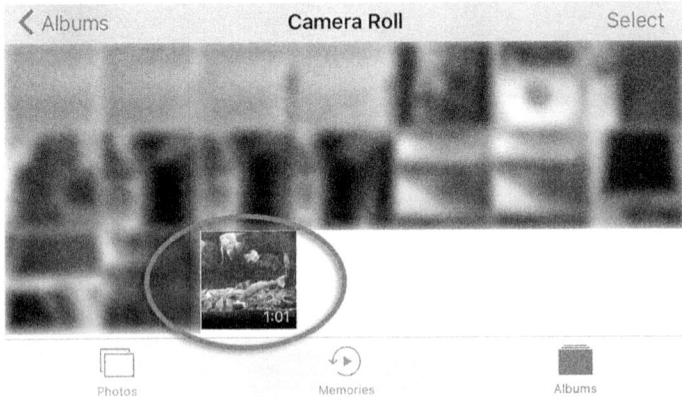

This works the same for other files too, just select the file and tap the share icon. Files will appear in the relevant apps; music will go to iTunes and files will be stored in Files app. If iOS doesn't recognise the file type, then it will ask you what app you want to open the file with.

# To Receive a File from Someone using AirDrop

Make sure your AirDrop is enabled on your device.

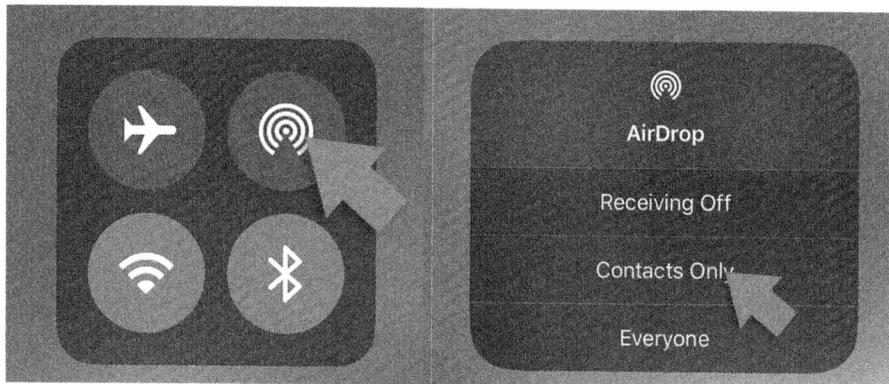

AirDrop will try to negotiate the connection with near by devices.

More often than not, the file will automatically download. If you get a prompt, tap on Accept when the photo comes through

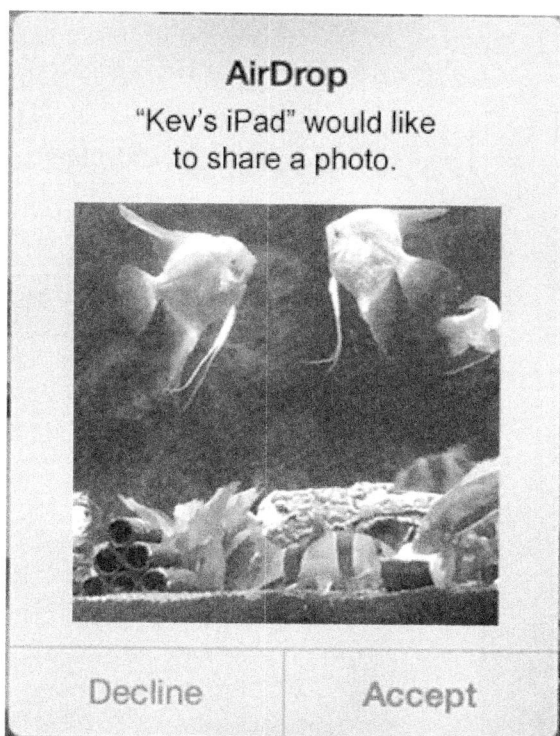

Go into your photos app and the photo will be stored in there.

# Using Multimedia

Your iPhone is a multimedia rich device, meaning you can take photos and record videos. You can even edit and enhance your photos, correct colour and brightness.

You can post your photographs to your favourite social media account for the world to see.

You can create slide shows, edit your videos, download and watch TV programmes and films.

You can download and play any kind of music you can think of, all from your iPhone.

So lets begin by taking a look at the Photos App.

# Photos

Using the photos app, you can import photos from a memory card or digital camera, edit and share photos taken with the on board cameras on your iPhone.

## Import Photos

There are two adapters available to accomplish this: the Lightning to SD Card Reader, or the Lightning to USB Adapter.

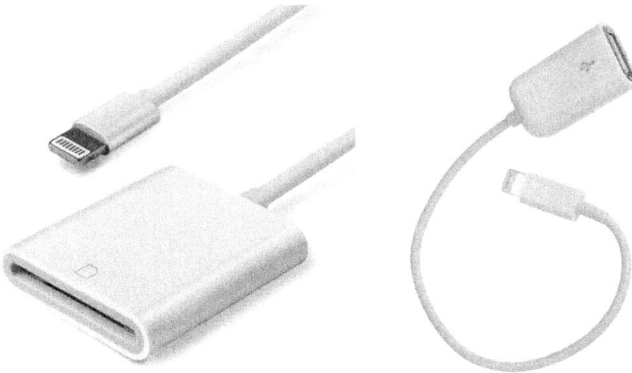

The card reader enables you to insert the SD card from your camera and copy images from it.

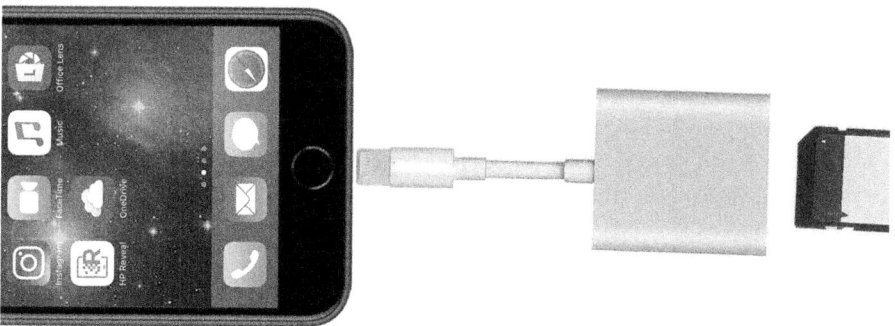

The card reader plugs into the docking port on the bottom of the iPhone. Launch the iPhoto app. Tap on camera or card.

**149**

You can also connect your camera directly using a lightning to USB connector. Plug the connector into the bottom of your iPhone, then plug the USB cable that came with your camera into the other end of the lightning to USB adapter.

When iPhone detects your media, it will prompt you with an import screen. Tap the photographs you want to import and then tap import to copy the photos across.

Once the photos have been imported, you will see a prompt asking you whether to keep the images or delete them.

If you select keep, this leaves all the photos intact on the memory card. If you select delete, this deletes the photos you just imported off the memory card.

Once all the photos have been imported it is safe to delete the photos off the card.

# Editing Photos

You can do some basic editing on your iPhone. You can lighten up dark images, crop and rotate your photos.

To do this tap on the photograph in the photos app.

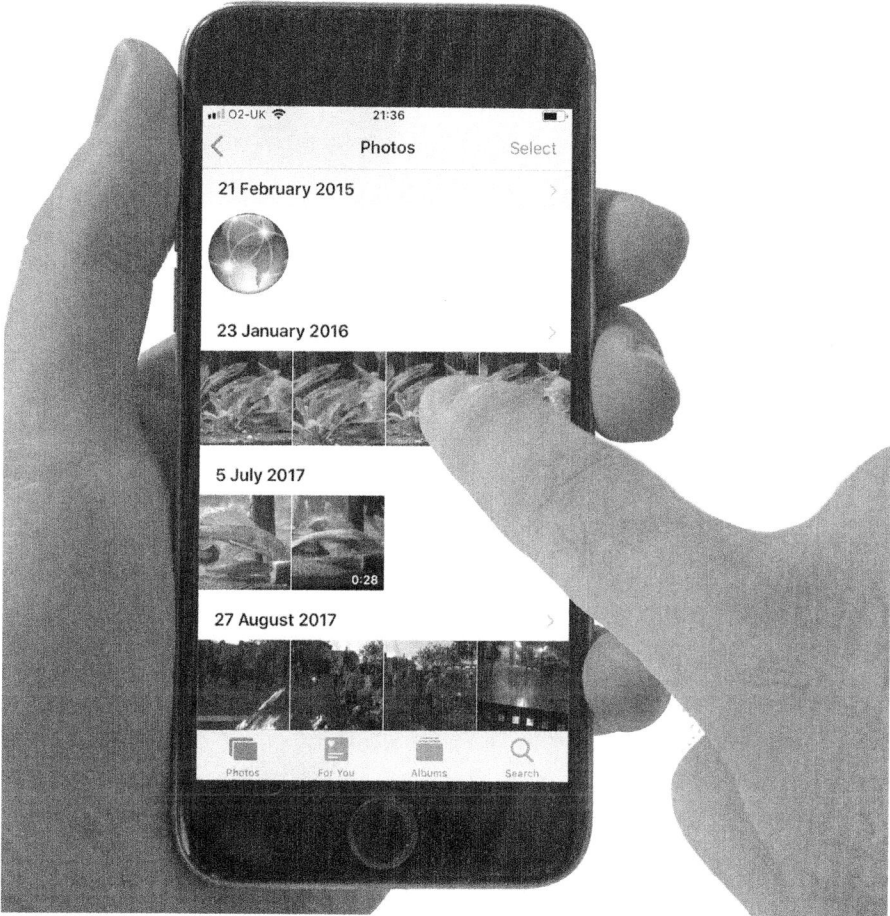

The image will open up full screen. Tap on the edit icon on the top right of the screen.

Along the bottom of the screen you'll see your editing icons.

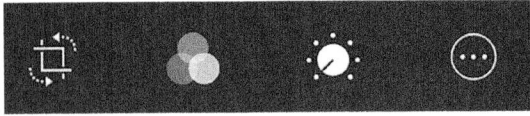

Reading the icons in the centre from left to right we have:

**Image crop and rotate,** this allows you to rotate images that may have been taken at an angle or crop parts of the photo you don't want.

**Effects,** allows you to add black and white, fade, sepia effects to a photo.

**Adjustments,** allows you to adjust colour, brightness, contrast, bring up shadows, reduce highlights in bright areas of a photo.

Tap the three dots icon for more options such as markup.

## Crop Image

To crop the image, click the crop & rotate icon on the bottom left of the edit screen. You'll notice a white crop box appear with resize handles around the edges. Tap and drag the box around the bit of the photo you want.

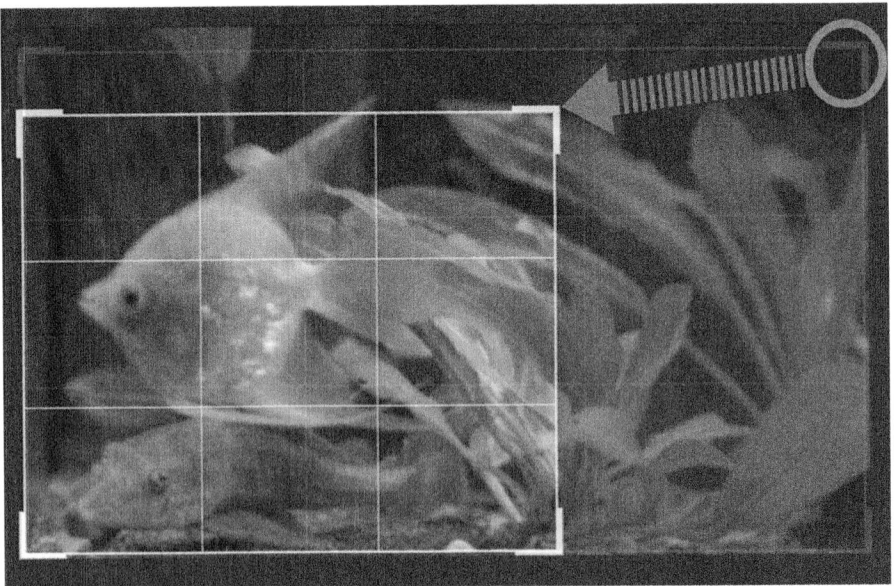

In this example, I want to crop the image to the fish in the corner.

# Rotate Image

If you want to rotate the image, tap the crop & rotate icon from the bottom left of the edit screen.

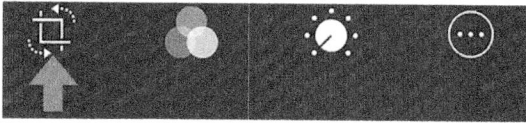

Drag the rotation protractor underneath the image to the left or right.

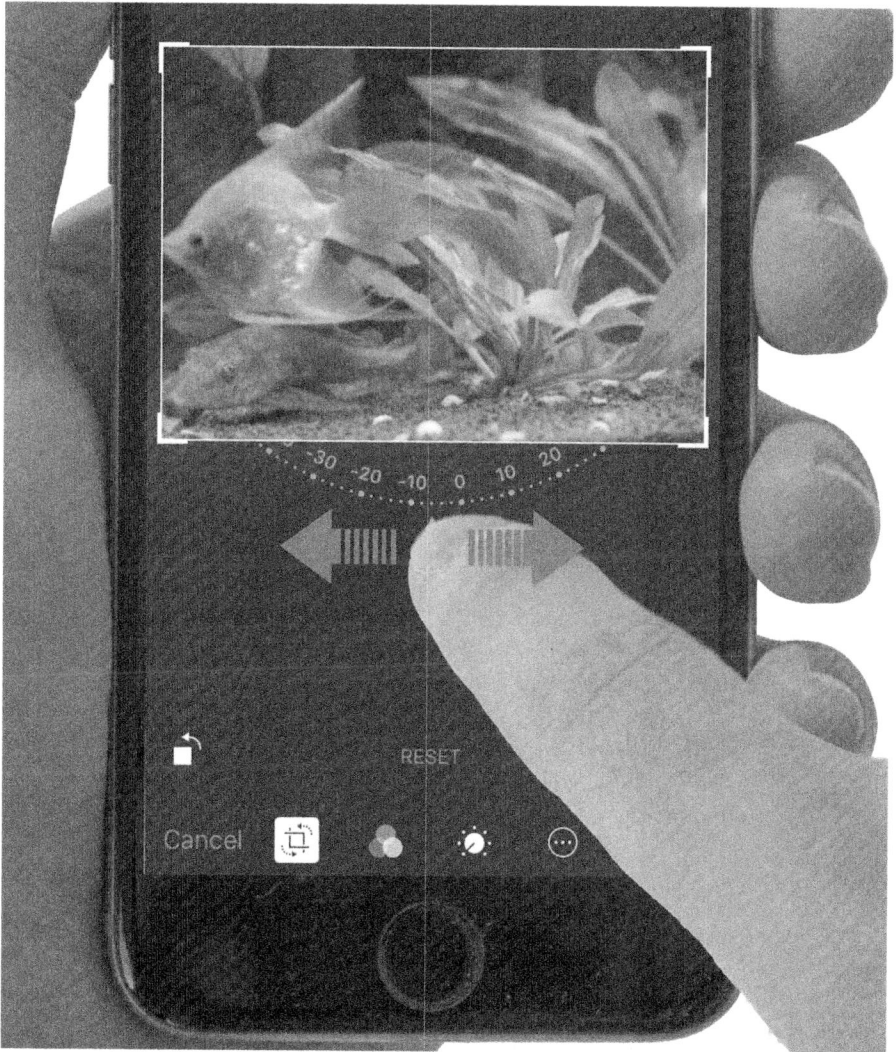

Tap 'done' on the bottom right when you're finished.

## Adjusting Images

If you want to correct colour, contrast, or brightness, tap the adjustments icon on the bar along the bottom of the edit screen.

You'll see three options appear.

- 'Light' contains all the controls for adjusting brightness, contrast, highlights, and shadows.
- 'Colour' contains all the controls for adjusting colour saturation.
- 'B&W' creates black and white image effects.

In this example I am going to adjust the brightness of the photo. So tap on 'light'. This opens up the 'light' group.

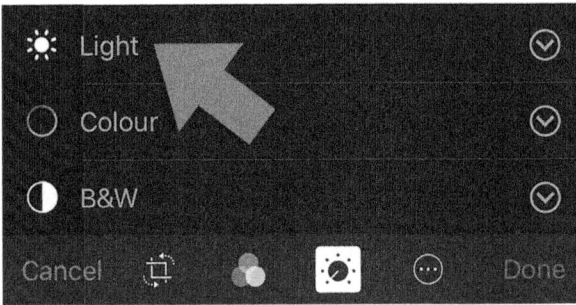

Drag the slider with your finger, left and right, to adjust the overall brightness.

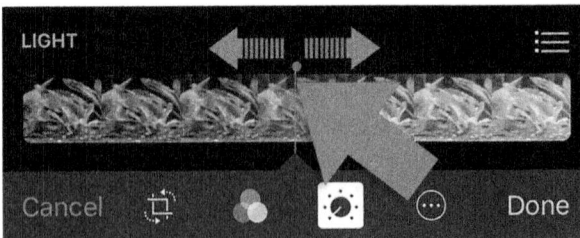

To change contrast, shadows, or highlights, tap the hamburger icon to the right.

**154**

From the menu, select the one you want to change - try adjusting highlights - this is the bright parts of the image. Also try adjust the contrast.

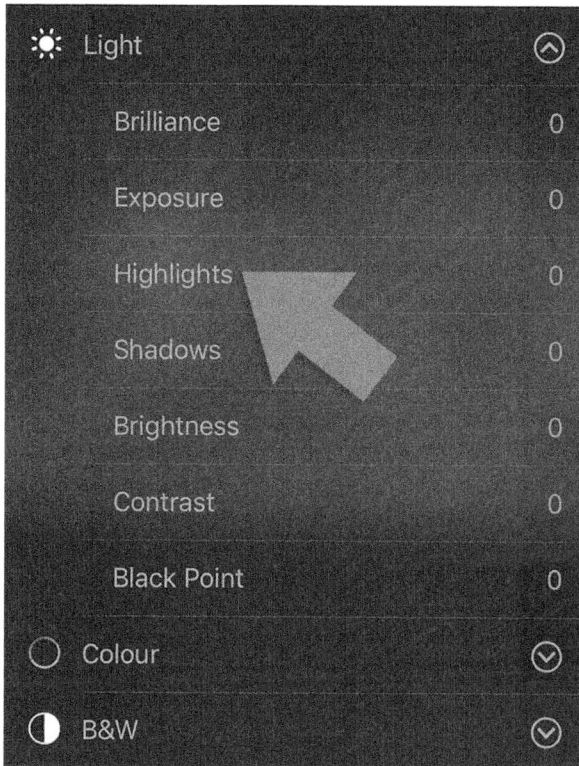

Use the slider to change the setting.

Tap the hamburger icon to the right again to select another adjustment, eg shadows.

# Taking Pictures with Camera App

Tap the camera icon on the home screen.

You can use your iPhone as a camera to take photos and record video.

Along the left side of your screen you have some icons. With the top icon, you can apply a filter. Next down is a timer delay (can set to off, 3 or 10 seconds). The third icon you can enable HDR (this is good for scenes where you have dark shadows and bright areas such as sky). The bottom icon enables and disables the flash.

On the right hand side you can select the type of video or photo you want to take: time lapse, slomo, video, photo, square photo and panoramic photo. You can select them by swiping your finger over them.

You can adjust the zoom using the slider on the right hand side of the image, or use your forefinger and thumb to zoom - just spread your two fingers out over the glass using a pinch & spread gesture, as shown in the illustration below.

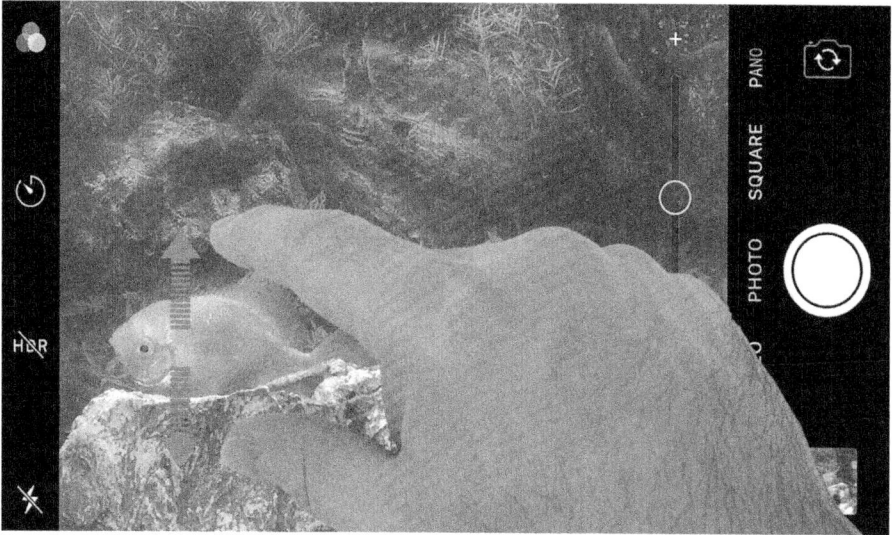

If you're having trouble focusing, tap and hold your finger on the object you want to focus on. This will lock the exposure and focus on that object, so it doesn't change, making it easier to take the photo.

Tap the white circle on the right hand side as normal to take the photo

You can also adjust the brightness before you take a photo. To do this tap on the screen and you'll see a yellow square show up with a vertical line with a slider on it.

Drag the slider upward to brighten up the image, slide it downward to darken the image.

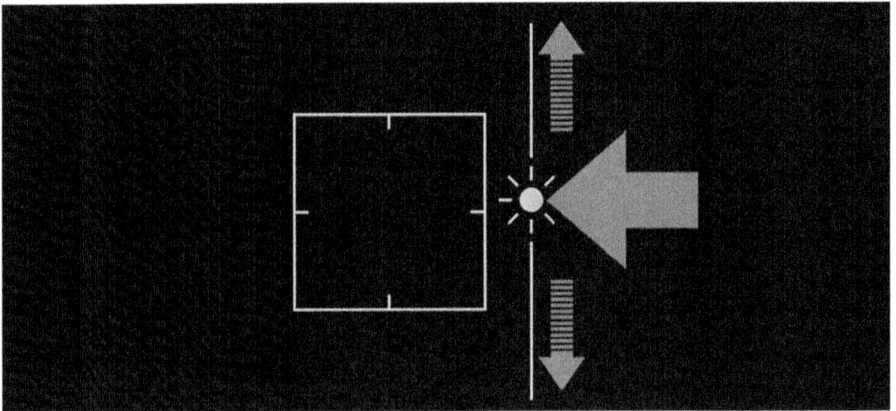

Tap the white circle on the bottom to take the photo as normal.

# Adjusting Photos

Once you have taken your photo you can you can crop or rotate the image. Rotating an image is good for straightening up photos.

To crop the image, tap the photo icon on bottom left hand side of the screen, to open the photo you just took.

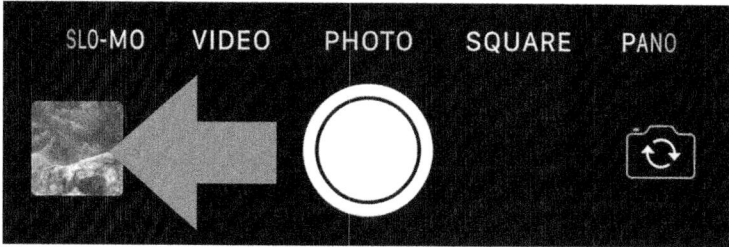

Tap edit on the bottom right, then select the crop tool, from the toolbar along the bottom of the edit screen.

Use the grid shown below to highlight the section of the photograph you want to keep. Drag the edges of the box inwards to the point you want to crop

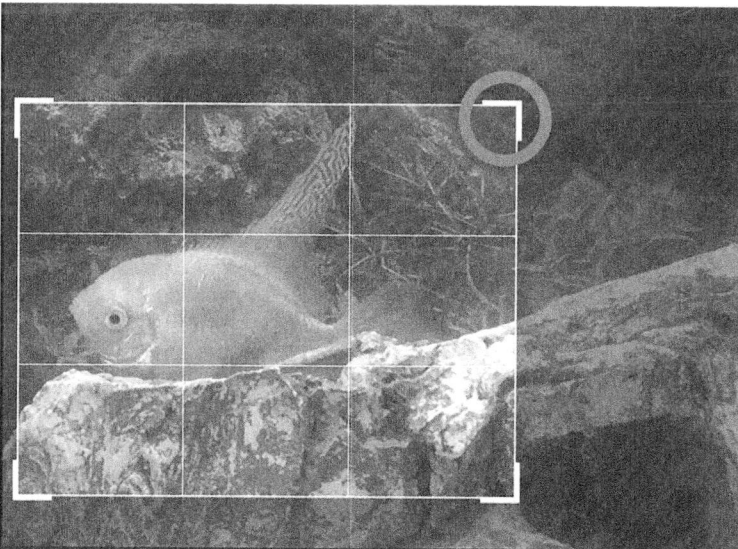

# Chapter 5: Using Multimedia

You can straighten a photograph by rotating it a number of degrees. To do this drag the dials up and down on the left hand side of the screen.

You can also change the shading and tonal effects of the image, making your image black and white, a sepia effect or boost the colours.

Tap the photo icon on the bottom left hand side of the screen, to open the photo you just took.

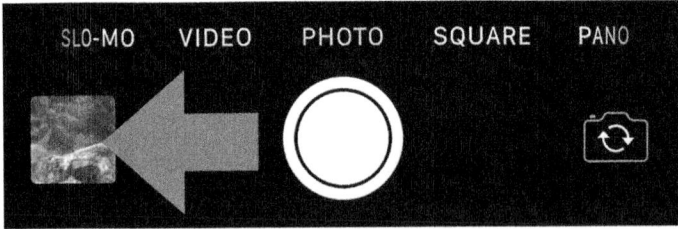

Now tap edit on the bottom right of your screen. To add tonal effects, tap the colour icon at the bottom of your screen.

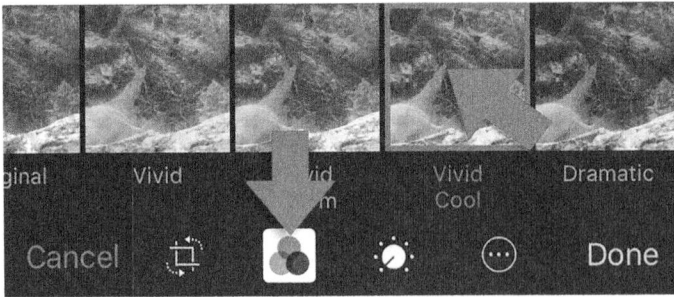

You can adjust the brightness and contrast or highlight shadows where photographs have come out dark in places.

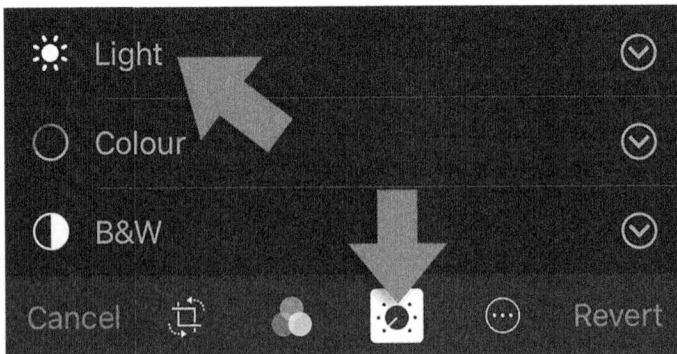

You can do this by tapping on the light adjust icon. This is the same as adjusting your photos in the photos app.

From the options, select the attributes of the photo you want to adjust, this is the exposure, highlights, shadows, brightness, contrast, or black point.

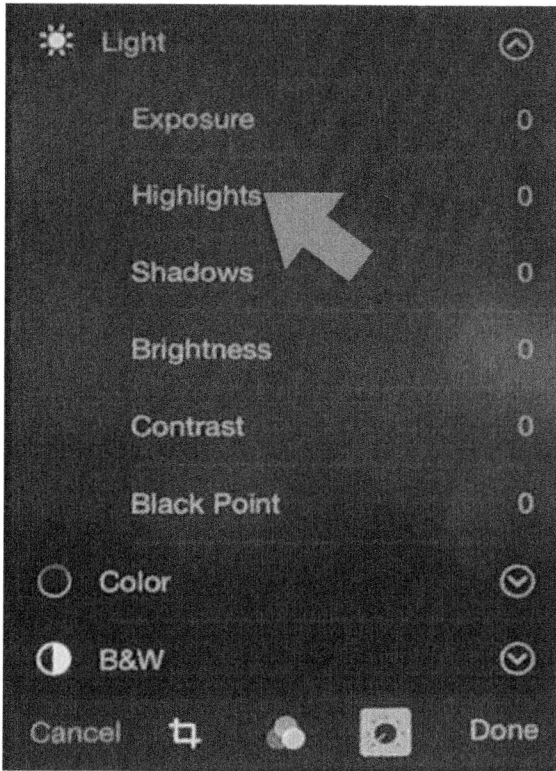

For example, tap on highlights to darken some of the bright parts in your image.

Drag the bar left and right to change the highlight.

Also try exposure or brightness to lighten a dark image or shadows to lighten up dark parts of an image.

## Panoramic Photos

Panoramic shots are great for scenery and landscapes. Photos app allows you to automatically take a series of photos and it stitches them together into a long panoramic image.

To take panoramic photos, open your camera app, select pano from the bottom of the screen. You might need to scroll down the selections if it isn't visible.

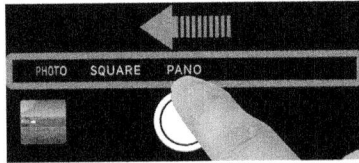

Now, move your iPhone to the start of the scene and tap the white circle. You'll notice in the centre of the screen a rectangular box, this will start to fill as you move your iPhone across the scene. In this demonstration, I'm taking a panoramic photo of a mountain range.

Position your iPhone camera at the beginning of the mountain range on the left, tap the white 'take photo' icon on the right of your screen. Now move your camera along the mountain range until you get to the end. You'll see the rectangular box in the centre of the screen fill up as you do so. Tap the white circle again to finish.

Make sure you stand in one spot, the panoramic photos don't work if you walk along with it.

**162**

## Recording Video

You can record video using the camera app. Select 'video' from the list on the bottom right of your screen.

To take the best looking video, use your iPhone in a horizontal orientation as shown below.

Tap the red circle icon on the right hand side of the screen to start recording.

Tap on any part of the screen to focus on that point during the video.

Use a pinch & spread gesture to zoom in and out.

Tap the red circle icon on the right hand side to stop recording.

## Live Photos

Live Photos capture 1.5 seconds of motion before and after the photo. They are only available on the iPhone 6s and later.

To take a live photo, from the Camera app, tap the Live Photo button, right at the top of the screen to turn it on, indicated with the red arrow below.

Tap the Shutter button to take your Live Photo.

They animate when you press firmly and hold your finger on the photo. To see your live photos in the photos app, tap on the photo thumbnail in the main screen.

Then when the photo opens up, press your finger firmly on the photo to see the animation.

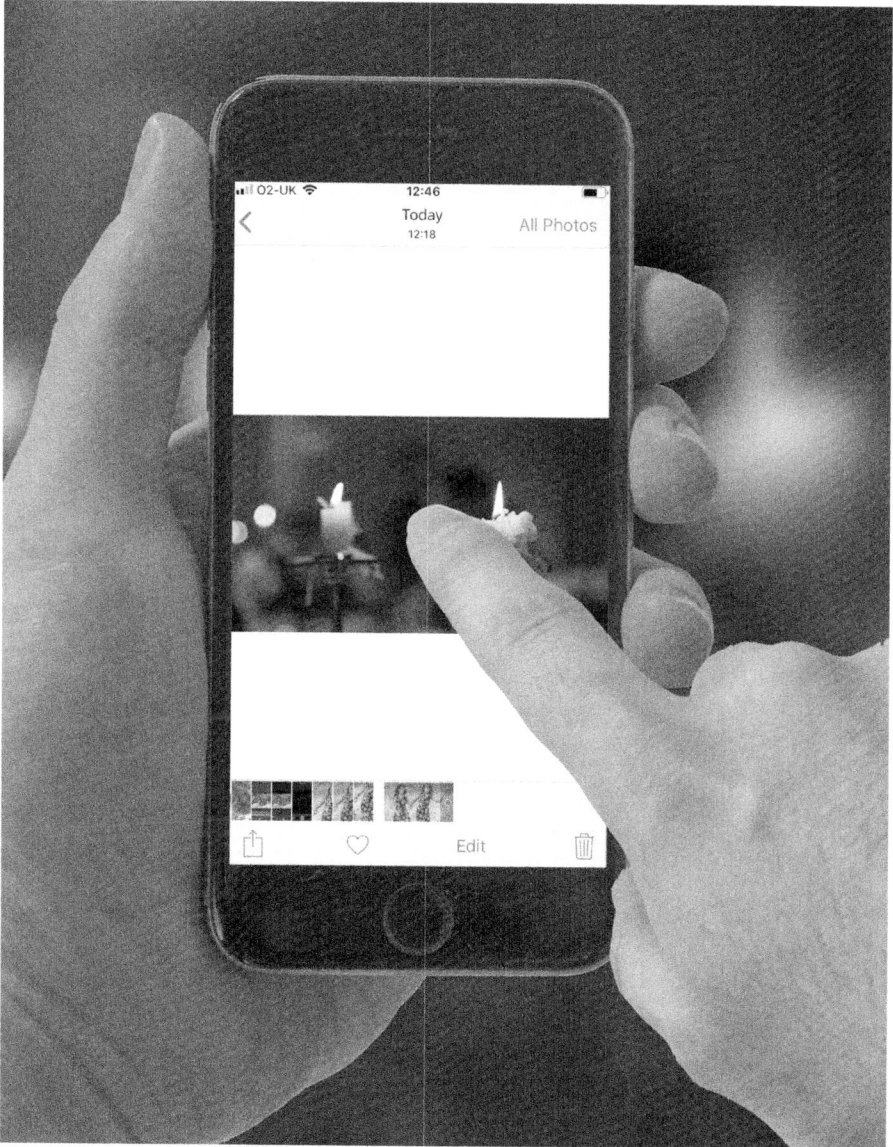

You can share photos via email, iMessage, Facetime in the usual way using the share icon.

## Share Pics on Social Media

You will need to be logged into, and have the appropriate app from the app store such as facebook, instagram, or twitter installed.

In this example I'm going to share a photograph on Facebook of the two girls.

If you have taken the photo using your camera, tap the small thumbnail in the bottom right hand corner.

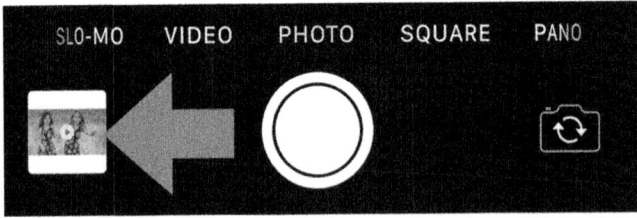

If you're in the photos app, tap on your photograph thumbnail to open it up

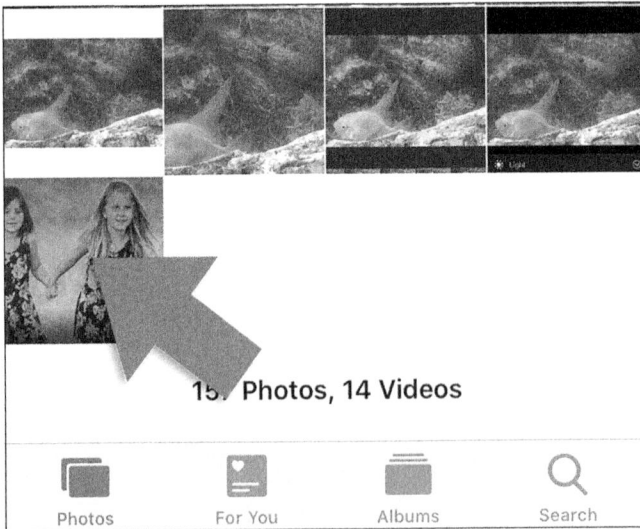

Once the photo opens up, tap the share icon in the bottom left corner.

Select 'Facebook' from the list of social media icons.

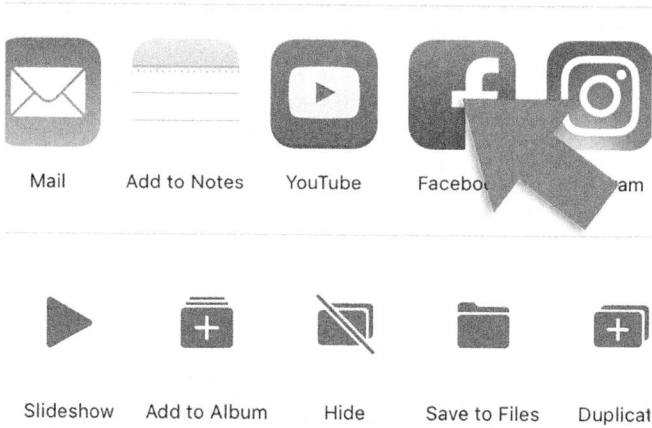

Type a message in your post, then hit 'post'.

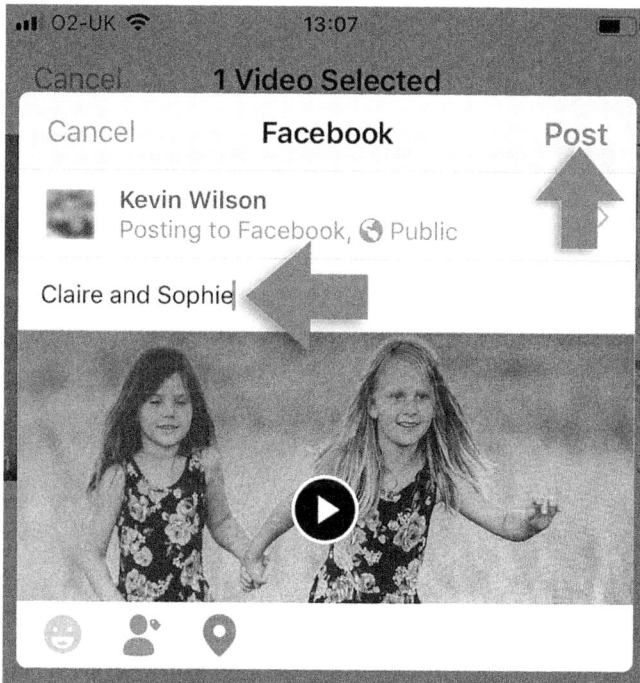

You can use the same procedure for Instagram, Twitter, email, iMessage, and any other social media you use. Just select the icon from the social media icons list on the previous page.

# Music App

You can start the music app by tapping on music icon on the main screen.

Once music app has loaded, you'll see all the songs and albums that are currently on your iPhone.

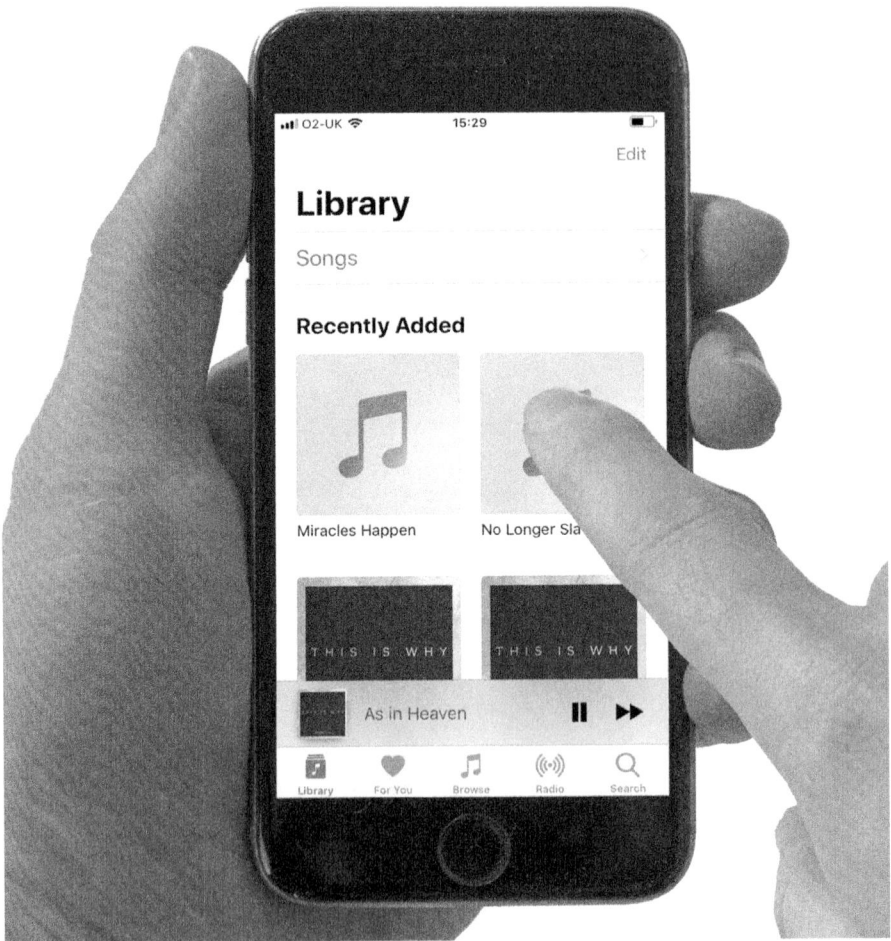

Tap on any album cover to see a list of tracks on that album. Tap 'songs' to view the songs on your iPhone as a list.

# Connecting to your Computer

To get music onto iPhone you can purchase and download from the iTunes Store, or sync with iTunes on your computer by connecting your iPhone using the USB lightning cable.

Open iTunes on your computer, then click the iPad/iPhone icon on the top left of the tool bar.

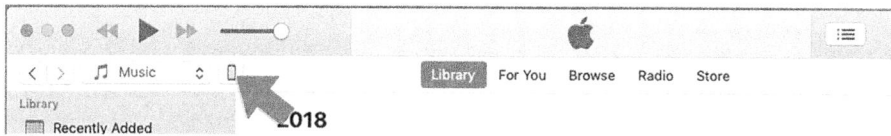

Click 'summary' on the left hand side. Here you can update your iPhone's iOS software, just click 'check for update'. Press the option key and click 'check for updates' if you have downloaded a restore image (IPSW).

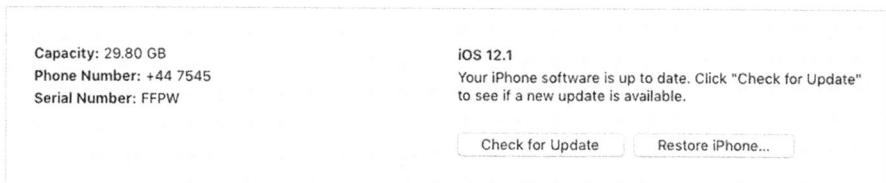

You can restore your device to its factory settings if you have problems with it. To do this click 'restore iPad/iPhone'. This will wipe your data, apps, music and settings, so you'll need to restore from a backup if you do this.

# Chapter 5: Using Multimedia

Further down the options, you can set backups. By default, your data is automatically backed up to your iCloud account, but you can also set it to backup to your computer - this means you'd have to plug your device into your computer to allow this. Most of the time leaving this backing up to iCloud is sufficient.

**Backups**

Automatically Back Up

○ iCloud
Back up the most important data on your iPhone to iCloud.

○ This Computer
A full backup of your iPhone will be stored on this computer.

Manually Back Up and Restore
Manually back up your iPhone to this computer or restore a backup stored on this computer.

[ Back Up Now ]  [ Restore Backup ]

Latest Backup:
05/01/2019, 17:23 to iCloud

Scroll down to the bottom of this page and select **'manually manage music and videos'**. This allows you to select the songs or albums you want to transfer instead of syncing your whole library.

**Options**

☐ Automatically sync when this iPhone is connected
☐ Sync with this iPhone over Wi-Fi
☐ Sync only ticked songs and videos
☐ Prefer standard definition videos
☐ Convert higher bit rate songs to [ 128 kbps ⌄ ] AAC
☐ Manually manage music and videos
[ Reset Warnings ]
[ Configure Accessibility... ]

**Automatically sync when this iPhone is connected:** iTunes opens and syncs your phone whenever you connect to the computer.

**Sync with this iPhone over Wi-Fi:** Your iPhone will sync automatically over your wifi network. Your phone and computer will need to be on the same wifi network for this to work.

**Prefer standard definition videos:** Syncs standard definition videos instead of HD in order to save space on your iPhone.

**Convert higher bit rate songs to 128 kbps AAC:** Converts high quality tracks to a lower quality 128 kbps AAC format during syncing, in order to save space on your iPhone.

**Manually manage music and videos:** Disables auto syncing and allows you to manually add and remove tracks.

**Configure Accessibility:** Options for people with hearing or visual impairments.

# 170

# Transferring Music from a Computer

Enable your sidebar in iTunes, if it isn't already open. I find this helps when transferring songs or albums to an iPhone. To do this, open the view menu and select 'show sidebar'.

Also your iPhone will need to be set to 'manually manage music and videos' - see previous section on how to do this.

Now, under the 'library' section of the sidebar on left hand side, select 'songs'. This is music that is stored on your computer.

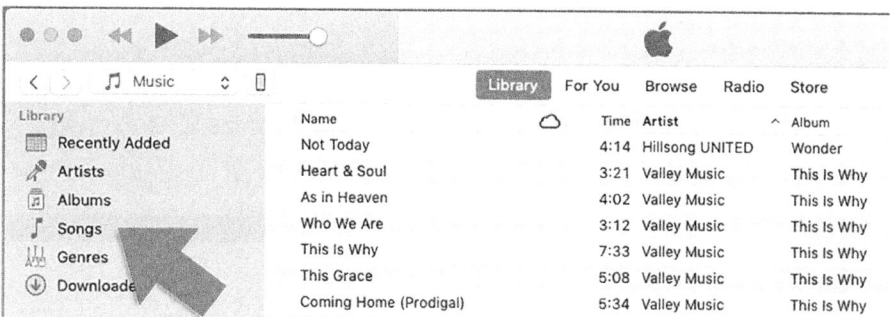

To add any music to your iPhone, just drag and drop a track or album from the main window, onto the iPhone device under the 'devices' section on the left hand sidebar.

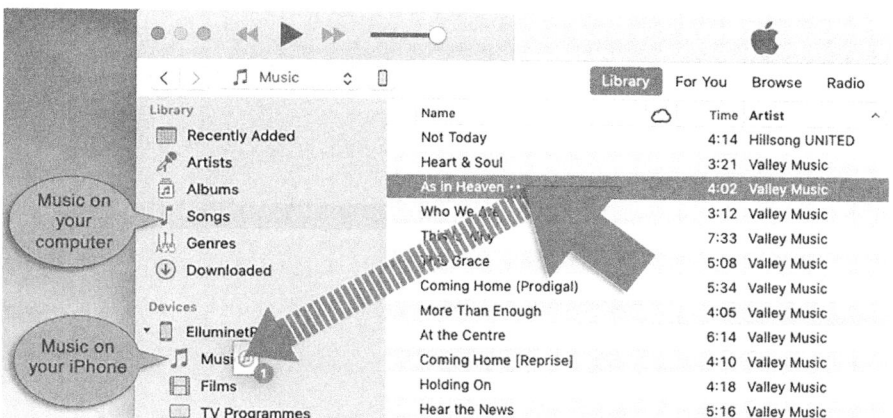

**171**

# Setting Up Apple Music Streaming

Apple Music is a music streaming service that allows you to stream music from the iTunes music library for a monthly subscription fee.

- £4.99 a month gives you full access to the iTunes music library and is only available for University/College students.

- £9.99 a month gets you full access to the iTunes music library and many radio stations available. This is an individual account and allows only one account access to the iTunes Store.

- £14.99 a month gets you full access to the iTunes music library and radio stations and allows up to 6 people to sign in and listen to their music. This is ideal for families.

To set up Apple Music, first open the music app, tap the app on the home screen.

From the list of icons along the bottom of the screen, select 'for you'.

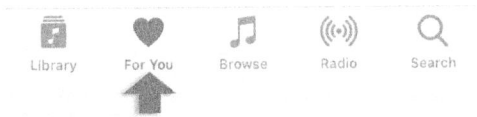

To get started, tap 'choose a plan'.

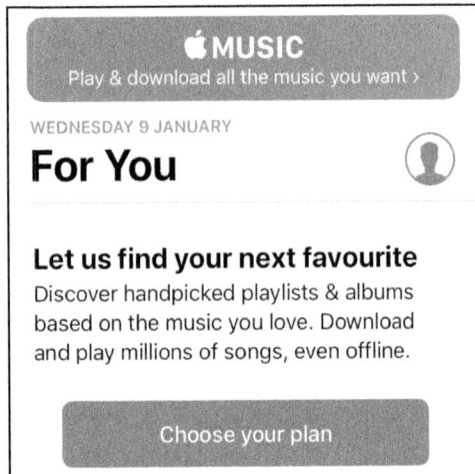

Choose a membership programme, then tap 'join apple music'.

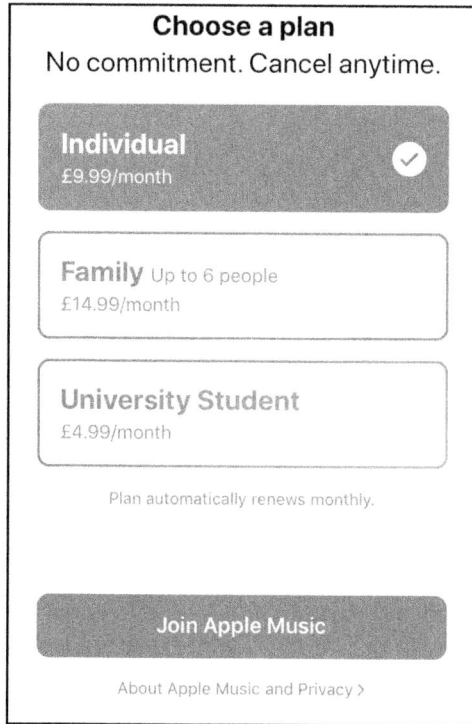

**Choose a plan**
No commitment. Cancel anytime.

**Individual**
£9.99/month

**Family** Up to 6 people
£14.99/month

**University Student**
£4.99/month

Plan automatically renews monthly.

**Join Apple Music**

About Apple Music and Privacy >

Enter your Apple ID username and password, or confirm with touch ID, if you have this enabled, by placing your finger on the home button.

Tap the genres you like. Tap 'next' when you're done.

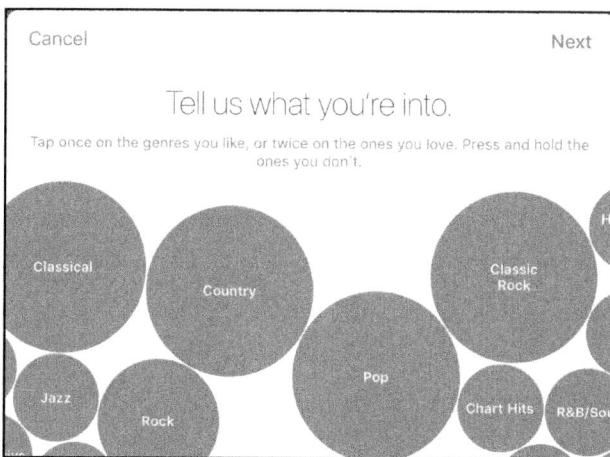

Cancel                                        Next

Tell us what you're into.

Tap once on the genres you like, or twice on the ones you love. Press and hold the ones you don't.

Classical    Country    Classic Rock    Hi

Jazz    Rock    Pop    Chart Hits    R&B/Sou

Now you can stream any music you like directly to your iPhone.

## The Main Screen

You can use the icons along the bottom of Apple Music to navigate around.

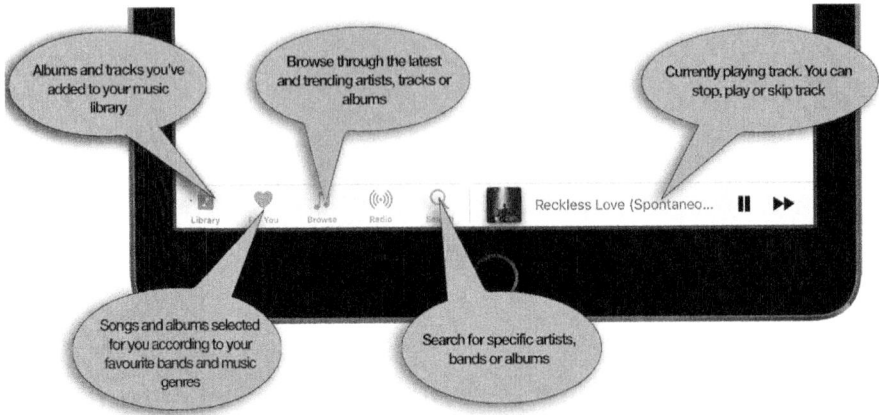

Albums and tracks you've added to your music library

Browse through the latest and trending artists, tracks or albums

Currently playing track. You can stop, play or skip track

Reckless Love (Spontaneo...

Library    You    Browse    Radio    Search

Songs and albums selected for you according to your favourite bands and music genres

Search for specific artists, bands or albums

Tap the currently playing track to reveal the album or track details

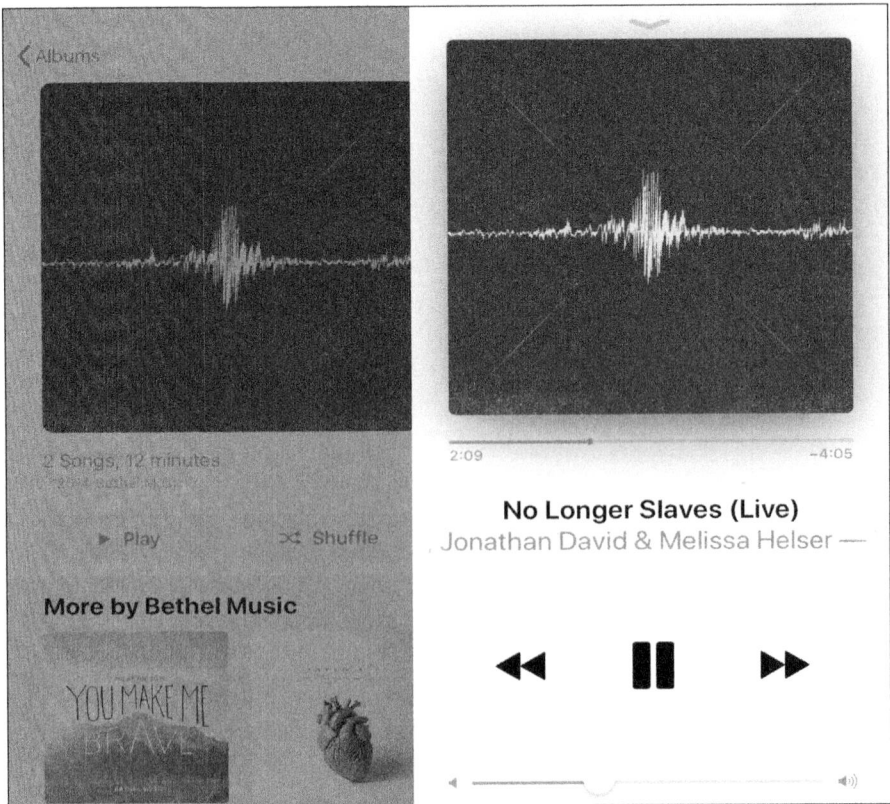

Albums

2 Songs, 12 minutes

▶ Play        ✕ Shuffle

**More by Bethel Music**

YOU MAKE ME BRAVE

2:09                                    ~4:05

**No Longer Slaves (Live)**
Jonathan David & Melissa Helser —

◀◀        ❚❚        ▶▶

# Searching for Music

Select the artists you like. If you don't see all the ones you like, tap 'more artists' on the bottom left. If the artist you're looking for isn't there, you can add them. To do this tap 'add an artist' and enter their name.

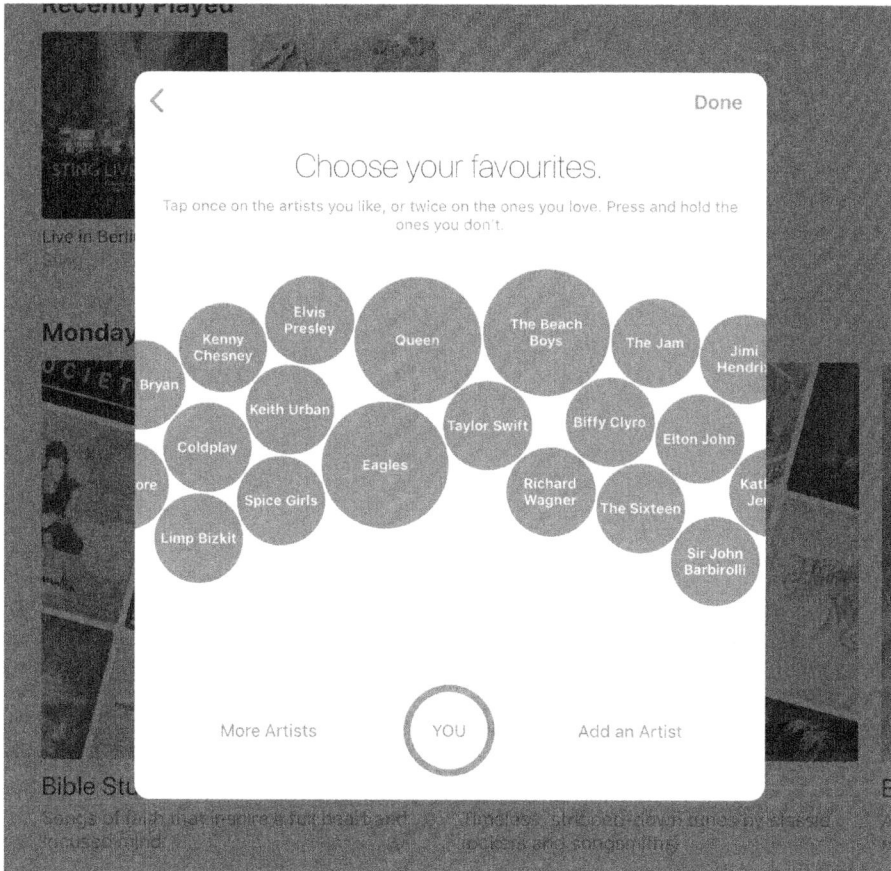

Now, you can search for any artist, band or song you can think of. To do this, on Apple iTunes Music's home screen, select 'search' from the icons along the bottom of the screen.

# Chapter 5: Using Multimedia

Type an artist's/album name into the search field at the top.

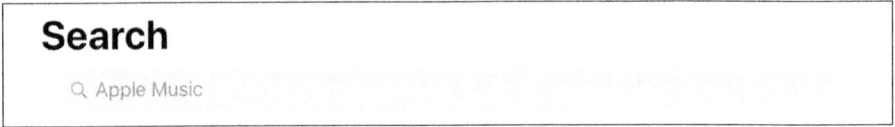

---

## Search

🔍 Apple Music

---

Select the closest match from the list of suggestions.

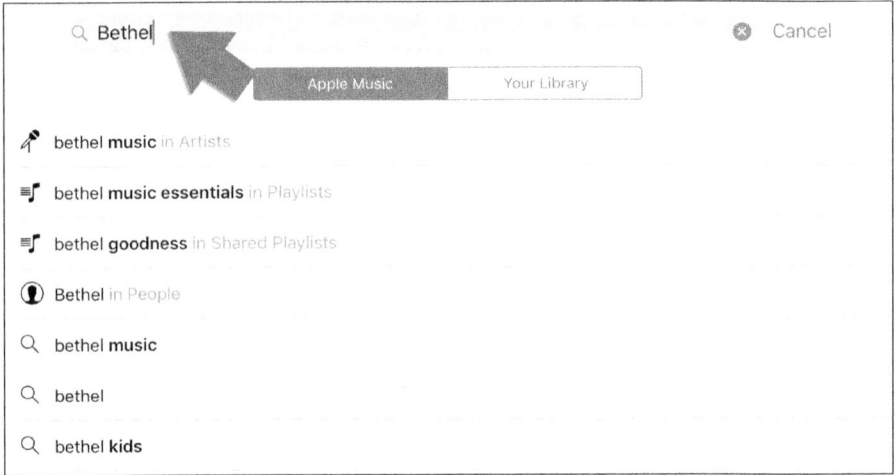

🔍 Bethel|                                    ⊗ Cancel

| Apple Music | Your Library |

🎤 bethel **music** in Artists

🎵 bethel **music essentials** in Playlists

🎵 bethel **goodness** in Shared Playlists

👤 **Bethel** in People

🔍 bethel **music**

🔍 bethel

🔍 bethel **kids**

---

From here you can tap on a song to listen to it, open an album, add to your music library, or you can build your own playlists.

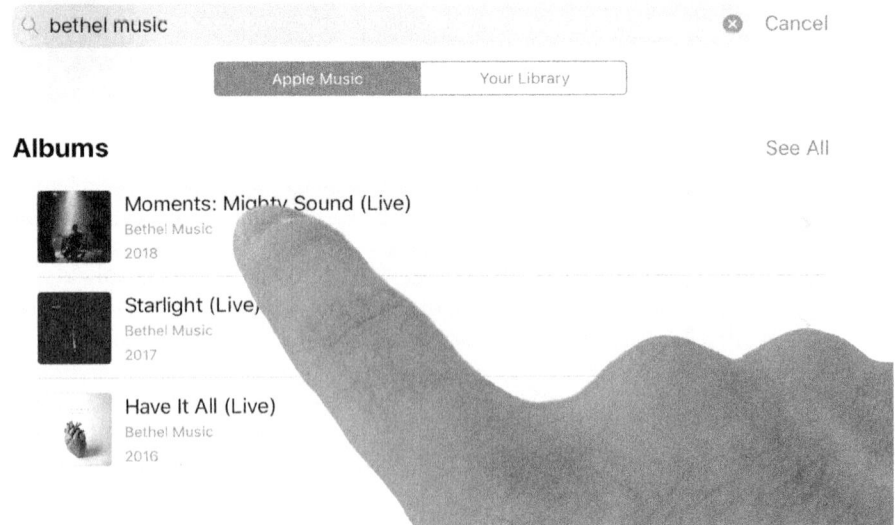

🔍 bethel music                                    ⊗ Cancel

| Apple Music | Your Library |

## Albums                                    See All

Moments: Mighty Sound (Live)
Bethel Music
2018

Starlight (Live)
Bethel Music
2017

Have It All (Live)
Bethel Music
2016

Tap on an album to open it.

**176**

# Add to Library

You can start to create a library of your favourite music, so it's easy to find. To do this, tap the + sign next to the song you want to add to your library. If you want to add the whole album tap '+add'.

‹ Search

Moments: Mighty Sound (Live)

Bethel Music

Christian & Gospel • 2018

+ ADD  ...

| 1 | Mighty Sound (Spontane...<br>Bethel Music, Brian Johnson &... | + | 9:13 |
|----|---|---|---|
| .... | Reckless Love (Spontan...<br>Bethel Music & Steffany Gretzin... | + | 9:59 |
| 3 | Spirit Move (Spontaneou...<br>Bethel Music & Kalley Heiligent... | + | 9:59 |
| 4 | Catch the Wind (Sponta...<br>Bethel Music & Melissa Helser | + | 9:49 |

12 Songs, 1 hour, 55 minutes

2018 Bethel Music

You can access your music library using the 'library' icon on the bar along the bottom of the screen.

# Albums

3 Albums                                    ▶ Play        ⤬ Shuffle

Moments: Mighty So...        Wonder        This Is Why
Bethel Music                        Hillsong UNITED        Valley Music

Library    For You    Browse    Radio    Search        Reckless Love (Spontaneo...    ❚❚    ▶▶

Tap an album to open it, tap on a track to play it

# iTunes Store

The iTunes Store is where you can buy individual tracks, albums, tv shows and movies. To open the iTunes Store, tap the app on your home screen.

Once the app has loaded you can browse through music, movies and tv shows. To do this, tap on the icons on the toolbar along the bottom of the screen.

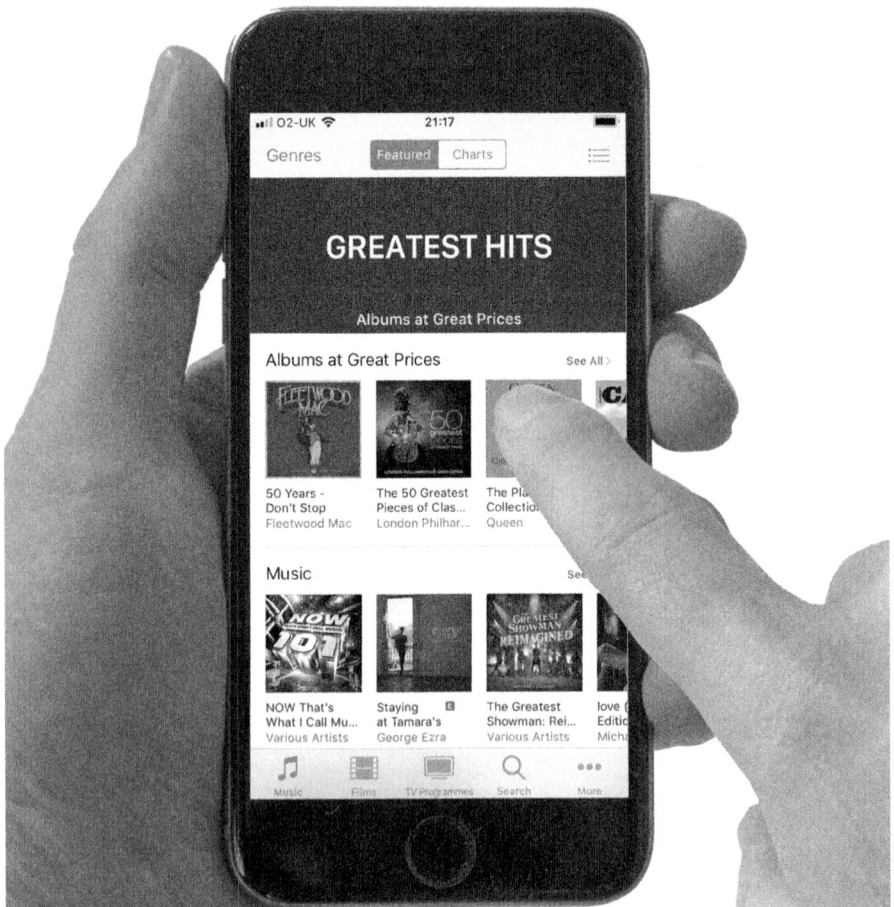

Tap on the album covers to see more information. To buy any of the tracks or albums, tap your finger on the price tag.

# Music

Within the music section of the iTunes Store, you can browse through the latest releases, charts and different genres.

To search for your favourite tracks, artists and albums, select 'search' from the toolbar along the bottom of the screen.

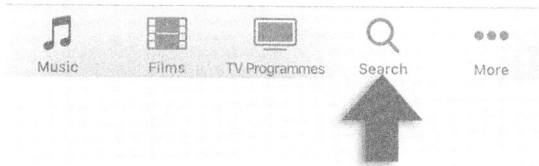

Type your search into the field at the top.

Along the top of the search results, you can view by song or album. Scroll up and down the list to see the songs and albums.

Tap on the price tag to download the song. Once the songs are downloaded you will find then in your recently added playlist.

## Chapter 5: Using Multimedia

## Films & TV

You can stream films and TV programmes directly to your iPhone from the iTunes Store. You can buy or rent what you want to watch. To to this, select 'films' or 'tv programmes' from the toolbar along the bottom of the screen.

Browse your favourite genre, tap 'genres' on the top left, then select one from the list.

Scroll up and down the screen to see the latest releases, trending title. Tap on a film to see details. Tap the buy or rent price tag to watch the film.

To search for a film or TV programme you want to watch, tap the search icon on the toolbar along the bottom of the screen. Then type your search into the field at the top.

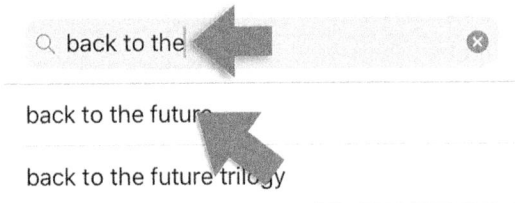

Scroll down the search results until you come to the 'films' section. Tap on the thumbnail cover of the film you want, to view the details.

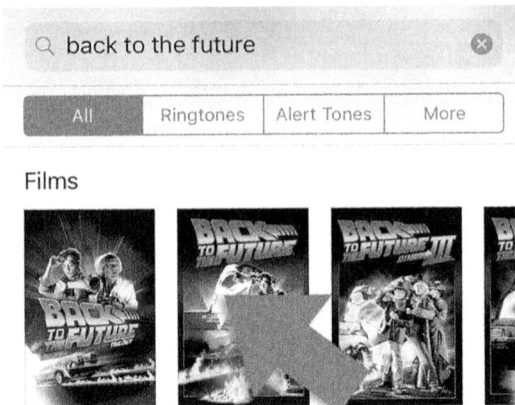

On the film details screen you'll be able to read details about the film, reviews and ratings. Tap 'rent' or 'buy'. Verify your purchase using the Touch ID, or your Apple ID username and password.

You'll find your downloaded films and TV programmes in the library section of the TV App.

## Apple TV App

If the TV app is not on your iPhone, go to the App Store and search for 'Apple TV App'. The Apple TV App is where you'll find all your purchased or rented films and TV programmes. You'll find the app on your home screen.

Select 'library' from the panel along the bottom of the screen.

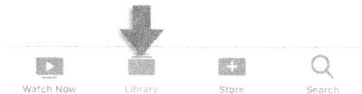

Tap on the film or tv programme to begin playback.

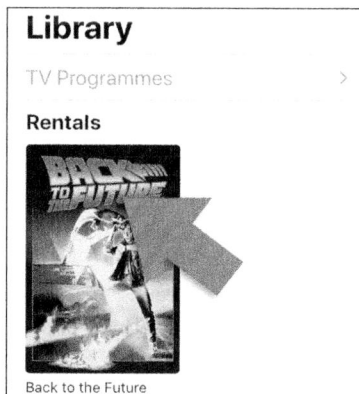

# Airplay

Airplay allows wireless streaming of audio and video data to an Apple TV or compatible receiver on your TV.

For this to work, both your iPhone and Apple TV will need to be on the same WiFi network. This is usually the case in most homes.

To mirror your iPhone, open your control centre - swipe upwards from the bottom edge of your screen.

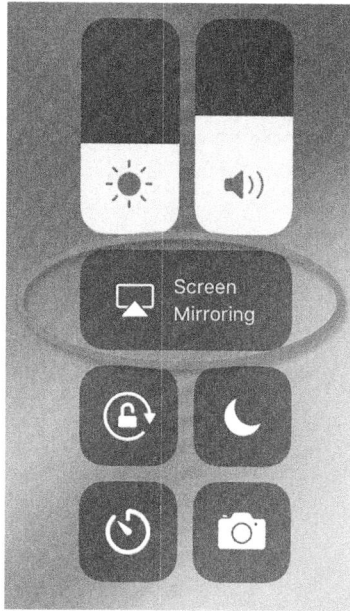

Tap on 'screen mirroring' or 'airplay mirroring' and select your Apple TV from the list. Enter your passcode if prompted.

If you don't know the Apple TV passcode, go on your Apple TV, then go to settings > Airplay, select 'Onscreen code'.

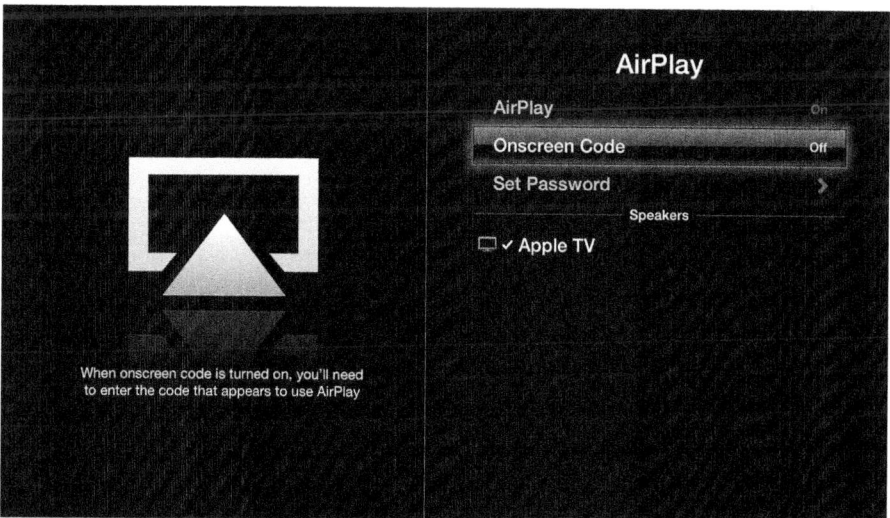

You can turn off the code or set a new one.

# Document Scanner

Within the Notes App, you can scan documents. You'll find the notes app on your home screen.

Open a new note. Tap the new note icon on the bottom right of the screen.

**Mission statement**
12/06/2017   To help people use comput

14 Notes

Tap the + sign on the toolbar on top of the on screen keyboard.

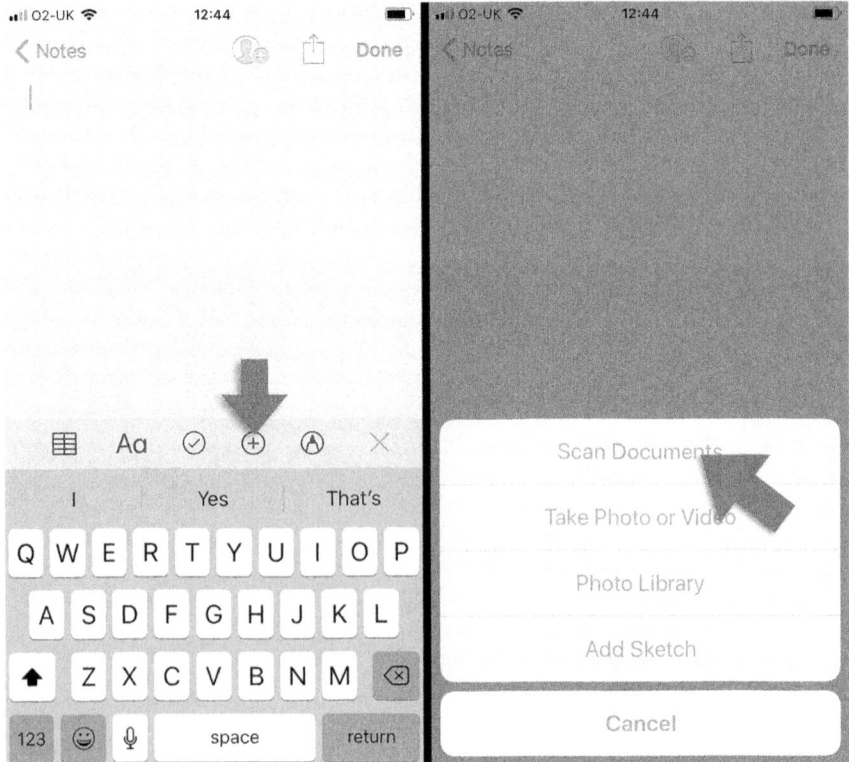

Tap 'scan document' from the popup menu

**184**

Line up the document in the window as shown below, make sure the yellow box covers the whole document.

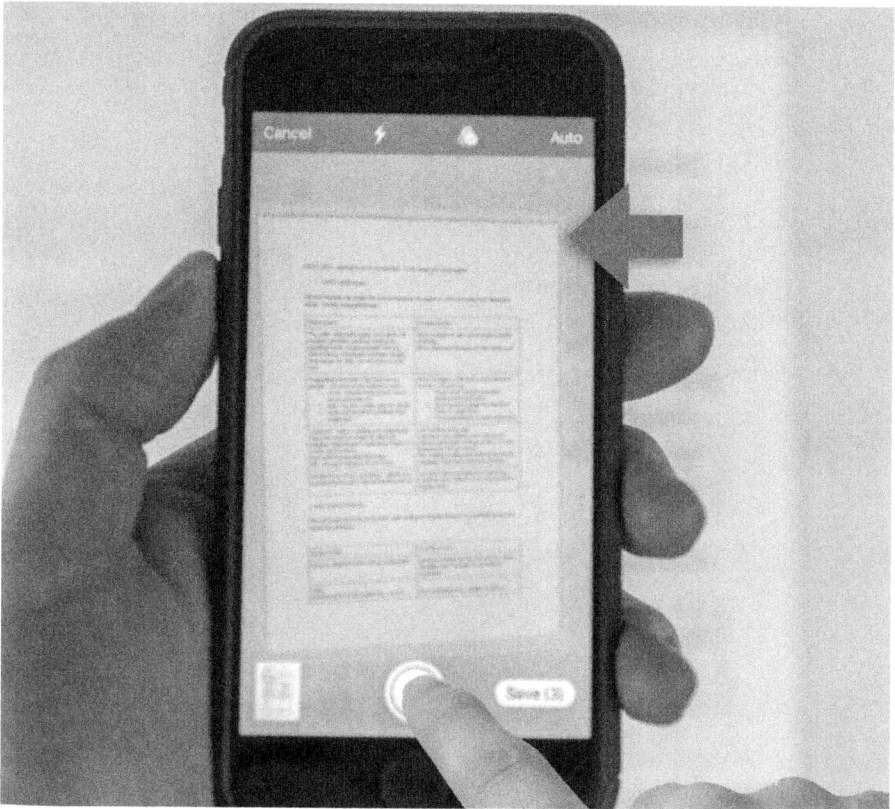

Tap the white button on the bottom to 'scan the document'. Adjust the corners by dragging the handles, if any edges of the page have been cut off, then tap 'keep scan'.

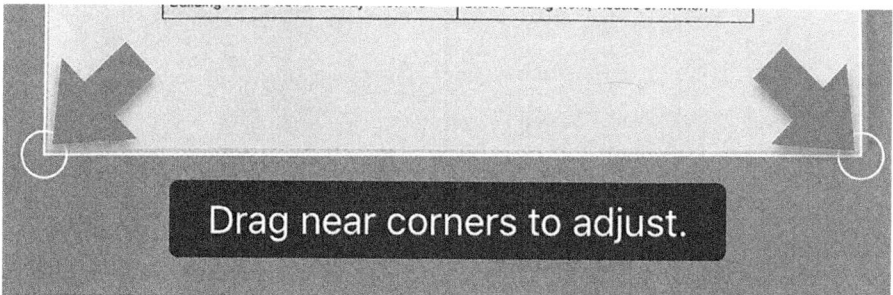

Drag near corners to adjust.

Retake                                                    Keep Scan

If you have more pages, repeat the process and 'scan' them as well using the white button on the right hand side. Once you have 'scanned' all your pages, tap 'save' on the bottom right corner.

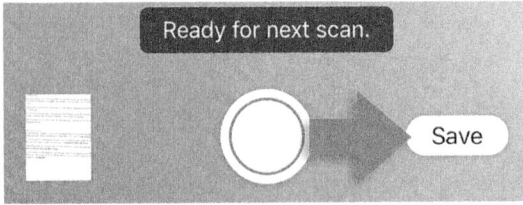

Now you can send the document via email, safe it as a PDF, print it and write directly onto the scan with markup.

To share the scan with someone, tap 'share' icon on the top right of your screen. If you don't want to send the scan to anyone, just tap 'done'.

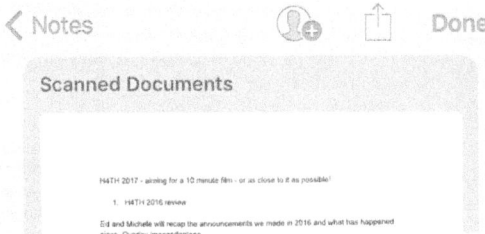

From the drop down, tap 'mail' to email it to someone or 'message' to send via iMessage. From here you can also save it to a PDF or print it if you have air print installed. In this example I'm emailing it.

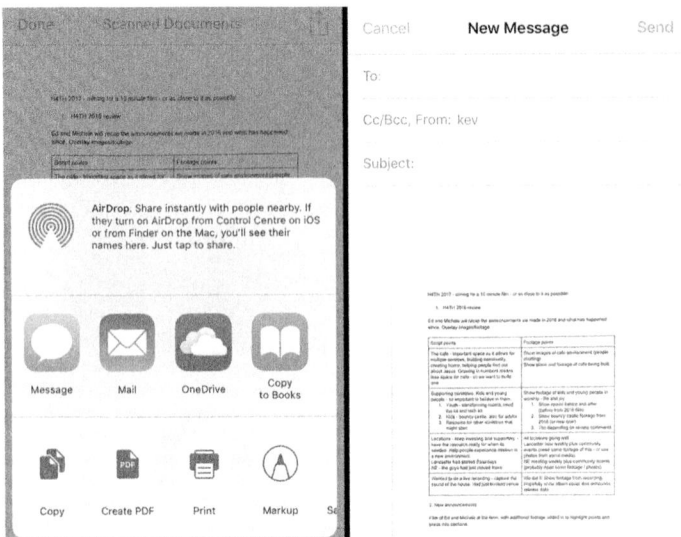

# QR Code Scanner

A QR code (or quick response code) is a 2D bar code used to provide easy access to information through your iPhone. This could be a link to a website. These codes are usually printed on signs, flyers, and other printed material.

To scan a QR code, open your camera app, point it at a QR code, tap the code on the screen to focus.

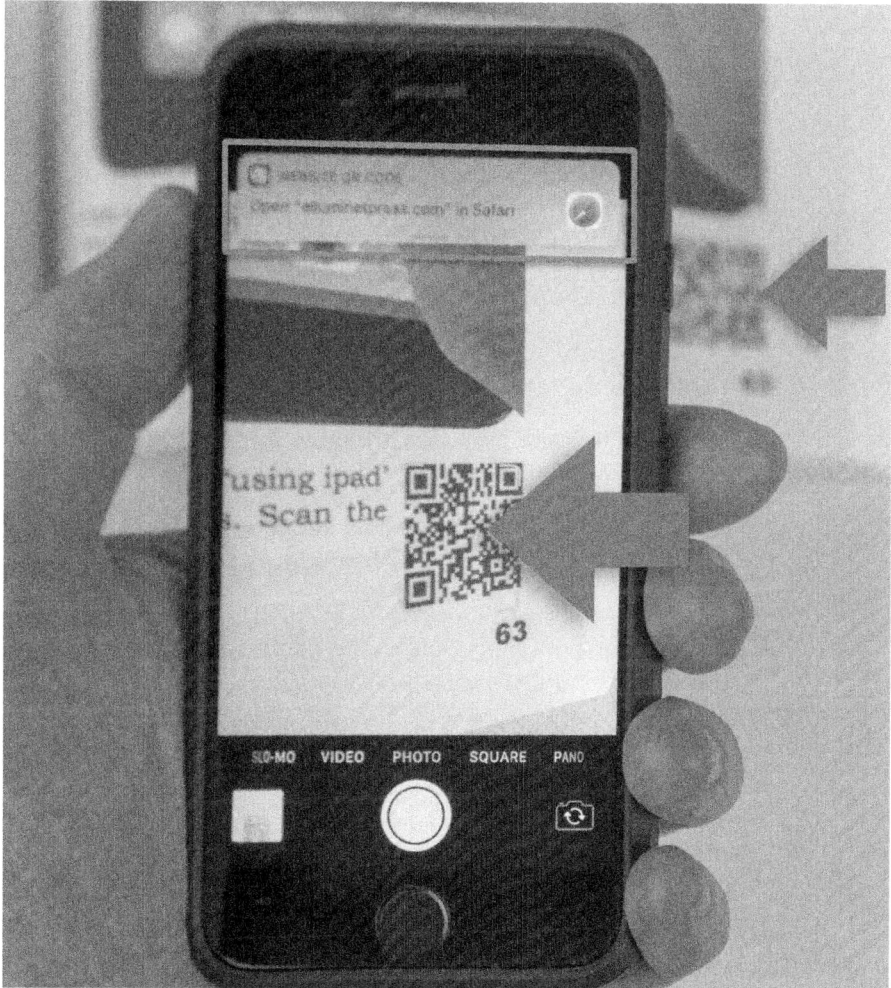

When the camera reads the code, you'll see a prompt at the top of the screen telling you what the code is and where it links to. Tap and drag the small handle, down to expand the window to see a preview of the website. Tap on the site to open it up in full screen.

**187**

# Common Apps

You can pretty much get an app for virtually anything, and these are all available from the app store. Some are free and others you have to buy.

There are games, productivity apps and apps just for fun.

Your iPhone comes with some apps build in but you can download millions more from the App Store.

Lets start by taking a look at the App Store in more detail.

The App Store has had a make over in this version of iOS and has a much easier to use interface.

# App Store

The app store has millions of apps available for download direct to your iPhone. To open the app store, tap the icon on your home screen..

Once on the app store's main screen, tap the icon on the top right to sign in with your Apple ID if you haven't already done so. If you are already signed in, your Apple ID will be displayed here, you won't need to sign in again.

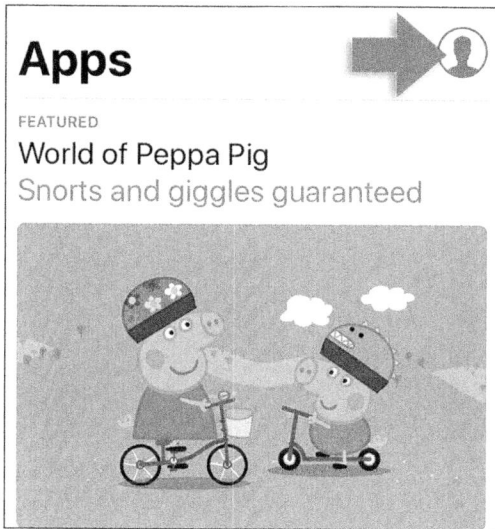

In the box that appears, enter your Apple ID email address and password.

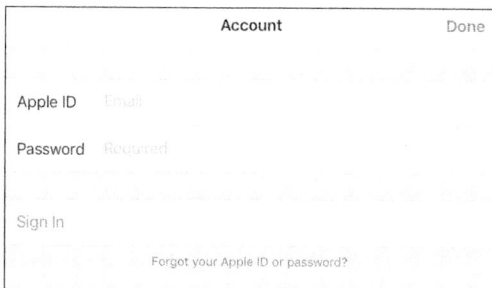

# Chapter 6: Common Apps

On the app store, you will find everything from games and entertainment to productivity tools such as word processing, drawing and photo apps.

These are split into games and app sections and you'll find these on the bar along the bottom of the screen.

Also along the bottom you'll find updates to your installed apps, it's worth checking this from time to time, as apps are updated all the time.

The last icon on the bar along the bottom allows you to search the app store for a specific app name or type/genre of app.

You can even find apps for recipes, travel details, maps. There is an app for almost anything you can think of.

# Search for Apps

To find an app, tap on 'search' on the bar at the bottom of your screen.

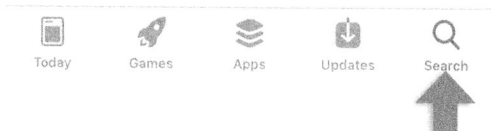

Type into the search field on the main screen, as shown below. In this example, I'm going to search for one of my favourite games called 'worms'.

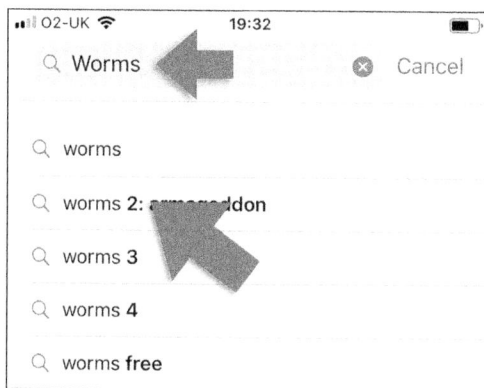

From the suggestions, tap on the closest match. Tap on the image to view more details about the app. Here you'll see reviews, price, screen shots and other info.

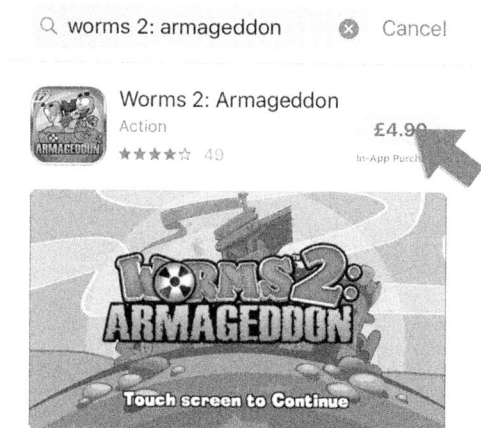

To download the app, tap 'get' next to the app if it's free, or tap the price tag if it's paid.

# Chapter 6: Common Apps

If it's a paid app, tap 'purchase' to confirm, if prompted.

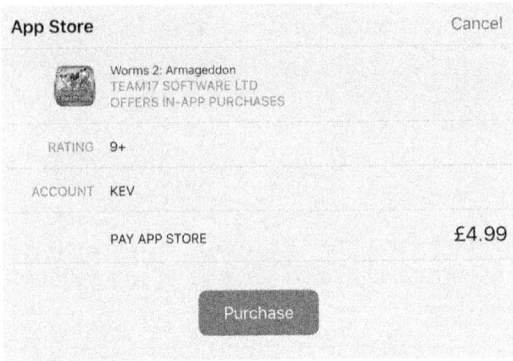

Authorise your payment with touch ID. Place your finger on the home button.

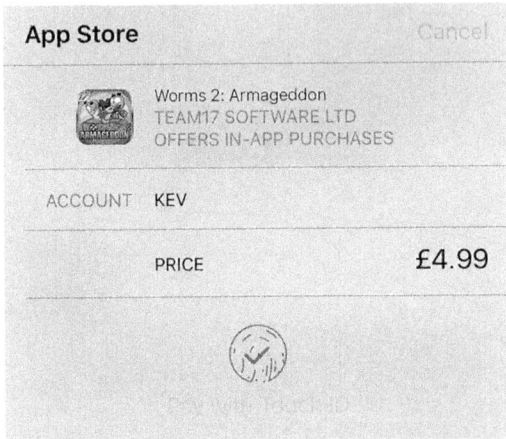

Authorise the purchase with your Apple ID password if required.

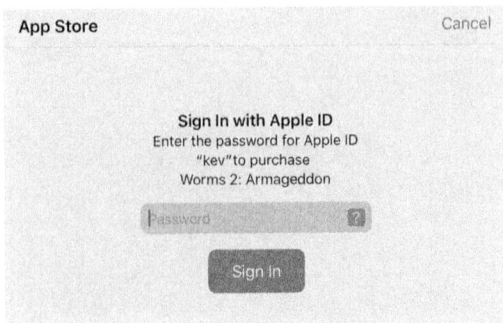

The app will appear on your home screen once it has downloaded and installed itself.

# Browsing the Store

If you are more the browsing type, app store has grouped all the apps into categories according to their use. Select 'apps' from the bar on the bottom of the screen.

Here you'll see some of the most popular apps, new apps and top selling apps. You can tap on any of these apps to view or download.

Tap on the app's image to view more details, Tap 'see all' at the top of each section to see all the apps in that section. Tap on 'get' or the price to download the app. Scroll down the page to see all the apps in the sections.

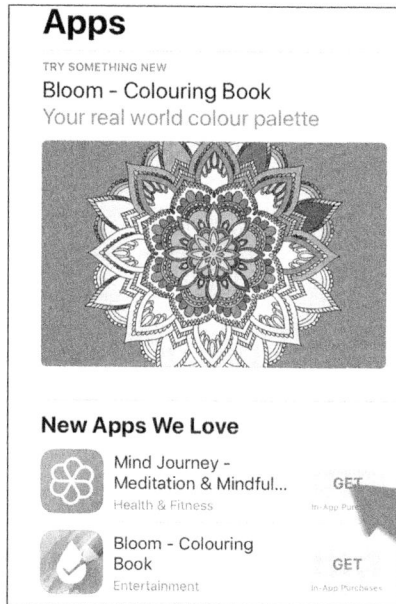

If you scroll down a bit, you'll see a section called 'top categories'.

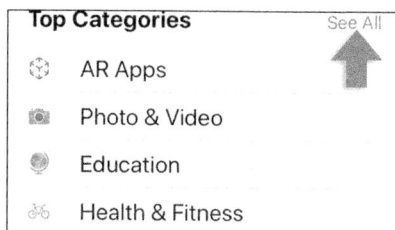

# Chapter 6: Common Apps

Tap on a category to browse the available apps. In this example, I'm going to explore the 'reference' category.

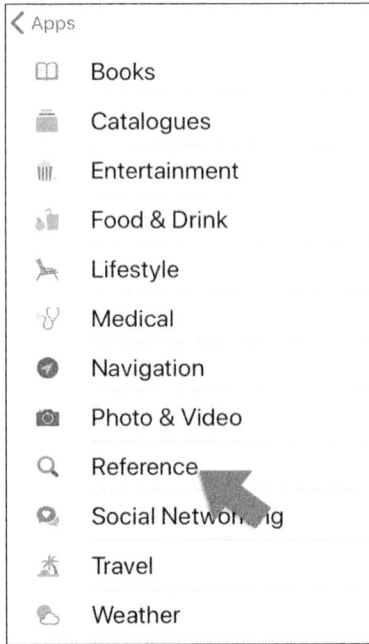

Here, you'll see a list of all the apps available for that category. Again, tap 'see all' on the top right to see the full lists in the different sections.

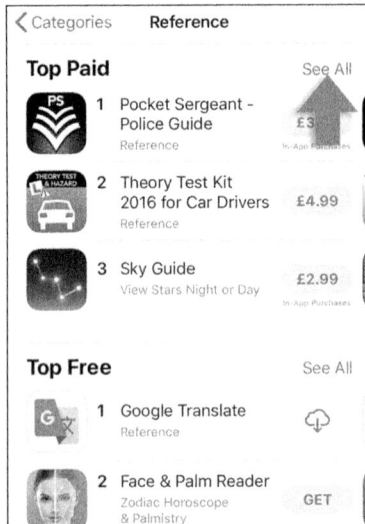

The categories are split into two sections: Apps you have to pay for, and apps that are free.

Claire is 18 and learning to drive, so an app that might be of use to her is 'Theory Test Kit'. Tap on the app's icon to view more details about.

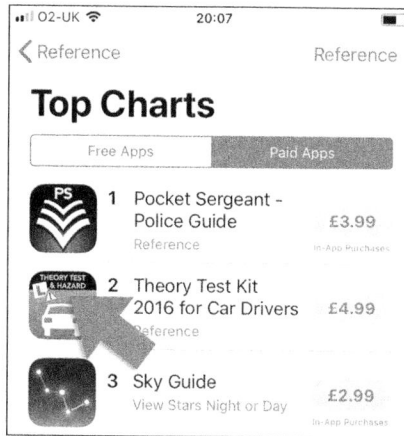

This gives information about what the app does, what it costs, some screen shots of the app in action, and the device requirements in order to run the app. Scroll down the screen to see all the information.

Tap the price tag at the top of the page to purchase, download, and install the app on your iPhone.

# Taking Notes

To start notes app, tap the icon on the home screen.

When notes has loaded, you will see a list of all the notes you have taken. Lets take a look at the main screen.

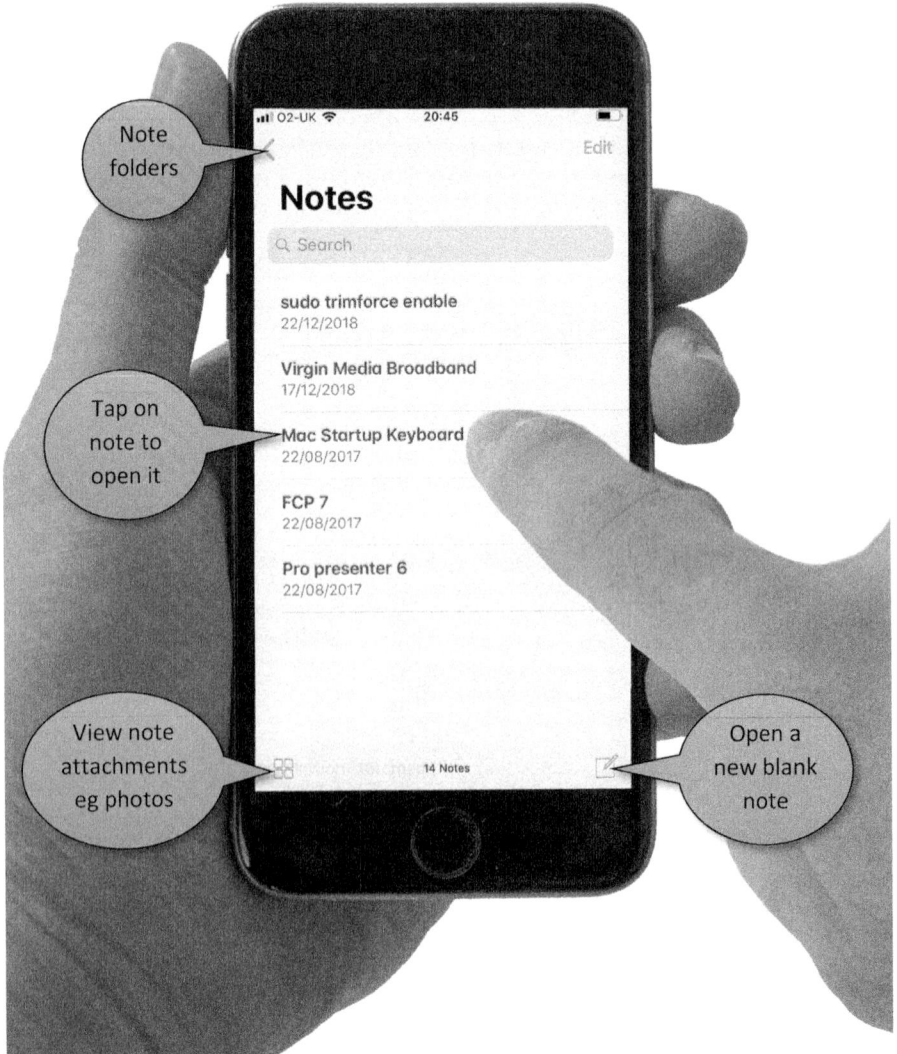

**Note folders**

**Tap on note to open it**

**View note attachments eg photos**

**Open a new blank note**

# Typing Notes & Inserting Photos

You can type your notes in as if it were a notepad, using the on screen keyboard. You can format your text using bold headings or font sizes - tap the text formatting icon.

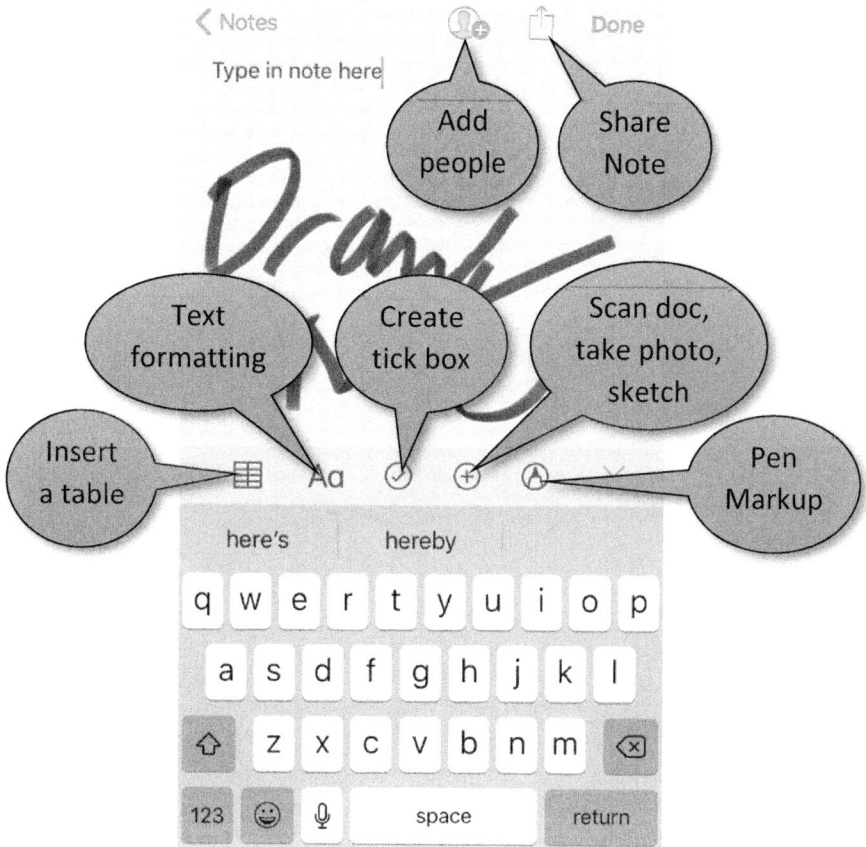

You can also write notes with your finger - to do this tap the 'pen markup' icon.

You can insert tables, and check/tick boxes for to do lists - tap the tick icon.

You can scan documents, and take photos - tap the '+' icon..

You can add people to your note. Adding them in this way allows other people to see your note as you create it. They'll be able to see any changes you make, photos you add, or documents you scan. Tap the 'add people' icon.

You can also share a copy of your note using the share icon.

## Dictating Notes

Instead of typing, you can dictate notes using the voice dictation feature. To do this, tap the mic icon on the bottom left of the on-screen keyboard.

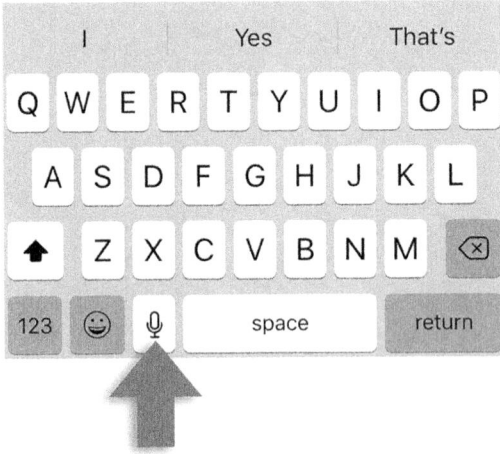

Record your notes using the voice recognition.

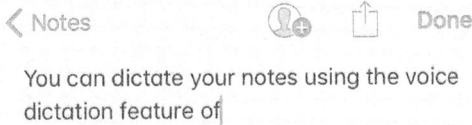

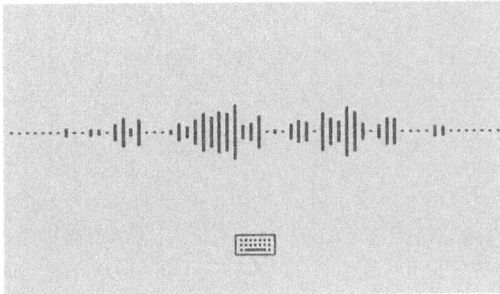

Tap 'done' at the top, when you are finished.

# Reminders

With reminders, you can create to do lists, and set alerts to remind you do to certain things. To start reminders app, tap the icon on the home screen

## Add a Task to List

To add a task, tap on a blank line on the paper then type your task.

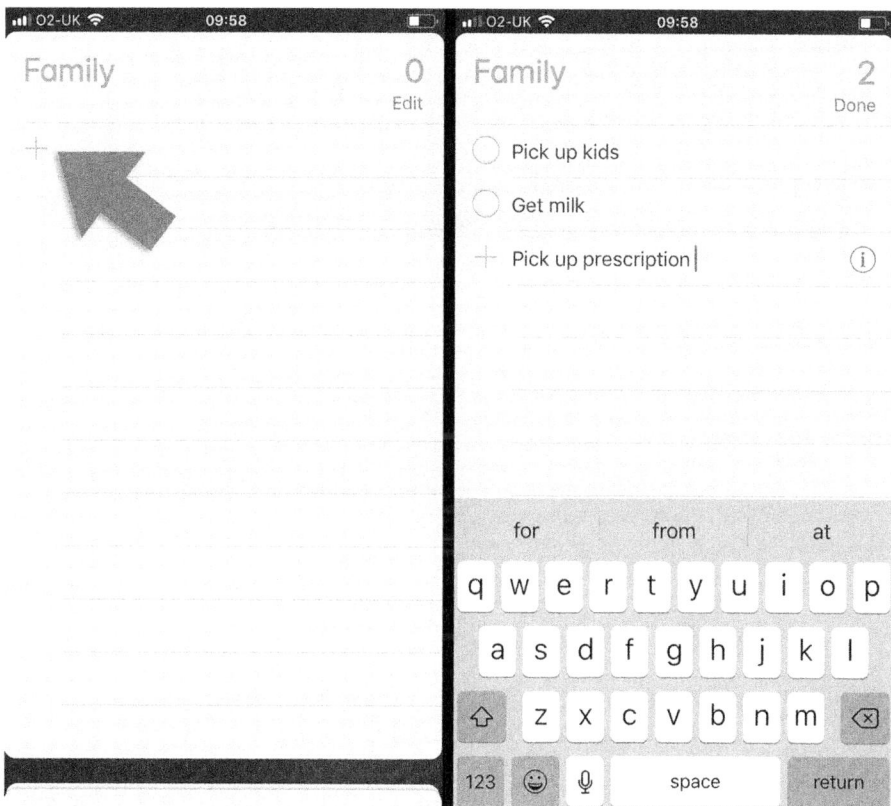

Tap return on the keyboard to add another reminder. These are reminders of tasks to do today.

Tap 'done' on the top right when you're finished.

## Edit a List

To edit your list, tap 'edit' on the top right corner of the screen.

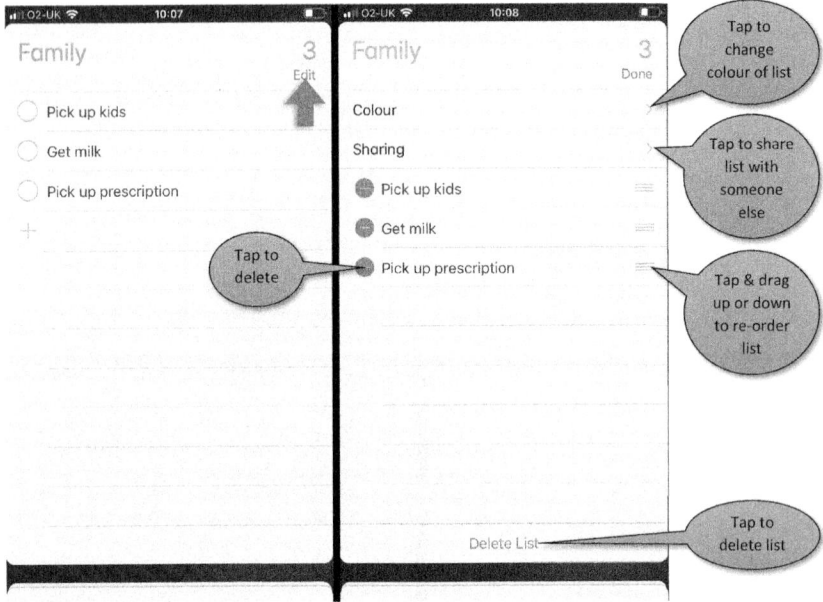

## Share a List

To share your list with someone else, tap edit on the top right corner of the screen, then tap 'sharing'.

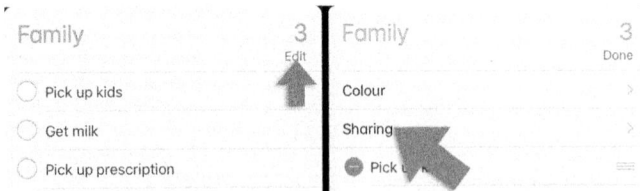

Tap 'add person', then type in the name of the person you're sharing with. Tap the '+' to add additional people. Tap 'add'

Tap 'done'. The person you shared with will get an invitation to view the reminder list.

# Schedule a Reminder

To schedule reminders, tap on the notes at the bottom of the screen. From the list tap 'scheduled'.

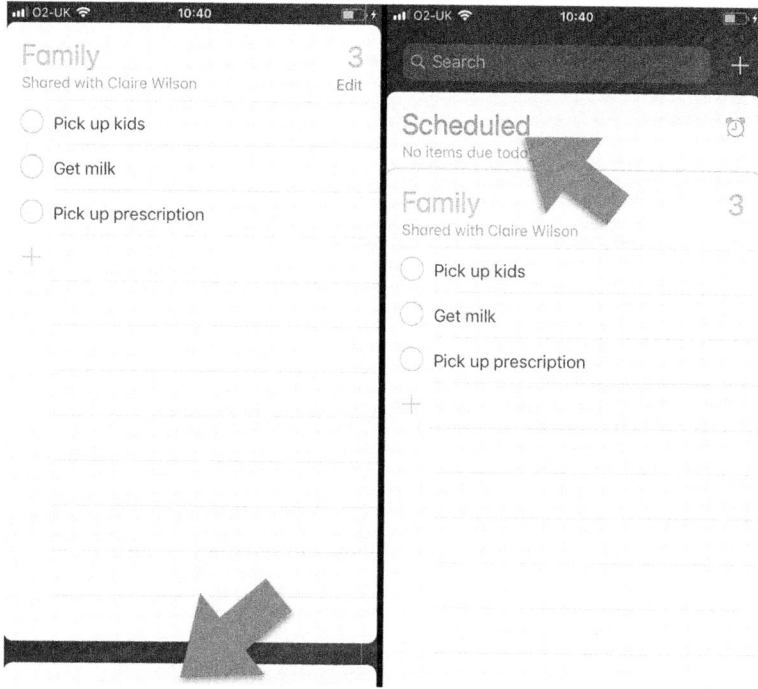

Tap on a blank line and enter a description of the task.

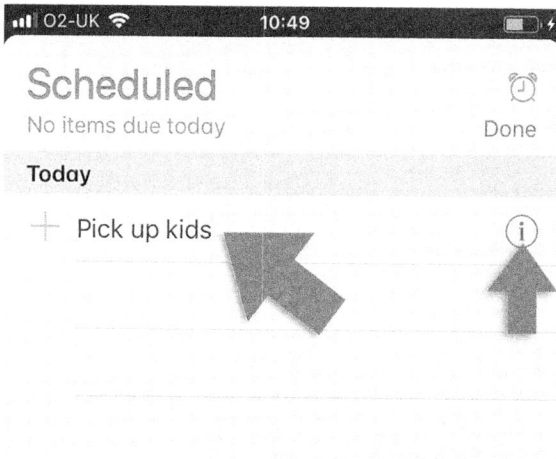

Then tap the 'i' icon on the right hand side of the reminder

This will allow you to enter the date and time. Tap 'alarm' then swipe up and down the days and times that appear, shown below.

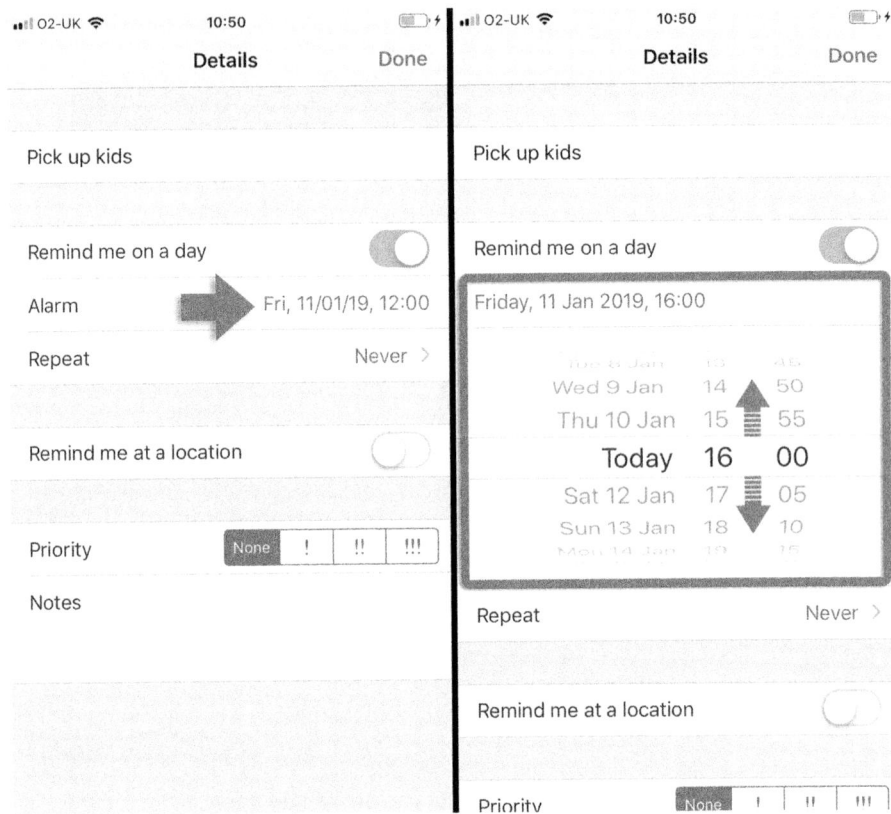

Tap repeat, here you can set a reminder to repeat every day, week, month, year, and so on.

Remind me at location, you can set a reminder to alert you when you reach a particular location. This could be your work address, home address, or anywhere else. For example, you could set your reminders to alert you when you arrive at work. Just tap 'remind me at location' and enter the address.

You can also set priorities. Some tasks could be important so you can select a high priority, eg select '!!', or top priority, select '!!!'.

You can also add notes at the bottom of the task. This could be details of the task that you've set a reminder to.

Tap 'done' on the top right when you're finished.

# Create New List

To create lists, tap the '+' sign on the top right of the screen.

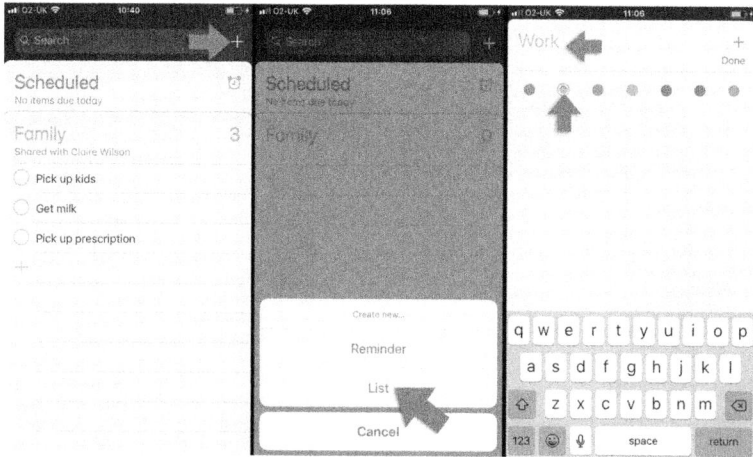

Select 'list' from the popup. Enter a name for the list at the top, eg 'work'. Tap 'done' when you're finished.

# Create New Reminder

To create lists, tap the '+' sign on the top right of the screen.

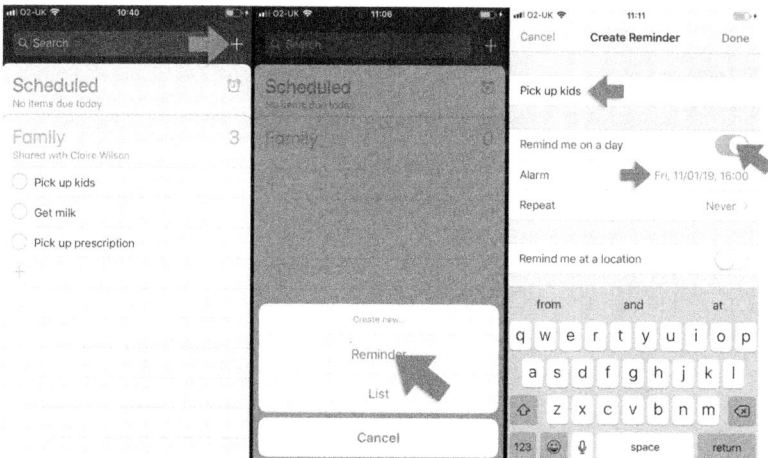

Select 'reminder' from the popup. Enter a task you want to be reminded of at the top, eg 'pick up kids'.

Turn on 'remind me on a day', tap 'alarm' and enter the day and time you want to be reminded.

# Maps App

Maps is an extremely useful app if you are trying to find out where a particular place is and need to find driving directions. It works like a SatNav/GPS giving you precise directions straight from door to door.

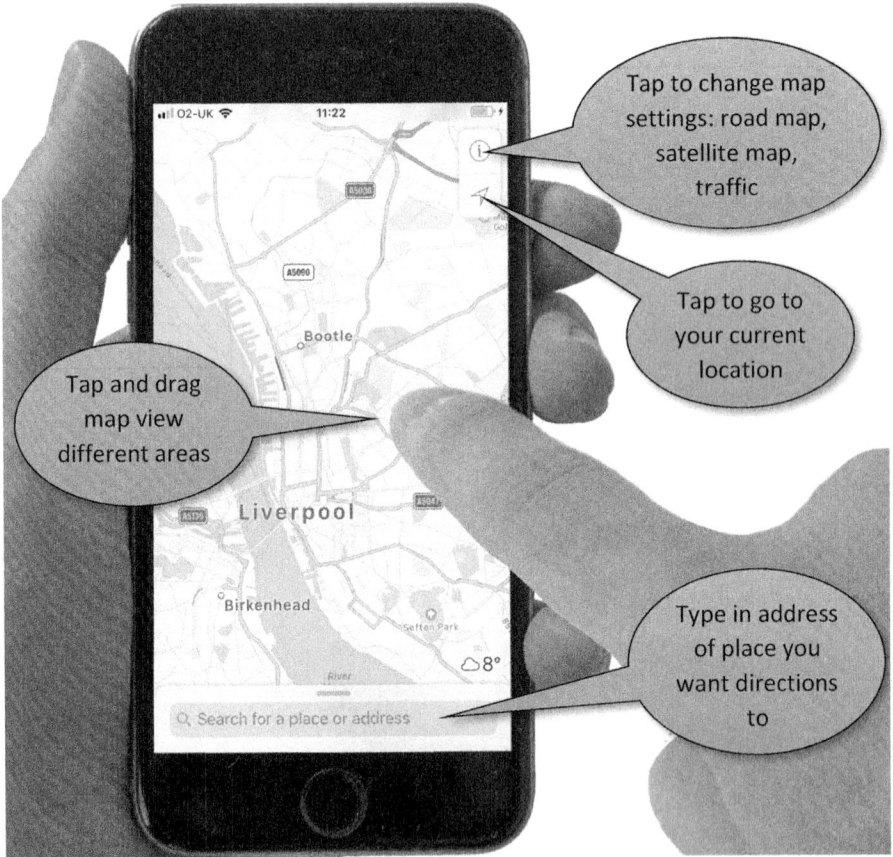

You can view the map in three different types - tap the 'i' icon on the top right of the screen to change this.

**Street maps** are great if you are using the maps app as a GPS/Satnav while driving, **transit maps** give you public transport routes in a particular location, and **satellite maps** are great if you are exploring a city or area of interest.

# Driving Directions

To find driving directions, type in your destination into the search field on the bottom of the screen.

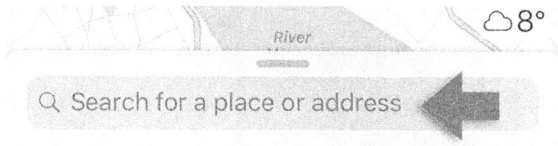

Select the destination from the list of suggestions. I'm going to go park in the car park. So I'd select this option.

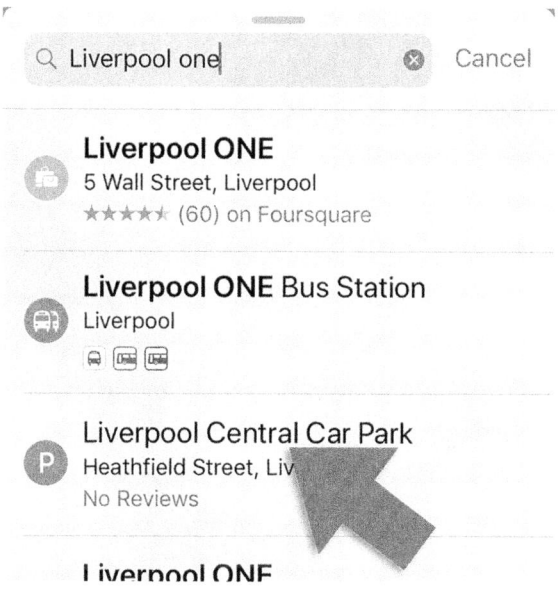

By default, the maps app will start the route from your current location - you can change this, just type in another location.

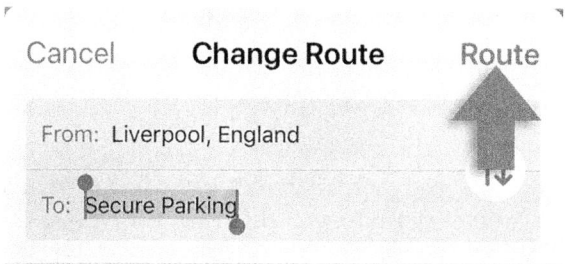

Tap on 'route' to calculate a route between your location and the destination you entered earlier.

**205**

Along the bottom of the screen, tap 'directions'.

On the screen you'll see an overview of your route. You can zoom in and out or move around the map using your finger to see details or roads.

Along the bottom of your screen you'll see 'drive', 'walk', 'transport', and 'ride'. This allows you to get different directions depending on what transport you're using. Eg if you're driving, select 'drive', if you're walking, select 'walk'.

What you're done, tap 'go'.

Here you'll see the start of your route, with turn by turn directions that will automatically change as you drive along the route. To see details of your route, tap and drag the small handle on top of the panel at the bottom of the screen, then tap 'details'. Tap a direction for more info. Tap 'done' when you're finished.

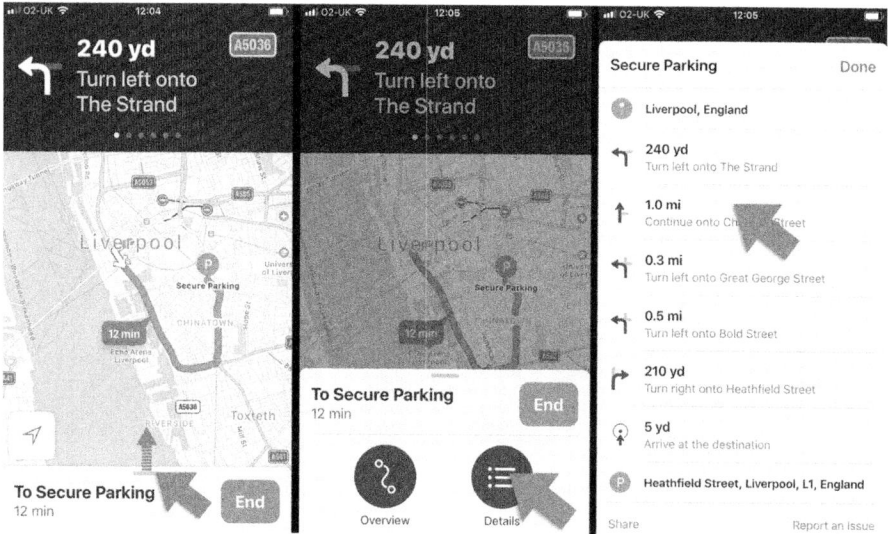

You can mount your phone to your windscreen and use it as a GPS SatNav.

Tap 'end' to stop the navigation.

## Chapter 6: Common Apps

# 3D Maps

3D maps are a great way to explore landmarks, major cities and areas of interest. You can flyover a city and explore what it has to offer.

To do this, first change your map to a satellite map if you haven't already done so. Then tap the 3D icon on the right hand side to switch to 3D mode.

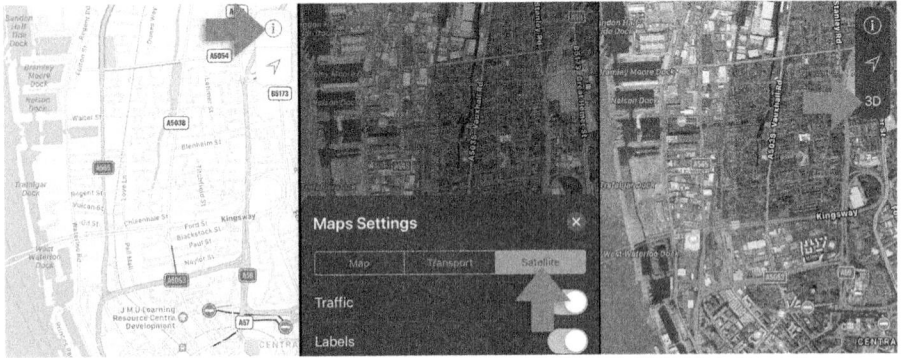

Type in a city name, place name or address into the search field on the bottom of the screen.

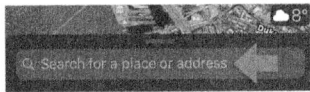

You can zoom in and out of the 3D map, and move around using your fingers.

# News App

The news app collects breaking stories from around the world and locally into one app, based on the topics you are interested in.

When you first start the app, you'll see a list of top stories, trending stories, and stories recommended for you.

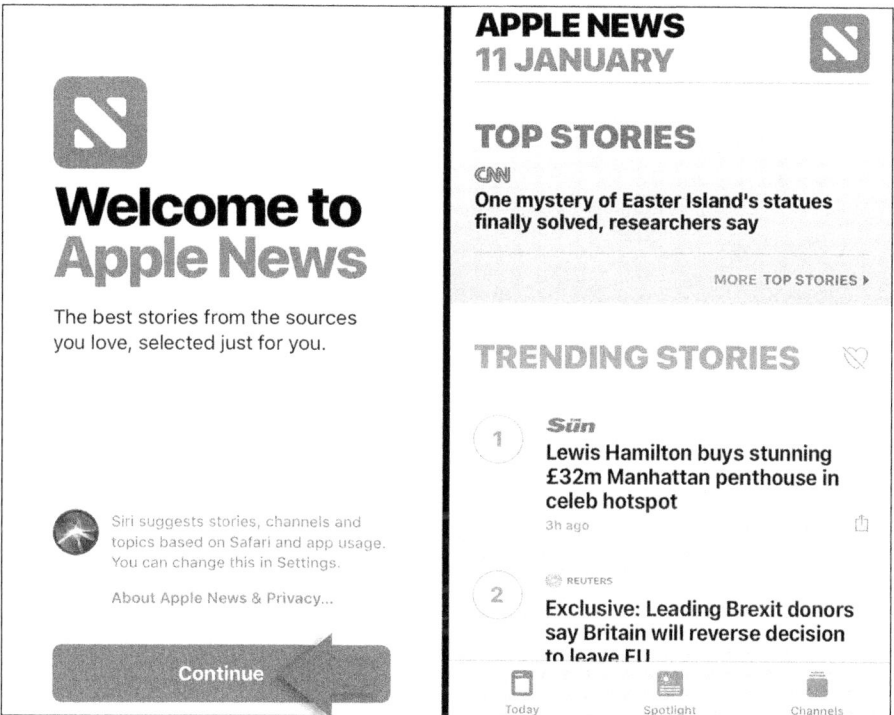

Scroll down the page, tap on a story to read the details.

Along the bottom of the screen, you'll see a panel with three icons. With these, you can select 'today' which will show you the latest top stories for the day.

Selecting 'spotlight' will show you stories of interest.

Selecting 'channels' allows you to select topics and channels you're interested in, so the news app will display stories according to your interests.

# Chapter 6: Common Apps

To personalise your news, tap 'channels' on the bar along the bottom of the screen.

From the channels list, scroll down to 'suggested by siri' and tap the heart icon next to the channels you're interested in.

Scroll down to the bottom, then tap 'discover channels & topics'.

From here you can select different news sources, magazines, newspapers and websites.

Tap 'done' at the bottom of the screen when you're finished.

# Apple Books App

Formerly known as iBooks, Apple Books is your electronic bookshelf and allows you to read ebooks. Tap the icon on your home screen.

You can download hundreds of different e-books that are available in the bookstore; from the latest novels, food, kids books or manuals.

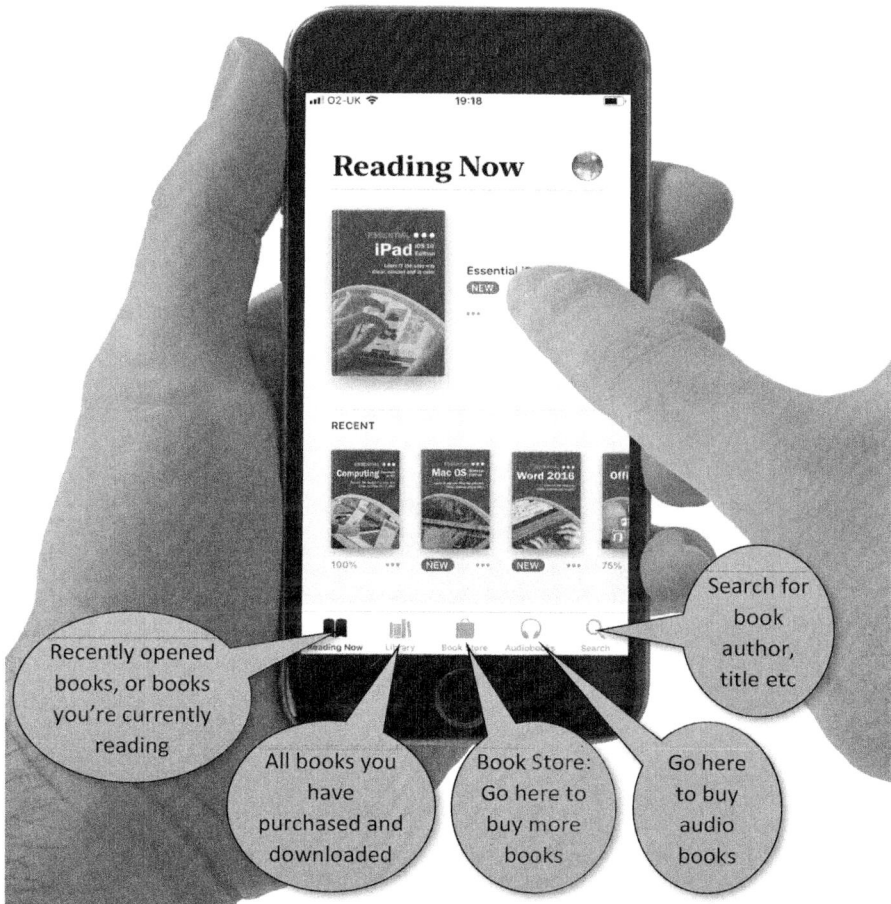

Recently opened books, or books you're currently reading

All books you have purchased and downloaded

Book Store: Go here to buy more books

Go here to buy audio books

Search for book author, title etc

Along the bottom of the screen you'll see some icons. Here you can see the books you are 'reading now', browse your library of books you've downloaded, browse the book store, look at audio books and search for a specific book title or author.

## Browse the Store

You can also browse through the book store. To do this, tap 'bookstore' icon on the panel along the bottom of the screen.

Scroll down the page, you'll see a 'for you' section. These are books that apple books recommends according to your interests. Scroll further down and you'll see new and trending books, latest releases, and so on. Tap on the book covers to see more information.

You can also browse by category or genre. To do this click the sections icon from the top right of the page.

Scroll down to 'genres' and select one. Perhaps you're into 'crime thrillers', 'fiction', or 'education'. Just tap on a category to view the available books.

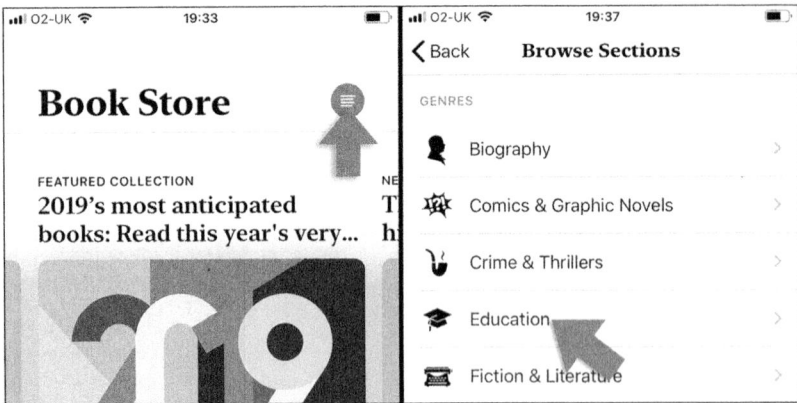

Scroll down the page, tap on the book covers to see more information.

# Search the Store

You can also search for specific authors or titles. To do this tap on the 'search' icon on the panel along the bottom of the screen.

Then type what you're looking for in the search field at the top of the screen.

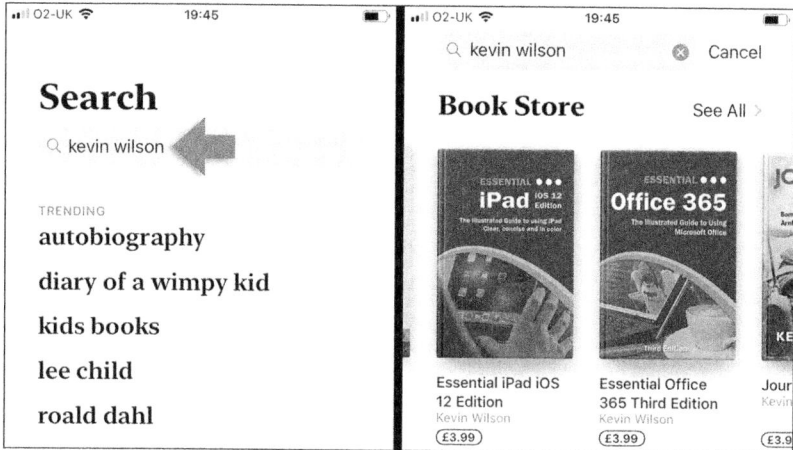

Tap on a book cover to see more details.

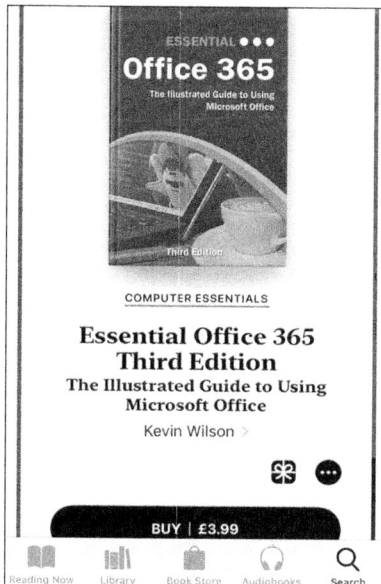

## Buying New Books

Once you have found the books you want either by searching or browsing the store, tap on the book cover to open the details page.

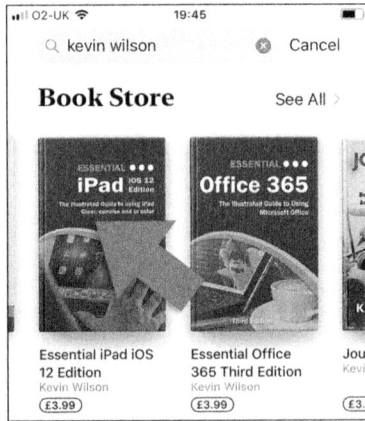

Here you can read reviews, write ups, and a free sample of the book. Tap 'get' if the book is free, or tap the price tag to download the book to your library. Authorise the payment with your Touch ID or password.

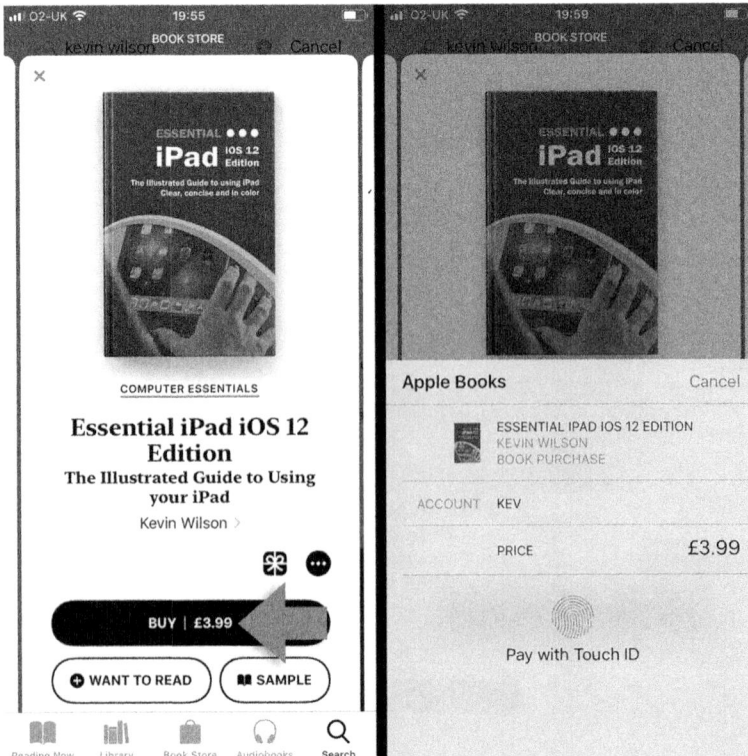

Once you've downloaded the book, you'll find it in your library. Tap the library icon on the panel along the bottom of the screen.

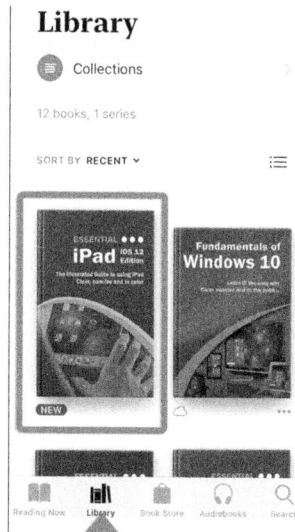

Tap on the book cover to begin reading.

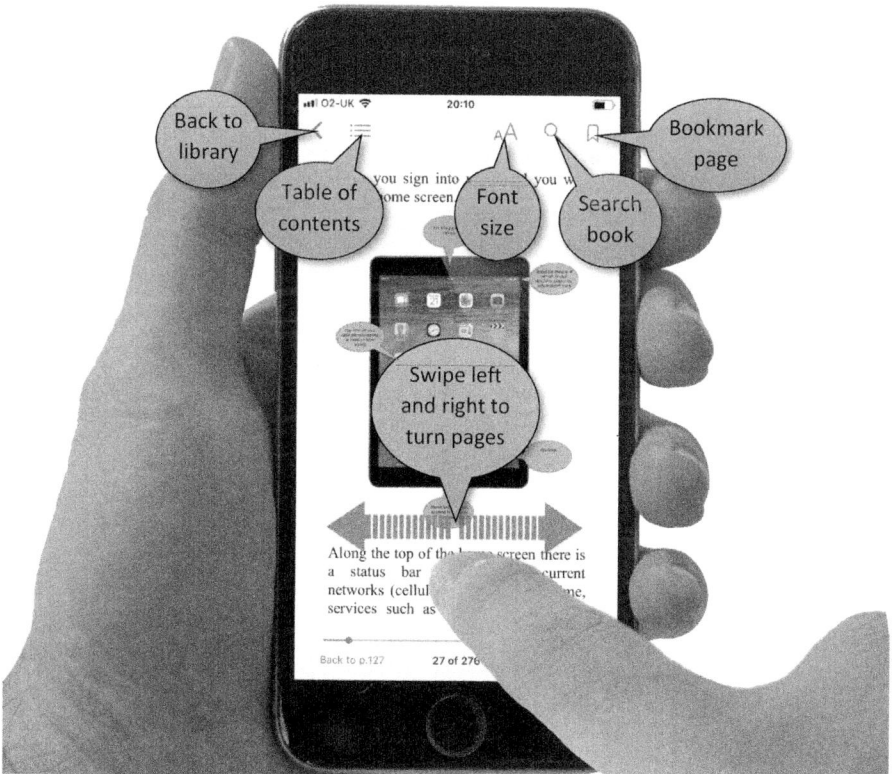

# Files App

The iCloud Drive App has been dropped and replaced with the Files App. You'll find the icon on your home screen.

In the Files App, you'll find all your files that are stored on your iPhone and iCloud Drive. When you first open the files app, you'll see your most recently opened documents.

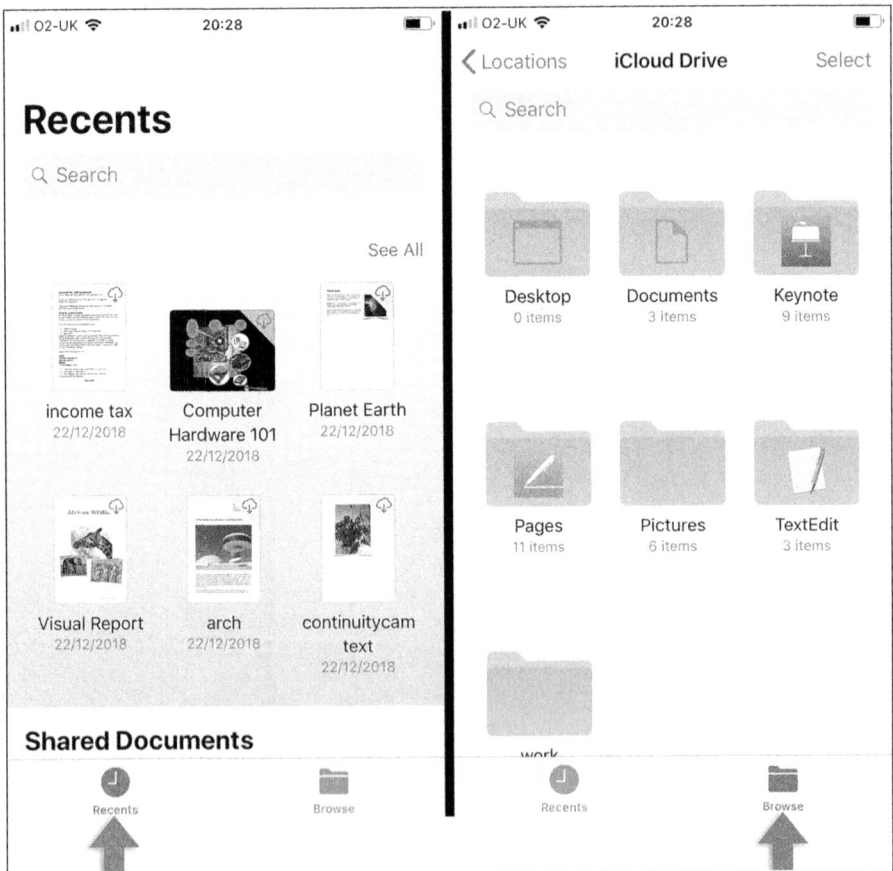

To see all the documents stored on iCloud, tap 'browse' from the panel along the bottom of the screen.

Tap on any icon to open the folder or file.

When working with any of Apple's productivity apps such as Keynote, Pages or Numbers, the files you create will be saved into the appropriate folders in the Files App.

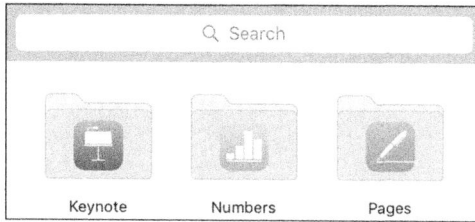

# Create New Folders

You can also create your own folders. To do this tap the 'new folder' icon on the top left.

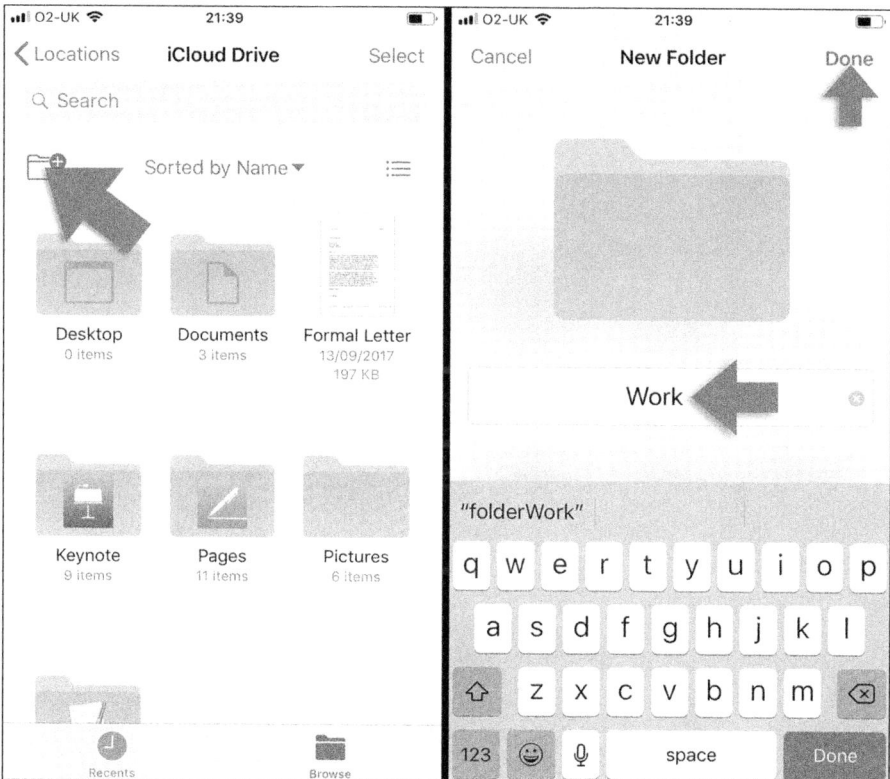

Enter the folder's name in the field, then tap 'done' when you're finished.

The new folder will show up in the 'browse' window.

## Drag Files into Folders

You can drag and drop files into these folders. Tap and hold your finger on the file, then drag your finger across the glass to the folder you want to put the file into. In this example, I'm going to drag and drop my letter into the 'work' folder.

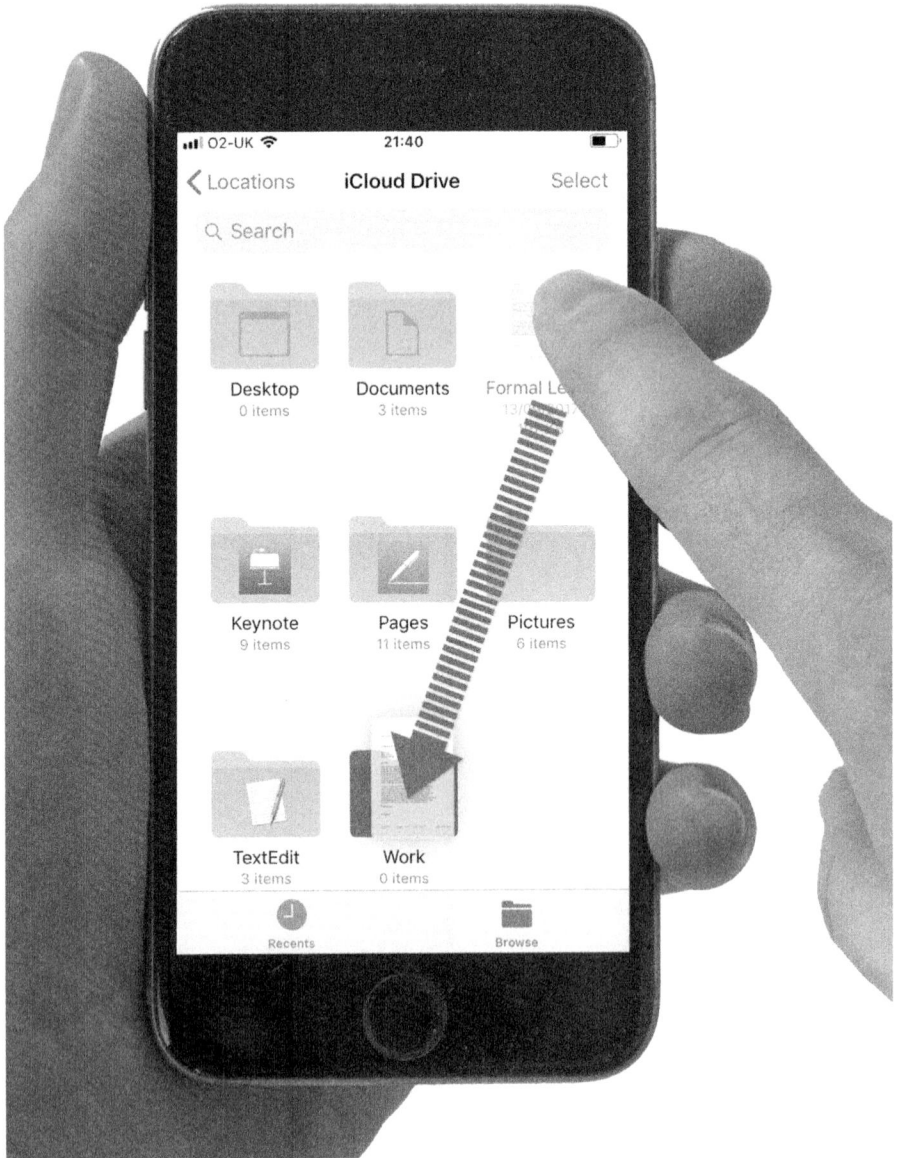

Tap on the folders to open them, tap on the file thumbnails to open the files.

# Delete Files or Folders

You can also delete files. Tap 'select' on the top right of the screen.

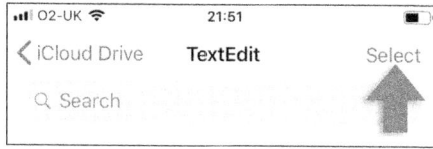

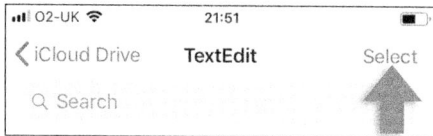

Tap on the files you want to delete.

Tap the delete icon on the toolbar along the bottom of the screen.

# Share a File

Tap 'select' on the top right of the screen.

Tap the file you want to share, then tap the share icon on the toolbar along the bottom of the screen.

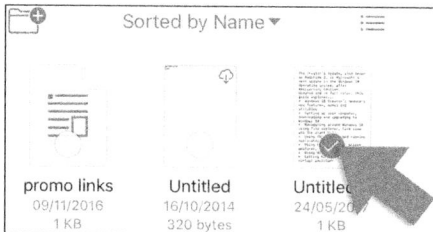

Select your sharing method from the options. You can share with iMessage, email, or airdrop.

# Apple Pay

Apple Pay allows you to keep digital copies of your bank cards, and lets you pay for things using your iPhone or iPhone. You can use this feature on an iPhone but it is more convenient with an iPhone.

*Apple Pay will run on iPhone SE, iPhone 6, iPhone 6 Plus, and later.*

## Setup

Make sure your bank supports Apple Pay. If so, go to your settings app, scroll down and tap 'wallet & apple pay'. Then tap 'add card'.

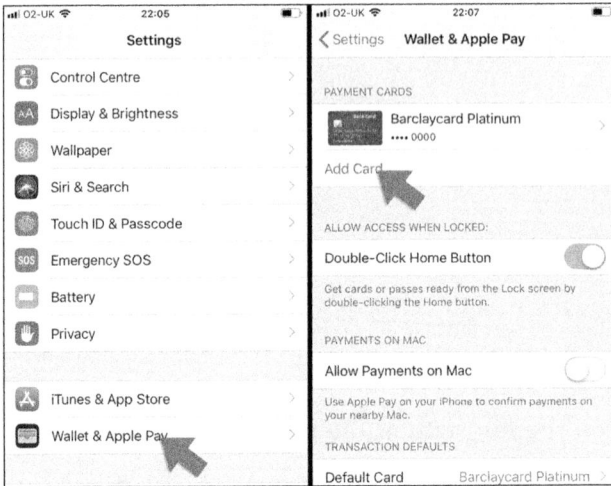

If you already have a credit/debit card registered with your Apple ID, then apple pay will ask you to add this one.

If this is the card you want to use, then enter the 3 digit security code and tap 'next' on the top right. Hit 'agree' on the terms and conditions. Your card will be added.

If you want to add a different card, tap 'add a different card' underneath.

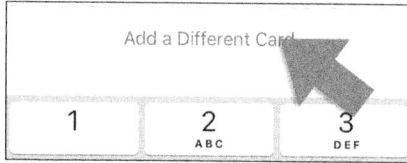

Position the card so it fills the white rectangle on your screen. Apple Pay will scan your card and automatically enter your details

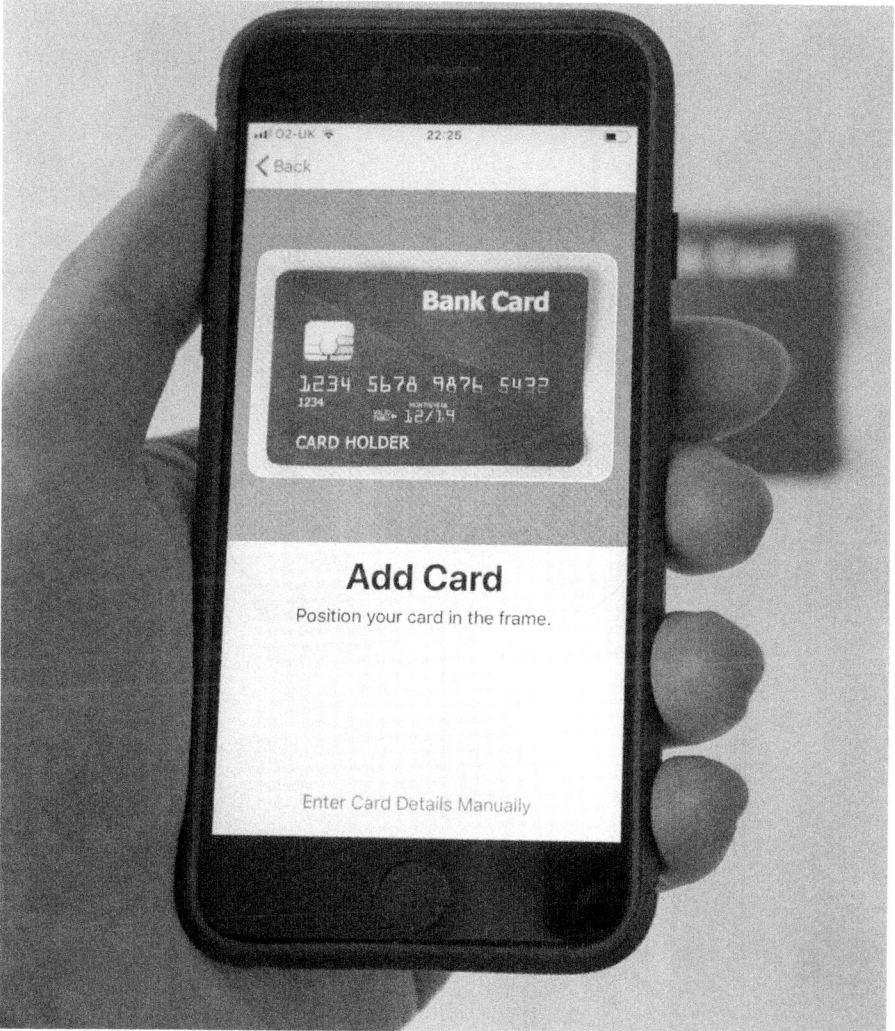

If you can't get the camera to scan the card, tap 'enter card details manually' then key in your card number, exp dates, and so on.

Tap next. Check and confirm your card details. Make any changes if necessary, so the details match those on your card. Tap next, then tap 'agree' to the terms and conditions.

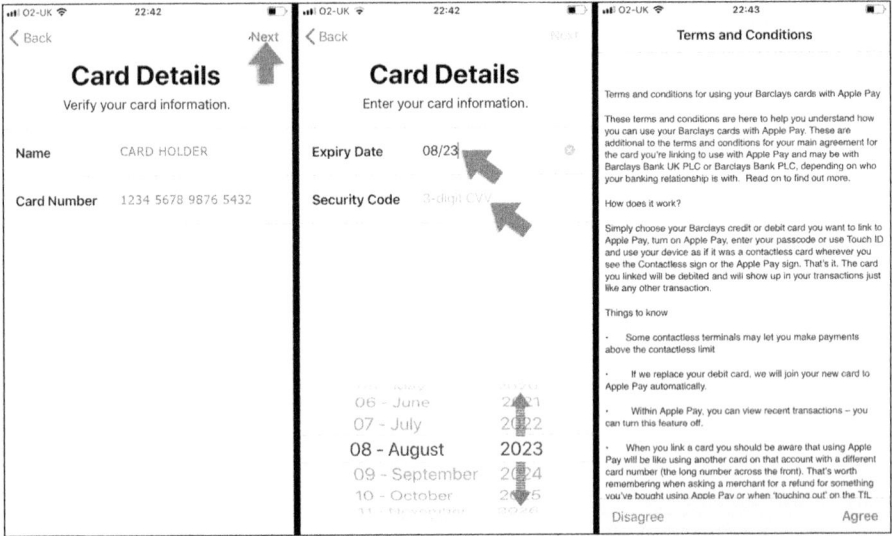

Now you'll need to verify your card. Some banks use different methods, so read the instructions on the screen. In this example, the bank will send a code via SMS to the phone number registered when the bank account was opened. Tap 'next'.

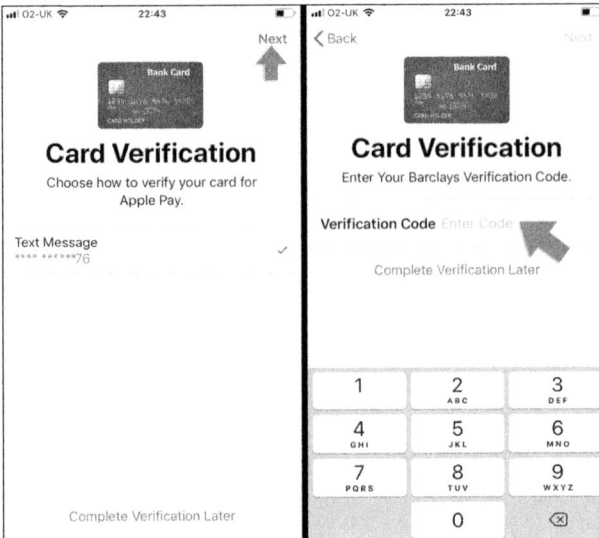

Check your SMS messages and enter the verification code in the field. Tap 'next'.

# Using Apple Pay

You can use Apple Pay at any store that supports this feature. You will usually see the logo displayed in store. You can also use Apple Pay on some online stores.

To pay with Apple Pay, place your iPhone above the reader. You'll see a prompt on your iPhone for the amount with your default card on the screen. Place your finger on the home button to authorise the payment with Touch ID.

You'll see a tick on your screen and a ping sound when the transaction is authorised successfully.

*If you want to pay with a card other than the default, hold the top of your iPhone near the contactless reader without touching the home button.*

*Tap the cards on the bottom of the screen. Tap the card you want to use from the popup selection.*

*Present your iPhone to the contactless reader with your thumb on the home button to complete payment.*

# Voice Memos

You can record audio using your iPhone's built in mic or a bluetooth external mic. You can record voice memos, meetings, and lectures.

You'll find the voice memo app on your home screen.

Lets take a look at the main screen. Here you can see your previous recordings listed down the middle.

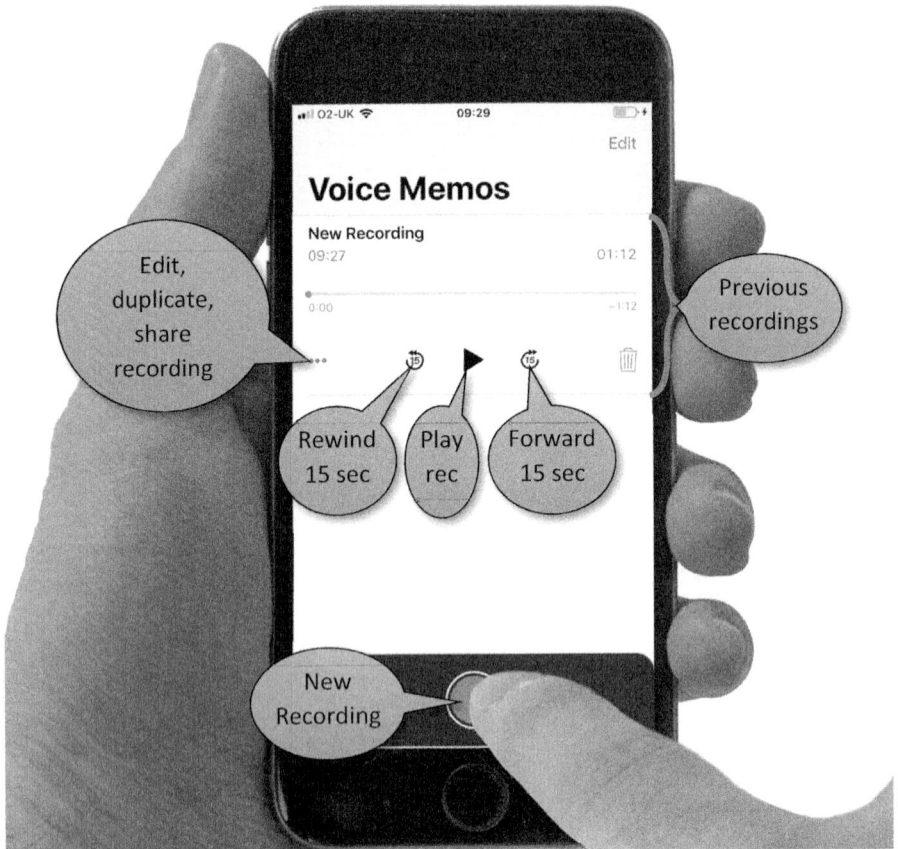

Tap the play button in the grey panel on the right to playback the recording. Tap red button to make a new recording.

# Recording Memos

To record a memo, simply tap the red record button on the bottom of the screen.

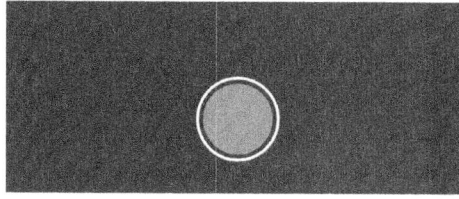

The memo app will start recording. You'll see a wave form appear in the middle of the screen to indicate the app is picking up audio.

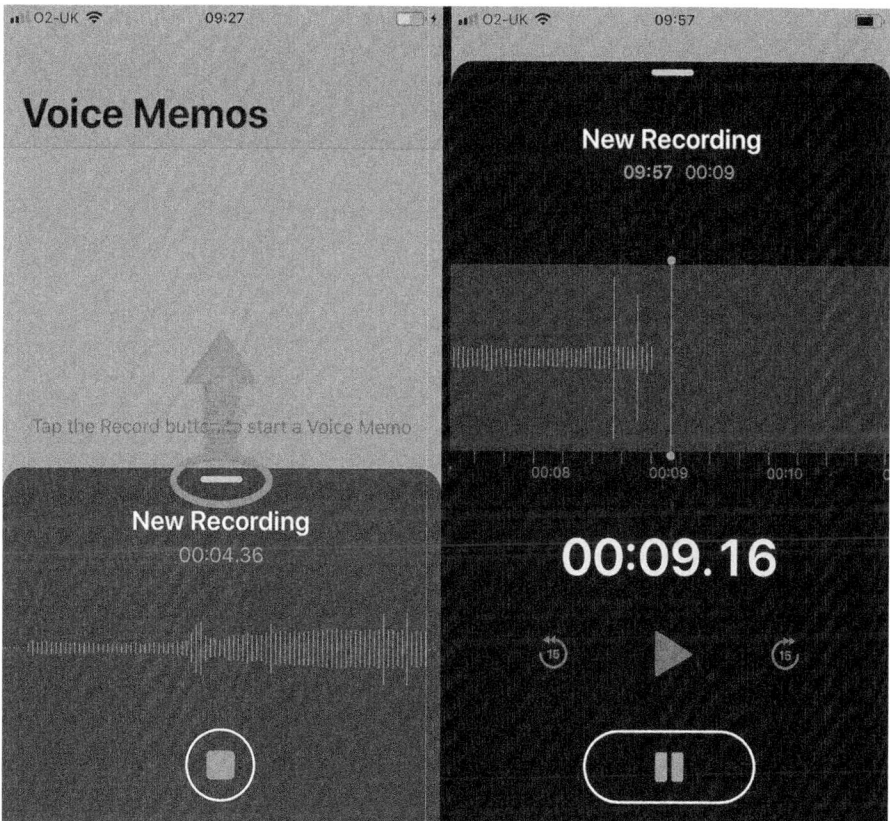

Tap and drag the handle on top of the lower window and drag it upwards to reveal all the controls. To pause a recording temporarily, tap the pause icon. To stop the recording, tap pause, then tap 'done'.

Your memo will appear in the list on the main screen.

## Renaming Memos

The first thing you should do with a new voice memo recording is give it a meaningful name. The last thing you want is every memo called 'new recording.

To demonstrate this, we'll rename the voice memo we just recorded. Then tap the title of the recording, the keyboard will pop up.

Delete the default text, then type in a meaningful name for the recording.

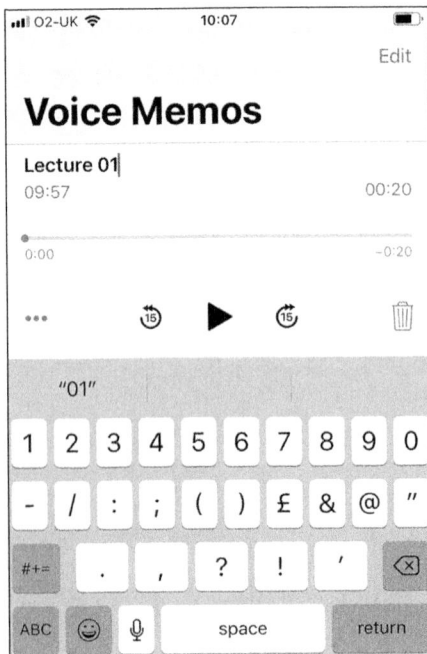

Hit return on the on screen keyboard to confirm the name.

## Trim a Memo

You can trim the beginning and the ends of the memo voice recording. To do this, tap the three dots icon on the bottom left of the recording in the main screen.

Tap 'edit recording', then tap the blue icon on the top right of the screen.

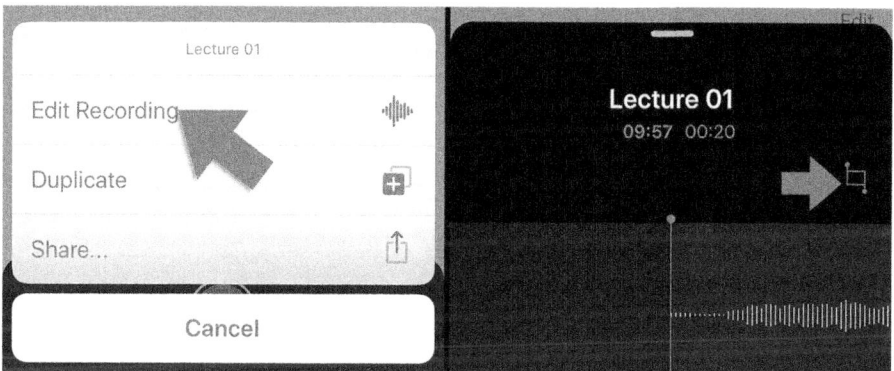

Now to trim the beginning and ends of the clip, drag the yellow handles along the track until you get to the start and end points you want.

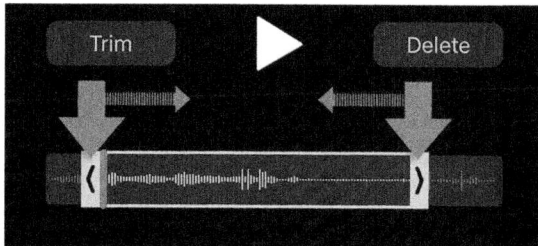

Tap 'trim' when you're done.

## Chapter 6: Common Apps

# Clock App

You can use the clock app to set alarms, timers, as a stop watch, and create time zone clocks so you can see the time in other countries.

You'll find the clock app on your home screen.

## World Clock

With world clock, you can create clocks for any city or country in the world. This is useful if you have friends or family in another country, so you know what time it is there and don't call them in the middle of the night. It's also useful if you're travelling.

To see the world clock, tap 'world clock' on the panel along the bottom of the screen.

To add a clock, tap the + sign on the top right of the screen.

Type in the name of the city or country you want to add

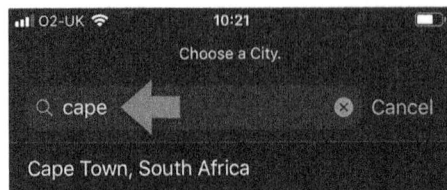

Tap the name of the city/country in the list of suggestions.

You'll see the clock appear on the list.

To remove a clock, swipe right to left over the clock and tap 'delete'.

**228**

# Alarm

You can also set multiple alarms. Eg one for wake up. To do this, select 'alarm' from the panel along the bottom of the screen.

This will display all the alarms you have set. To set a new alarm, tap the + sign on the top right.

Set the alarm to the time you want the alarm to go off eg 8AM. Tap 'repeat' to set what days you want the alarm, eg 'weekdays' - tap 'back'. Tap 'label' to name the alarm, eg 'AM Meeting', tap 'back'. Tap 'sound' to choose what your alarm sounds like - you can select a sound or a song from your music library. Tap 'save' on the top right when you're done.

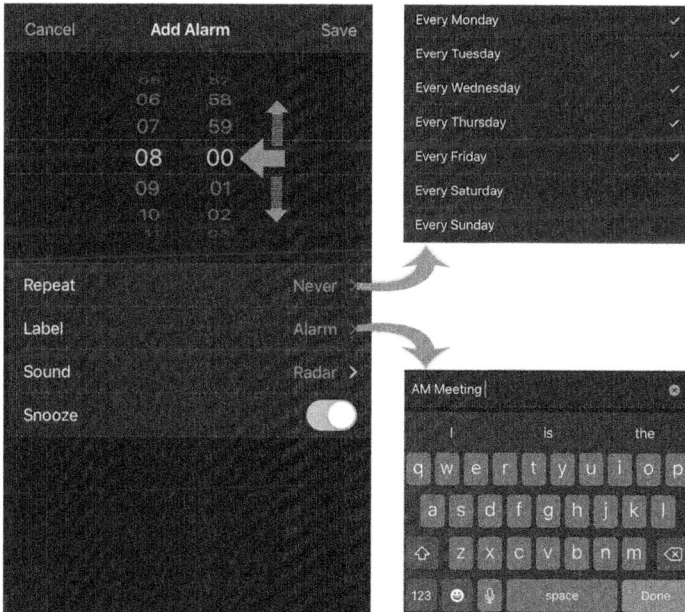

To delete an alarm, swipe right to left over the alarm in the main screen then tap 'delete'.

## Bed Time

Bed time allows you to create a sleep routine, allowing you to set a time to go to bed and a time to wake up, and the clock app will remind you.

Select 'bed time' from the panel along the bottom of the screen.

The first time you run this feature, you'll need to go through the setup. To do this tap 'get started'. Select the time you want to wake up using the sliders on the screen. Tap 'next'

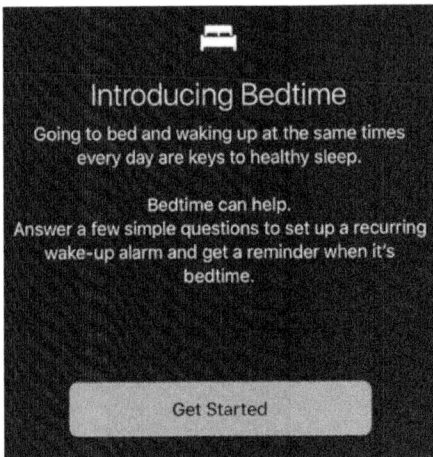

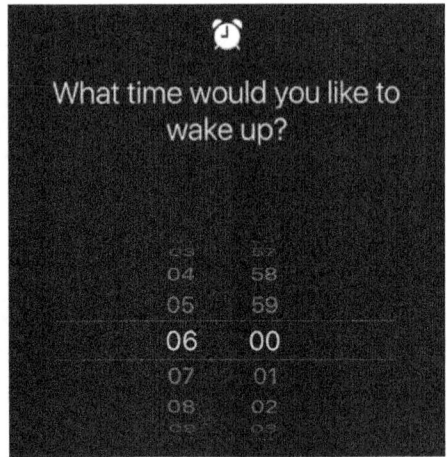

Select the days of the week, then select the number of hours sleep you need. Usually 8 hours. Tap 'next'.

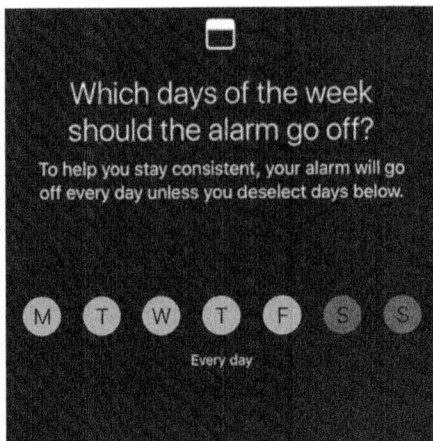

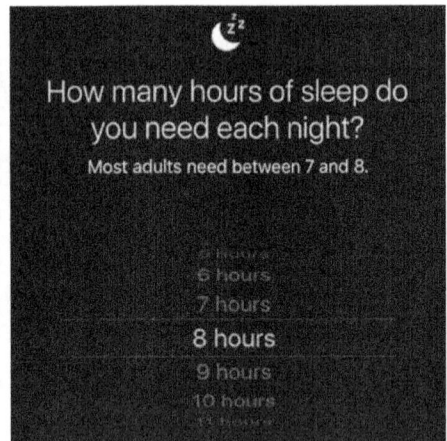

Set the days of the week you want to routine to be in force. Tap 'next'.

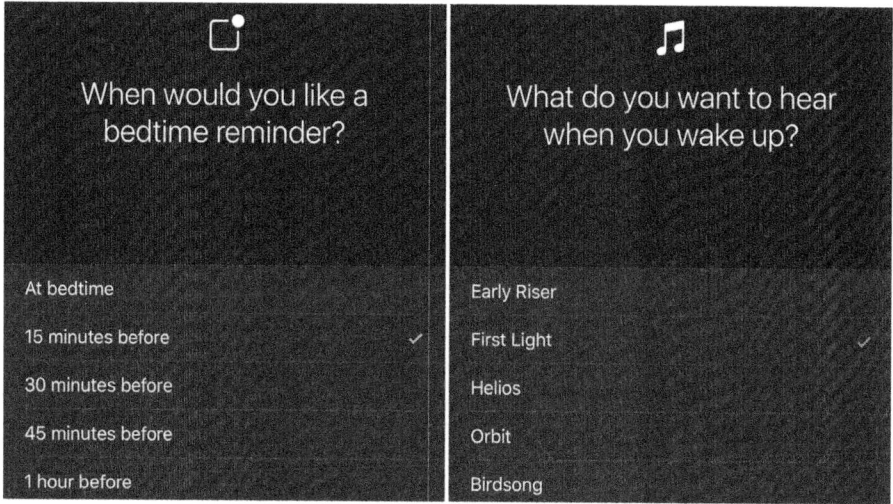

Once you've completed the setup, you can see your bedtime on the main screen. To adjust the bedtime time, drag the sleep marker around the clock. Similarly to adjust your wakeup time, drag the wake marker around the clock.

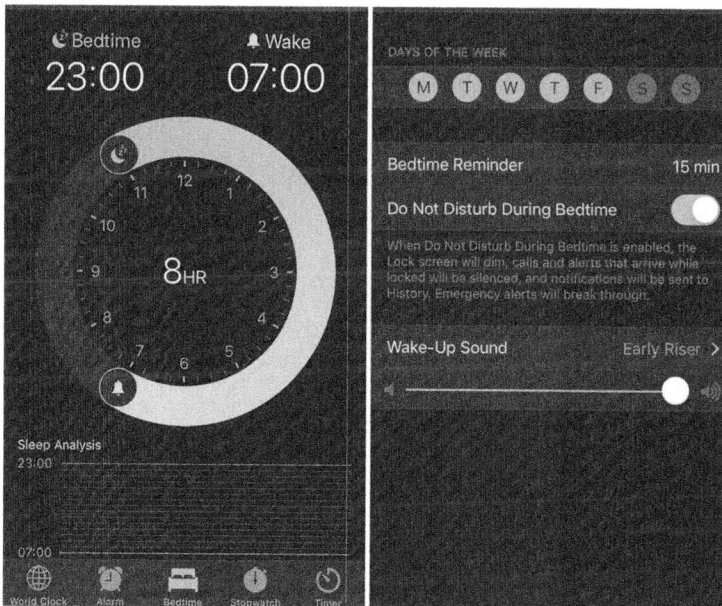

To change your options, tap 'options' on the top left of the screen. Here you can change the days of the week, set a reminder and set a wake up sound.

**231**

## Stop Watch

Use the stopwatch to time events. Eg an athletics event. Select 'stopwatch' from the panel along the bottom of the screen.

Tap 'start/stop' to start and stop the timer.

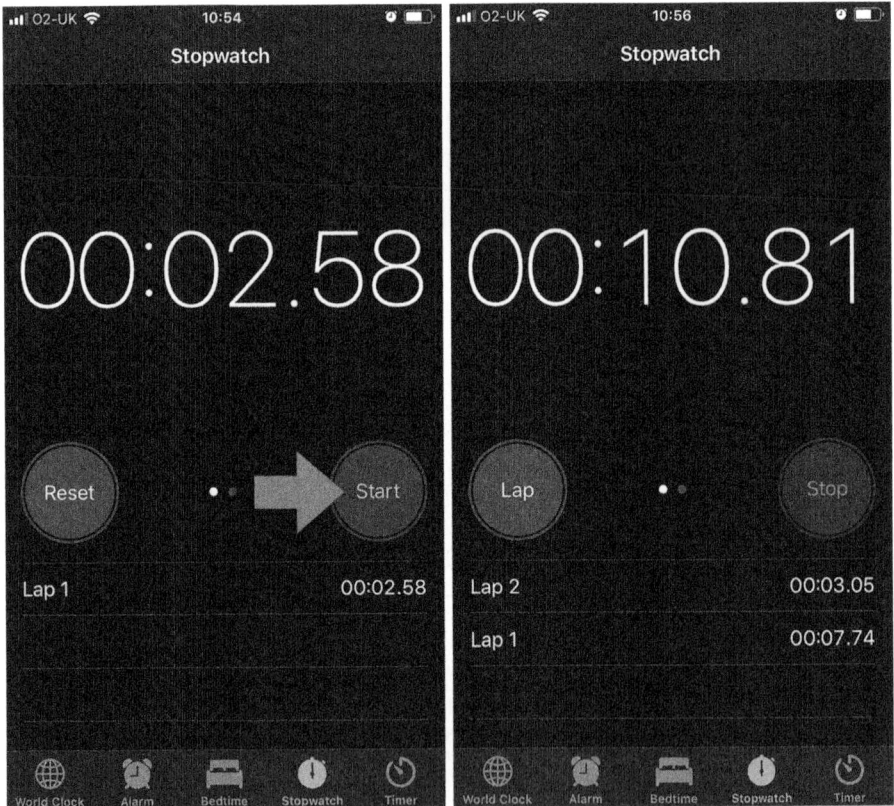

Tap 'lap' to count the number of laps if you are timing a sporting event such as athletics or racing.

# Timer

Use the timer to set a count down timer. Select 'timer' from the panel along the bottom of the screen.

Use the sliders to select the length of time in hours, minutes and seconds. For example, if you're playing a game or timing an egg, just set the amount of time allowed.

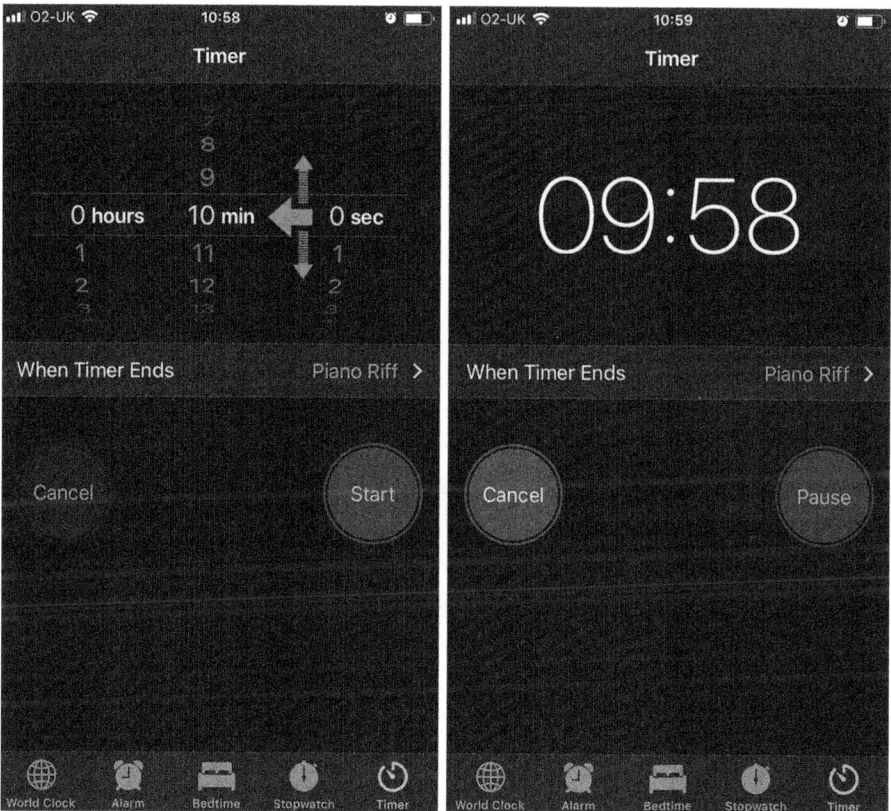

Tap 'start' to start the count down. Tap the iTunes icon next to where it says 'constellation' to change the sound the timer makes when the time runs out.

# Productivity
# Apps

Apple has developed two productivity apps that allow you to create documents and keynote presentations.

These apps don't usually come pre-installed, so you will need to download them from the app store.

You can do this by searching for 'essentials', then tapping on the 'get' icons for pages and keynote.

# Creating Documents with Pages

To launch Pages, tap the icon on your home screen.

Once Pages 6 has opened, tap 'continue' on the welcome page. If you are launched Pages for the first time, you'll be asked to use iCloud. Click 'Use iCloud'. This enables you to save your documents to your personal cloud space. Next, tap 'create a document'.

When you first open Pages, you'll see a list of your most recently opened Pages documents, as well as documents saved in your iCloud drive. Tap on the icons to open any of the files.

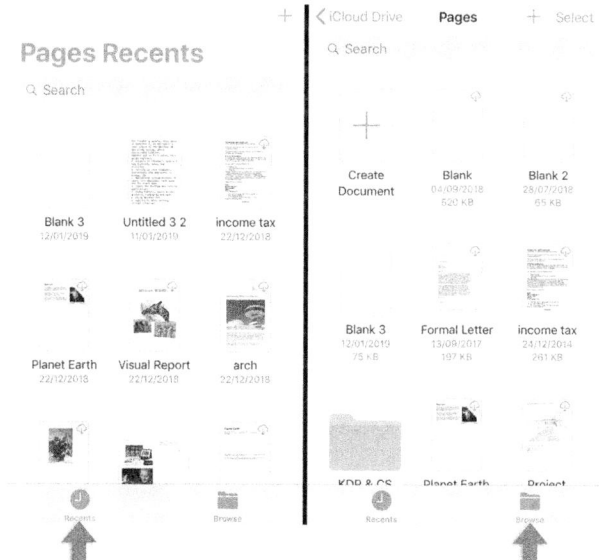

# Chapter 7: Productivity Apps

To open a blank document or a pre-designed template, tap the '+' sign, then select a template

Select a template, or tap 'blank document'. You can select pre designed reports, books, letters, flyers and so on.

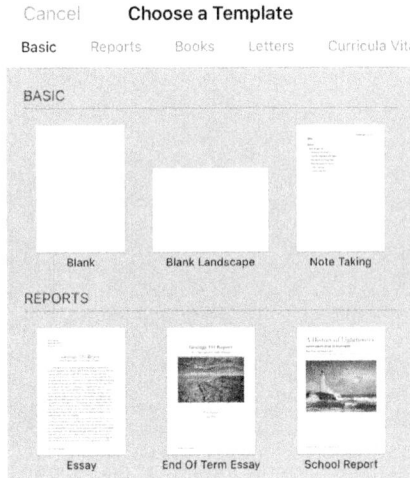

Once you have selected the template to use you will see the main work screen. Let's take a closer look at the main editing screen.

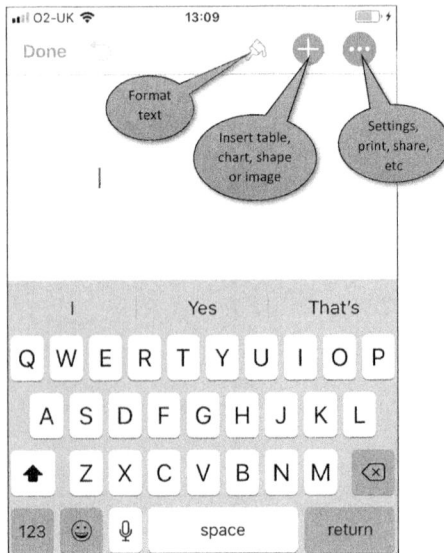

# Formatting Text

Begin typing in your text into the main window as shown above.

The text we entered before needs formatting. To add a heading type it in above the block of text.

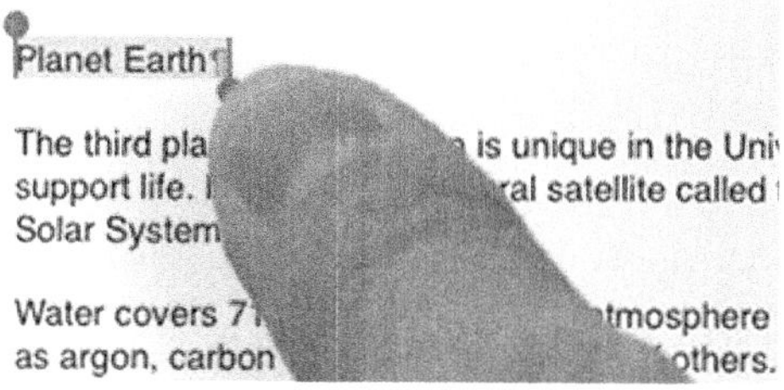

Planet Earth

The third pla... ...is unique in the Uni... support life. ... ...ral satellite called... Solar System...

Water covers 7... ...tmosphere as argon, carbon... ...others.

Highlight your text with your finger as shown above by dragging the blue dots over the text, then tap the paint brush from the toolbar.

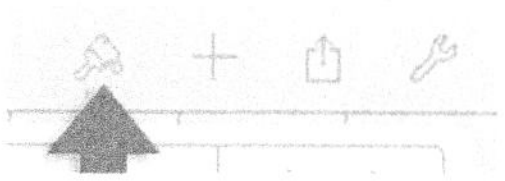

Tap on 'title' to apple the title style to the selected text

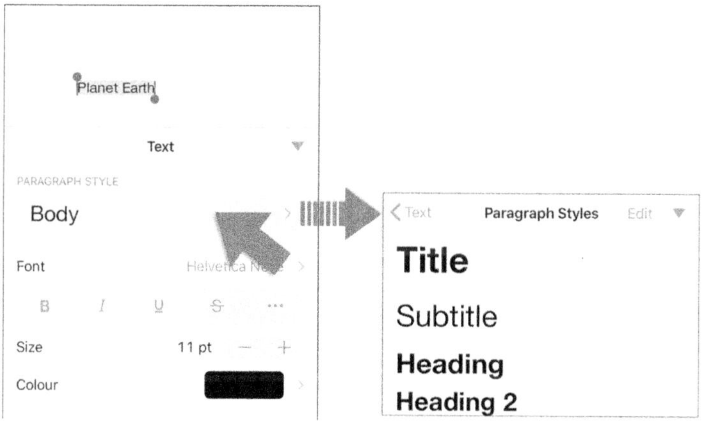

Planet Earth

Text

PARAGRAPH STYLE

Body

Font                    Helvetica N...

B    I    U    S    ...

Size              11 pt    —    +

Colour

< Text      Paragraph Styles      Edit

**Title**

Subtitle

**Heading**

**Heading 2**

Formatting your document means laying it out in a style that is easy to read and looks attractive. This could involve changing fonts, making text bigger for headings, changing colour of text, adding graphics and photographs, etc.

For each document template you choose from the Template Chooser there are a number of pre-set paragraph styles. These are to help you format your document consistently, eg so all headings are the same font, size and colour.

## Adding a Picture

The easiest way to add a picture is to tap the plus sign on the right hand side of the screen.

Tap image icon on the bar along the top. Select one of your albums if you want to insert a photo you took with your camera or tap 'insert from' if you have an image on your iCloud drive. Tap your pictures folder and select an image.

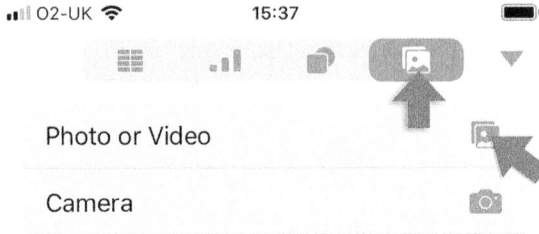

You can resize your image by clicking the resize handles, circled below, and dragging them.

support life. It has a single natural satellite called the Moon and is the fifth largest planet in the Solar System.

You can change the styles by adding borders and shadows by tapping on the paint brush icon on the top right of your toolbar.

# Keynote

Keynote allows you to create multimedia presentations. To launch keynote, go to your home screen and tap keynote.

Tap continue, and if you're running keynote for the first time, tap 'use icloud'.

When you first open Keynote, you'll see a list of your most recently opened presentations, as well as presentations saved in your iCloud drive. Tap on the icons to open any of the files.

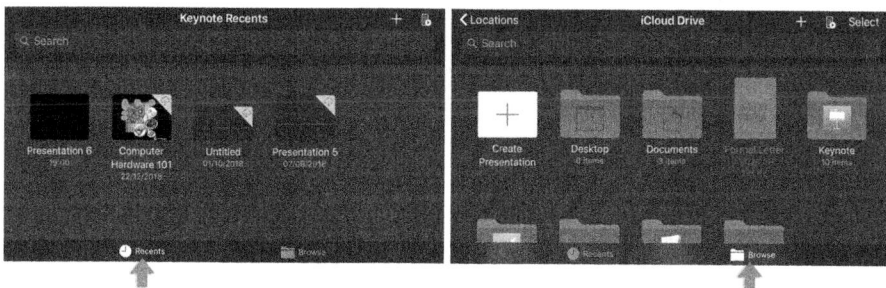

Select 'recents' to see your most recently opened presentations, or click 'browse' to browse through presentations saved on your iCloud drive.

To create a new blank presentation, or one from a template, tap the '+' sign on the top right of the screen.

# Chapter 7: Productivity Apps

Select a template from the designs. In this example, I'm going to select a blank 'black' presentation.

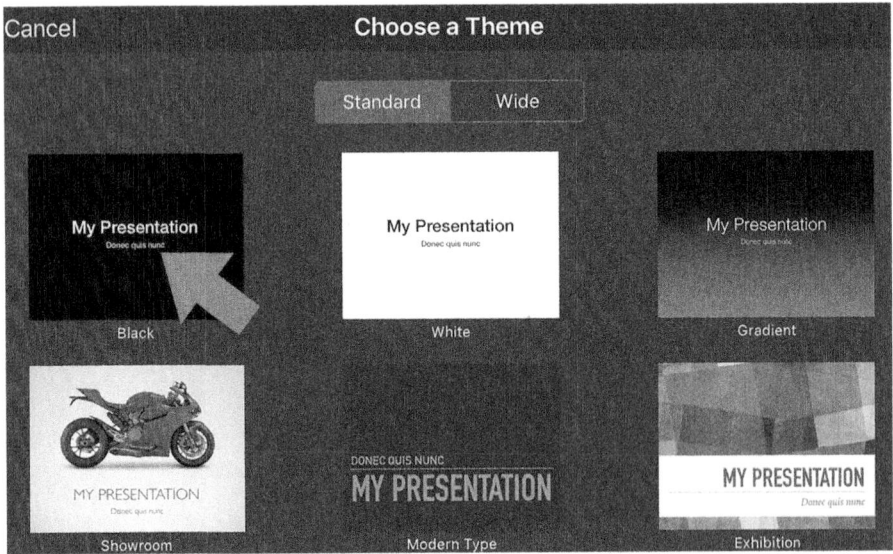

Once you have selected a template you will see the main screen as shown below.

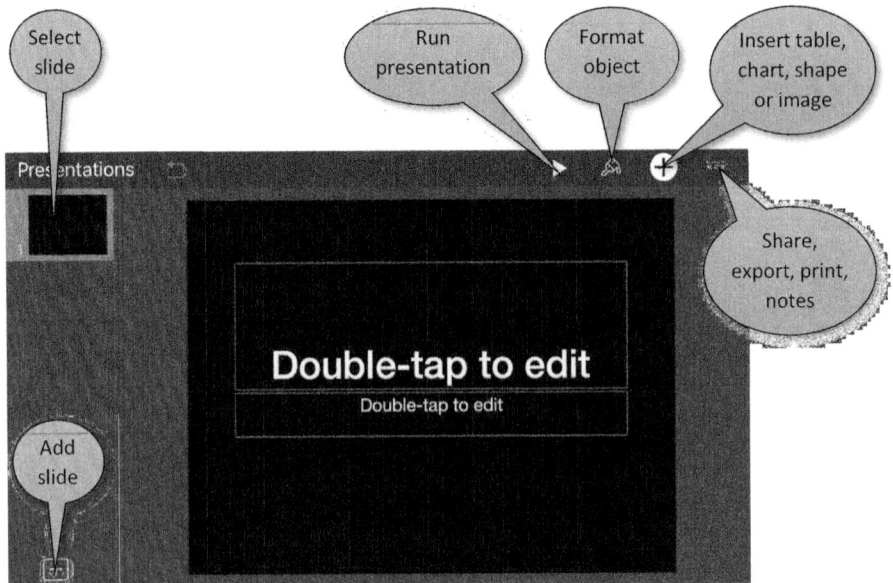

This is where you can start building your presentation.

## Editing a Slide

Double tap in the heading field shown below and enter a heading eg 'Planet Earth'. You can tap and drag the heading wherever you like.

## Adding a New Slide

Tap the new slide button located on the bottom left of the screen.

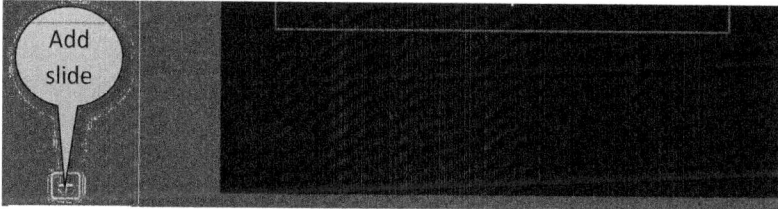

Tap a slide layout from the options that appear.

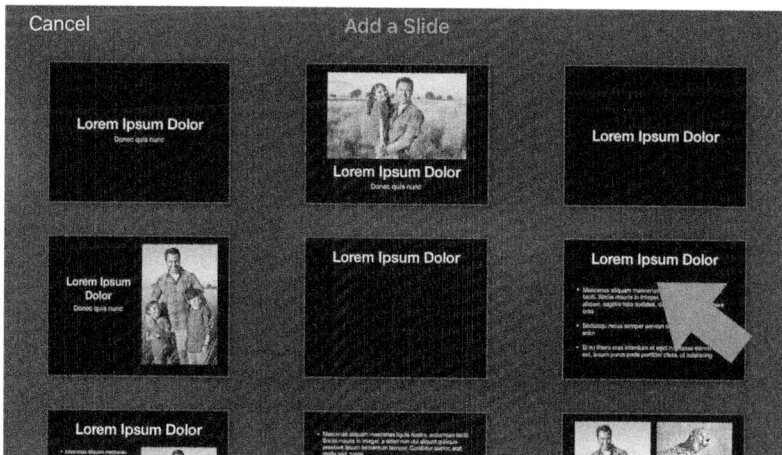

Add some text by double clicking on the text box that appears in the slide.

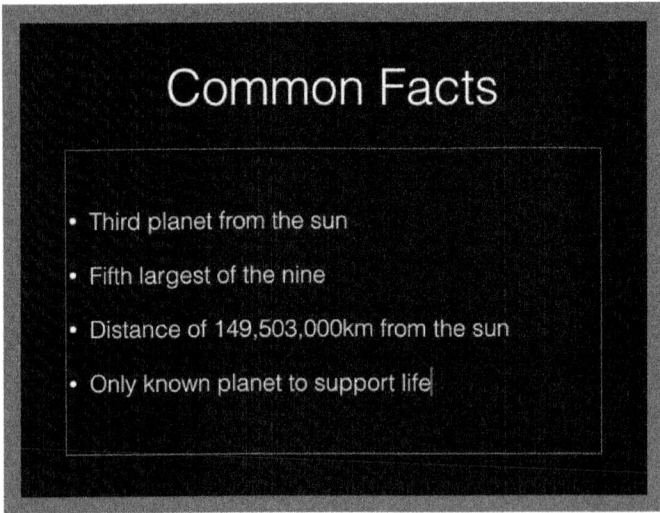

## Adding Media

To add images and media to your slide, tap the plus sign on your tool bar at the top right of your screen.

Then tap the image icon on the top right.

If you want to add one of your photographs from your photo library, tap on one of your albums and select a photo.

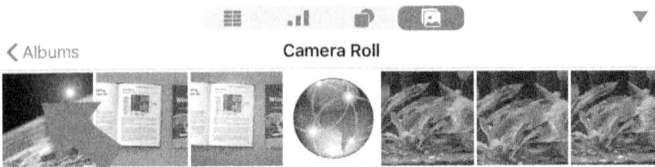

Tap on a picture.

# Animations

Animations allow you to make objects such as text or photographs appear...

Tap on your text box and select the animate icon located on the top right corner of your screen

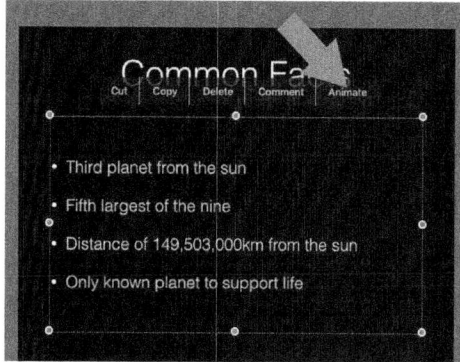

Then tap 'none: build in'

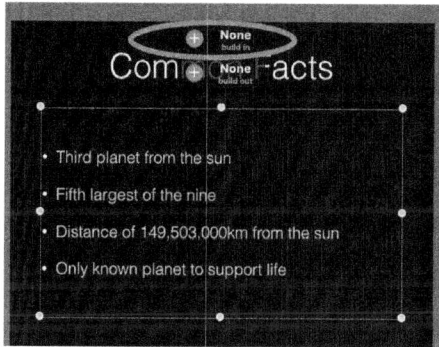

Then select an effect from the effects menu (shown below).

Then specify that you want the bullet points to appear one by one. Tap 'delivery'

select 'by bullet' from the drop down menu.

Tap 'done'.

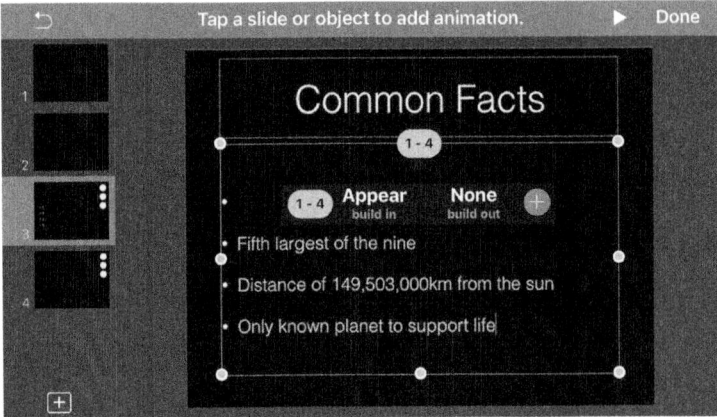

To see what the effect looks like, tap the play button on the top right of your screen.

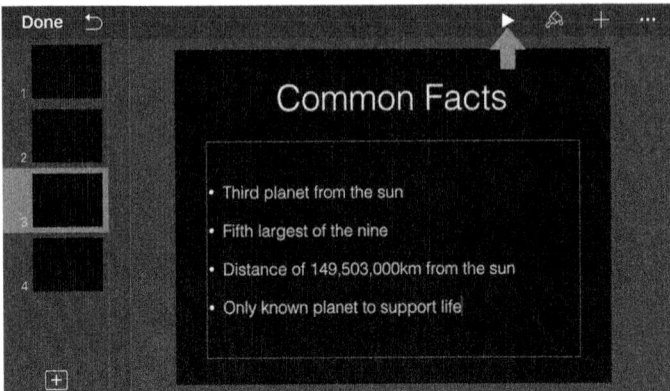

# Formatting Text Boxes

Tap on a text box you want to format. You can add borders to your text boxes, reflection effects or background colours.

To format the border and fill your text box, tap your text box.

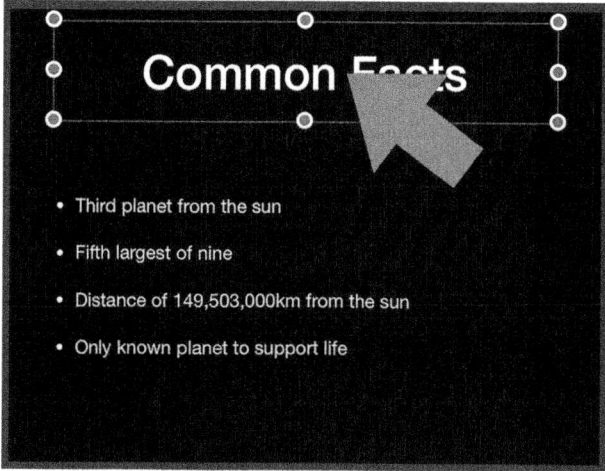

Tap the paint brush icon, on the top right of the screen

Tap fill to change the background colour of the text box. Then swipe your finger across the selections of effects and tap on one to select it. In this example, I am going for a nice blue fill.

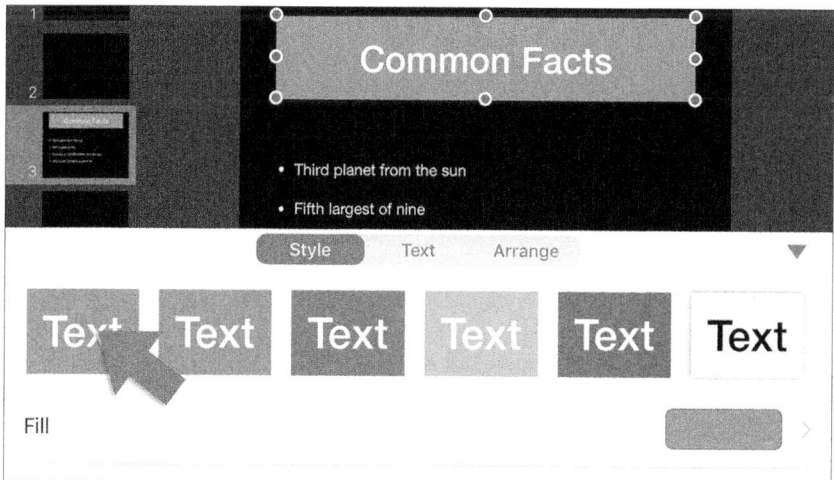

## Formatting Text Inside Textboxes

To change the formatting of the text, for example to change the colour of the text or make it bold.

First select your text in the text box you want to change. Tap on the text three times to select it all.

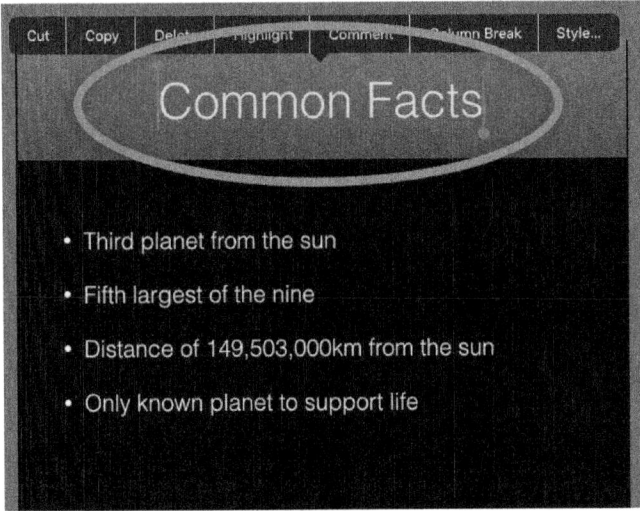

Tap the paint brush icon on the top right of your toolbar.

Select 'text' from the popup panel.

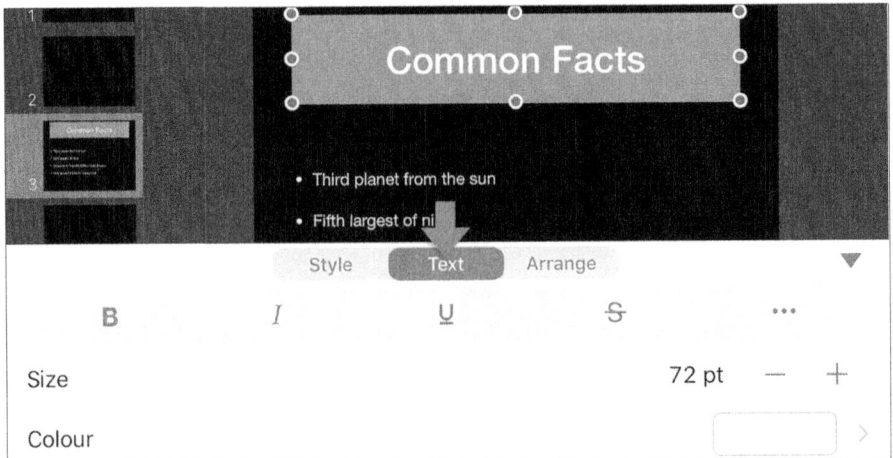

From here you can change the font, the font colour, size etc. As an example I have made it bold. Scroll down to see all the settings.

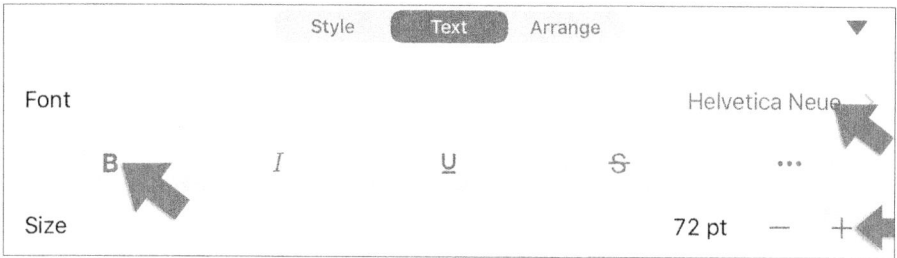

Tap on the font name, illustrated with the red arrows, then select a font.

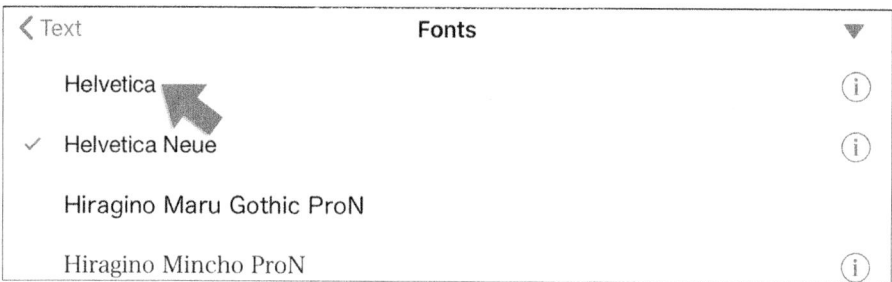

You can also change the colour, as well as the text alignment: left, center, right.

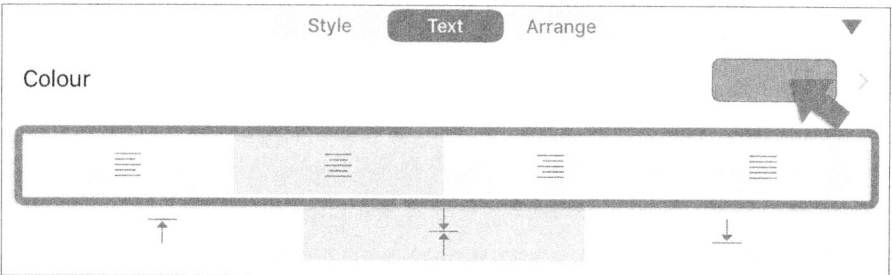

Scroll down to the rest of the settings.

Tap the slide, when you're finished.

# Printing Documents

To print documents from an iPad you'll need a printer that is compatible with Air Print. Most modern printers will have this feature included.

## Air Print

If your printer is Air Print enabled, then your printer will show up in the print dialog box automatically.

To print a document, select the share icon, then scroll along the circled icons until you see 'print'. *If you're using the Pages App, select the '...' icon and tap 'print'.*

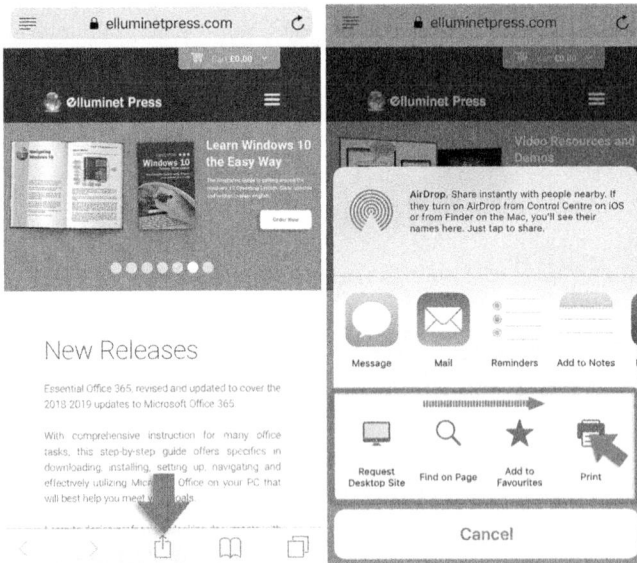

Select your printer from the printer field, enter the number of copies you want, and select the page range you want to print (eg pages 2-4), or leave it on 'all pages', if you want the whole document.

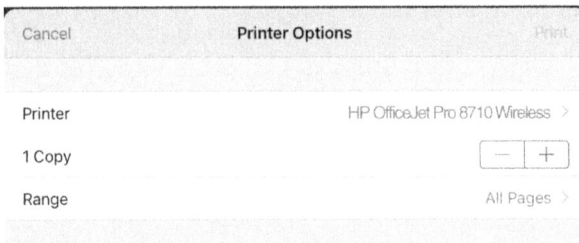

Tap 'print' on the top right when you're done.

# Older Printers

If your printer doesn't have the Air Print feature, you can download an app from the App Store for your printer.

- **HP Printers** download **HP Smart**

- **Samsung Printers** download **Samsung Mobile Print**

- **Epson Printers** download **Epson iPrint**

- **Canon Printers** download **Canon Print**

Open the app on your iPad and select the document you want to print.

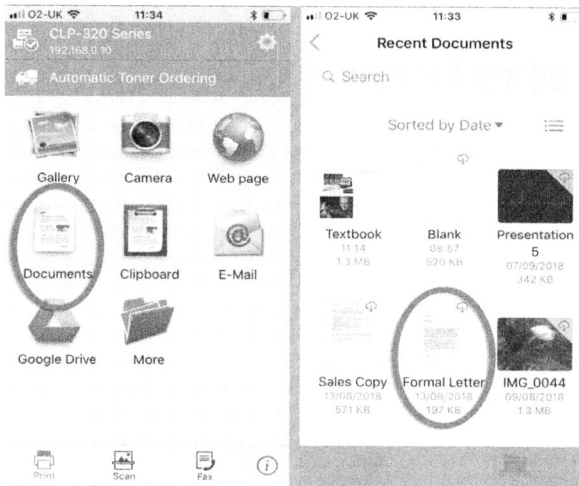

Select print.

# Chapter 8

# Maintaining Your iPhone

The new iPhones will ship with iOS 12, but if you need to update a previous model then you can do that here.

Apple has dropped support for iPhone 4s. iOS 12 will install on the following devices.

- iPhone X, 8, 7, 6, 5s

Before upgrading, make sure you have some time where you don't need to use your iPhone as it will be temporarily inoperative while the installation takes place.

# iPhone Backups

You can backup your settings, apps and files to your iCloud account.
Go to Settings, Tap on your account name, select 'iCloud', then sign
in if you haven't already done so. Scroll down until you see 'iCloud
Backup'.

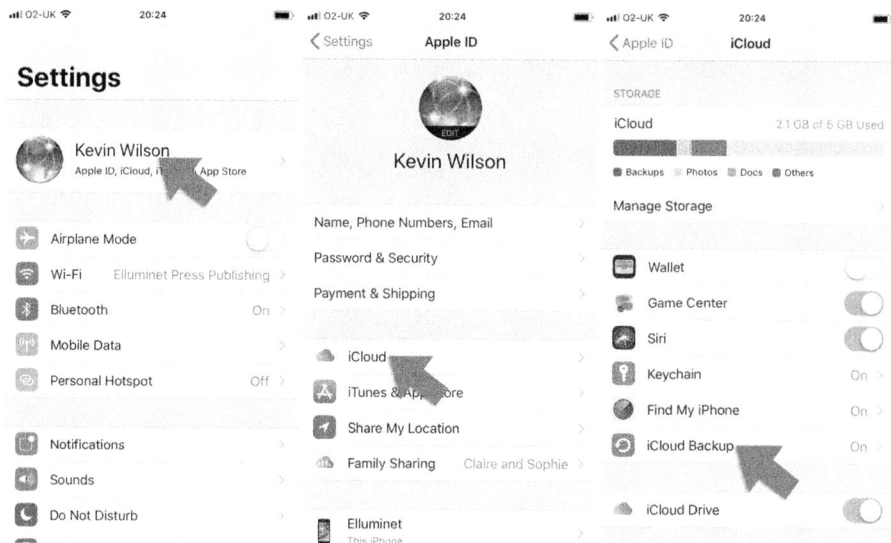

Tap 'Back Up Now'. This is usually the most common way.

*If you use iTunes, plug your device into your computer, select your iPhone
on the sidebar in iTunes, and select 'Back Up Now'. A backup will then
be saved onto your computer's hard disk.*

**251**

# System Updates

To run the update, on your iPhone open your settings app. Scroll down, tap 'general', then select 'Software Update'.

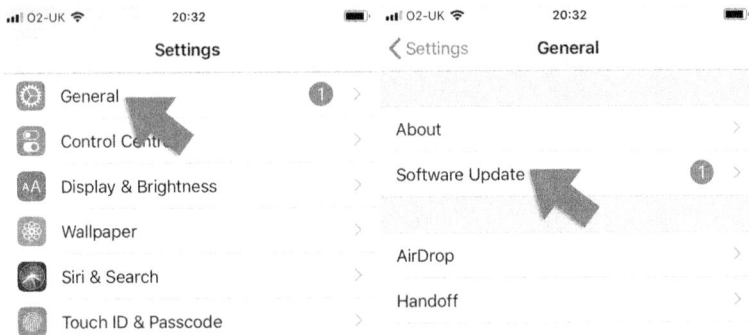

Make sure your device is connected to Wi-Fi and plugged into the charger, then tap 'download and install'.

Depending on your internet connection the installation might take a while.

If you prefer to update using iTunes. Connect your iPhone using the cable to a USB port and select your device from the sidebar under devices.

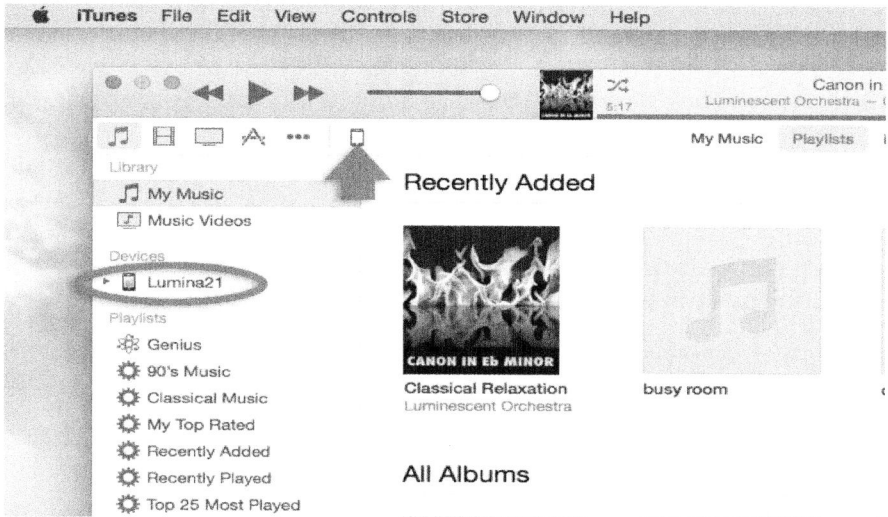

Under Summary, click 'Check for Update', then choose 'Download and Install'.

Confirm your iCloud details.

When updated, your iPhone will restart automatically. You may have to run through the initial setup again outlined in chapter 1.

After this, your newly updated device should be ready to use.

# App Updates

To check for app updates, tap the App Store icon on your home screen. From the bar across the bottom of the screen, tap updates.

Any available updates will be listed on this page. Tap and drag your finger downwards to check for new updates.

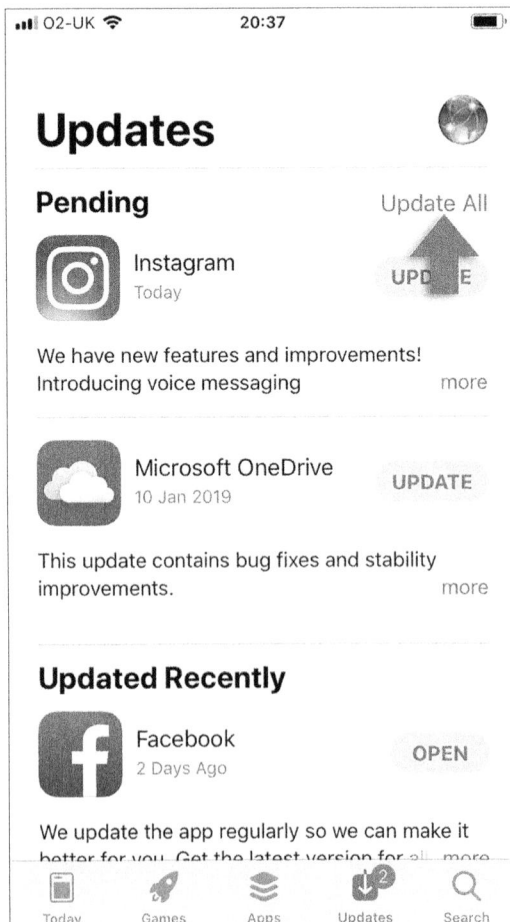

Tap 'update' to update that particular app, or tap 'update all' to apply all the updates.

# Deleting Apps

To delete apps, tap and hold your finger on an app, until the X appears on the icon.

Tap on the X to delete the app.

You can also delete any of the pre-installed apps you don't use, in the same way as above.

# iPhone Storage Maintenance

This gives you a view of the storage space available on your iPhone with some features for freeing up storage space automatically. You can set your iPhone to delete move your photos onto the iCloud photo library, empty your 'recently deleted' photos and albums, delete old conversations from iMessage, offload unused apps when your storage runs low and allows you to review large email attachments and messages and whether to keep them or move them off your iPhone and onto iCloud.

Open your settings app, tap 'general'

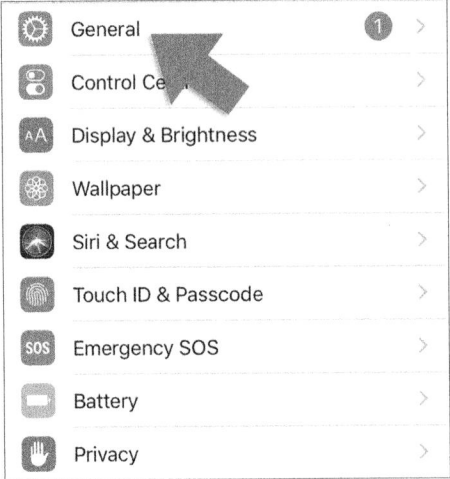

| | |
|---|---|
| ⚙ General | ① > |
| ▣ Control Ce | > |
| AA Display & Brightness | > |
| ✦ Wallpaper | > |
| ✦ Siri & Search | > |
| ◉ Touch ID & Passcode | > |
| SOS Emergency SOS | > |
| ▭ Battery | > |
| ✋ Privacy | > |

Tap 'iPhone storage'.

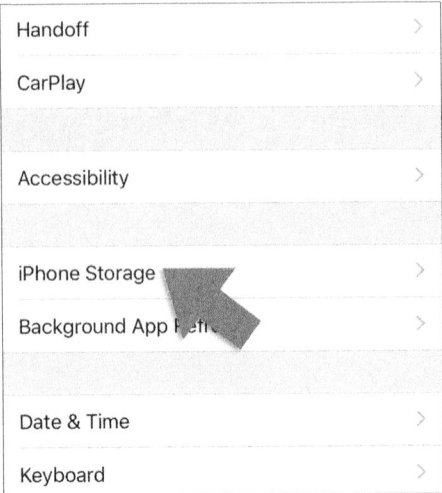

| | |
|---|---|
| Handoff | > |
| CarPlay | > |
| Accessibility | > |
| iPhone Storage | > |
| Background App | > |
| Date & Time | > |
| Keyboard | > |

Here you'll find a list of all the apps installed on your iPhone. If you scroll down the list, you'll see a list of individual apps that are currently installed on your iPhone. Tap on an app to view details about storage.

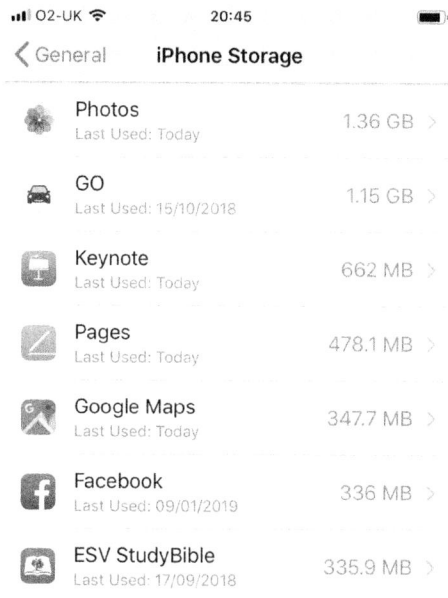

You can manually offload the app. Do this by tapping 'offload app'.

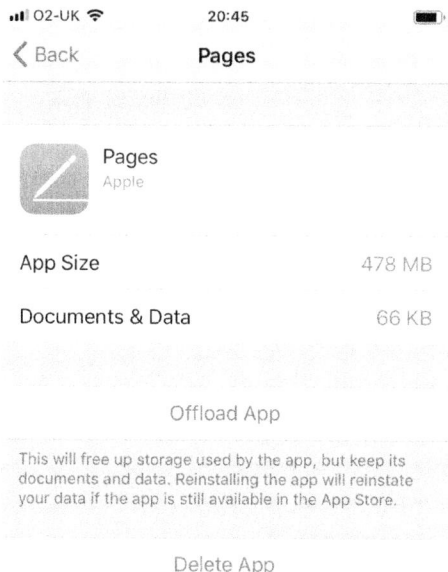

Or you can delete the app. Do this by tapping 'delete app'.

# Index

# Index

# Index

Printed in Great
Britain
by Amazon